The Road to

2015

Profiles of the Future

John L. Petersen

Waite Group Press™
Corte Madera, California

Publisher • Mitchell Waite
Editor-in-Chief • Scott Calamar
Editorial Director • Joel Fugazzotto
Managing Editor • Kurt Stephan
Content Editor • Heidi Brumbaugh
Production Director • Julianne Ososke
Cover Design • Ted Mader
Design • Kristin Peterson
Production • Deborah Anker
Illustrations • Ben Long, Pat Rogondino

© 1994 by John L. Petersen
Published by Waite Group Press™, 200 Tamal Plaza, Corte Madera, CA 94925.

Waite Group Press is distributed to bookstores and book wholesalers by Publishers Group West, Box 8843, Emeryville, CA 94662, 1-800-788-3123 (in California 1-510-658-3453).

Printed in the United States of America
94 95 96 97 • 10 9 8 7 6 5 4 3 2 1

Petersen, John L., 1943–
    The road to 2015 : profiles of the future/ by John L. Petersen.
        p.   cm.
    Includes bibliographical references and index.
    ISBN 1-878739-85-9 : $18.95
    1. Economic history—1990– 2. Social history—1970– 3. Economic forecasting. 4. Social prediction. I. Title.
HC59.15.P48   1994
330.9—dc20   94-22027
                                                 CIP

There is nothing permanent except change.
—Heraclitus (ca. 540–ca. 480 B.C.)

DEDICATION

For Diane
my best friend
who loves me
in spite of my explorations of life's edges.
And for
John
who will live
in the world this book describes.

ABOUT THE AUTHOR

John L. Petersen

John Petersen is a futurist who specializes in long-range thinking about national security. The Arlington Institute, the Washington, D.C.-area research institute that he founded, works with military leaders and others involved in the policy arena, encouraging them to develop new ideas of what might be on the horizon, how the concept of security is changing, and how the military might play a different role in our society in the future.

When he is not reading, writing, or lecturing, John leads seminars and workshops that help clients build new images of possible futures and visions for reaching their goals.

John also has worked in the Office of the Secretary of Defense and in the White House on the National Security Council staff, and has been a disk jockey, a salesman, a manufacturing executive, and a consultant. He has managed a national nonprofit organization, created advertising, provided marketing advice, produced musical concerts, developed real estate, and managed conventions. Many of these experiences were with firms that he started himself. He has also been involved in a number of presidential political campaigns.

In the Vietnam war he flew airplanes from aircraft carriers and spent part of his Naval Reserve career participating in the Gulf War. He is a private pilot.

John lives in the Washington area with his wife, Diane. Their son, John, is a member of the 82nd Airborne Division.

His e-mail address is 71650.144@compuserve.com

TABLE OF CONTENTS

TABLE OF CONTENTS

ACKNOWLEDGMENTS

You are holding the product of the diligent research and always friendly and insightful commiseration of my friend Xiaolin Li, the timely contribution of Elin Whitney-Smith, and the welcome and predictable resource material supplied by Joel Snell. Special thanks goes to Peter Schwartz of the Global Business Network, whose scenarios are the framework for the chapter on crosscuts and wild cards. John D. Rockfellow and the Institute for Future Studies in Copenhagen were kind to allow the use of some of their wild cards.

In an earlier incarnation, this book was a report commissioned by the Strategic Planning Staff of the Commandant of the U.S. Coast Guard. I am indebted to Captain Terry Sinclair, USCG, for his support in getting that project off the ground.

Many individuals were kind to allow me to use some of their original ideas and words. Thanks to the Worldwatch Institute; Hardin Tibbs of the Global Business Network; Wm. VanDusen Wishard at WorldTrends Research; John Sumser and the *Whole Earth Review;* Ira Kuhn, of Directed Technologies, Inc.; Amory Lovins and Eric Toler at the Rocky Mountain Institute; Hal Puthoff of the Institute for Advanced Studies at Austin; the Grumman Corporation; ABB Traction Corporation; Michael Rothschild of the Bionomics Institute; Doug Lenat and Judy Bowman at MCC Corporation; the University of Chicago's Marvin Zonis; and Barbara Abbott of the Jamestown Foundation.

Many good friends bless my life, and I have engaged a number of them over these issues during the past two years. In the process of my trying to pick their brains and steal their ideas, they have unwittingly (and materially) shaped the way I see the world and are therefore contributors to this project. I can remember particularly interesting discussions with Van Wishard, Jack Krings, Kazu Hamada, Tom Klutznick, Jack Sheehan, Dave Oliver, Bill Owens, Regis McKenna, Jack DuVall, Chris and Kirk MacNulty, Harlan Cleveland, and Willis Harman.

This book is also a tribute to the board of directors (both past and present) of The Arlington Institute, where I hang my hat. They have given their time, resources, and good counsel for years (with too little to show for their involvement), and for that I am in debt to Jack DuVall, Dick Sawdey, Paul Bracken, Bernie McMahon, Bob Morse, Neal Creighton, George Kuper, Jim Woolsey, and Chris MacNulty.

I am honored to have this volume included in the Waite Group Press catalog, and have appreciated the opportunity of working with Mitch Waite, Scott Calamar, and Kurt Stephan.

If, in giving birth to this book, I am its mother, then it had two fathers. David Kalish liked it so much in its original form that he took it to his publisher friend Mitch Waite. David then took the time from his busy life to edit this manuscript and contribute his always valuable insights.

The original idea of an "environment scan" came from Captain Dennis M. Egan, USCG. Mike was kind enough to sponsor the original report, shepherd it through a six-month wrestling match with the finest bureaucracy in the country, contribute his always deep and broad perspective to the original text, and then stay on to help update this version. That people as honest, open-minded, and charitable as he continue in the service of our government gives me hope for our nation's future.

Dear Reader:

What is a book? Is it perpetually fated to be inky words on a paper page? Or can a book simply be something that inspires—feeding your head with ideas and creativity regardless of the medium? The latter, I believe. That's why I'm always pushing our books to a higher plane; using new technology to reinvent the medium.

I wrote my first book in 1973, *Projects in Sights, Sounds, and Sensations.* I like to think of it as our first multimedia book. In the years since then, I've learned that people want to experience information, not just passively absorb it—they want interactive MTV in a book. With this in mind, I started my own publishing company and published *Master C,* a book/disk package that turned the PC into a C language instructor. Then we branched out to computer graphics with *Fractal Creations,* which included a color poster, 3D glasses, and a totally rad fractal generator. Ever since, we've included disks and other goodies with most of our books. *Virtual Reality Creations* is bundled with 3D Fresnel viewing goggles and *Walkthroughs and Flybys CD* comes with a multimedia CD-ROM. We've made complex multimedia accessible for any PC user with *Ray Tracing Creations, Multimedia Creations, Making Movies on Your PC, Image Lab,* and three books on Fractals.

The Waite Group continues to publish innovative multimedia books on cutting-edge topics, and of course the programming books that make up our heritage. Being a programmer myself, I appreciate clear guidance through a tricky OS, so our books come bundled with disks and CDs loaded with code, utilities, and custom controls.

By 1994, The Waite Group will have published 135 books. Our next step is to develop a new type of book, an interactive, multimedia experience involving the reader on many levels.

With this new book, you'll be trained by a computer-based instructor with infinite patience, run a simulation to visualize the topic, play a game that shows you different aspects of the subject, interact with others on-line, and have instant access to a large database on the subject. For traditionalists, there will be a full-color, paper-based book.

In the meantime, they've wired the White House for hi-tech; the information super highway has been proposed; and computers, communication, entertainment, and information are becoming inseparable. To travel in this Digital Age you'll need guidebooks. The Waite Group offers such guidance for the most important software— your mind.

We hope you enjoy this book. For a color catalog, just fill out and send in the Reader Report Card at the back of the book.

Sincerely,

Mitchell Waite

Mitchell Waite
Publisher

WAITE
GROUP
PRESS™

PREFACE

Waiting for a crisis to force us to act globally runs the risk of making us wait too long.

—Isaac Asimov

This book is probably not what you think it is. Although it raises the possibility of a number of profoundly important future events that are not commonly understood, and looks systematically at the forces that drive change in the major segments of human life, this is not a forecast of what will happen in the next two decades.

Rather, it is a tool that will provide you, the reader, with an example of an integrated framework from which you can develop your own models for thinking about the future. It is a mental device that will attempt to lead you down many paths, and in so doing convince you forever that effective thinking about the future is impossible without casting a very wide net. And as you will see, the task becomes quite complex and fraught with uncertainties. Simple suggestions become simple minded.

Above all, this book will paint pictures in your mind about what might happen in the next 20 years—mental images that are the key to thinking about the future. Only by building images of the intertwined driving forces and trends—images so complex and dynamic that only your mind is powerful enough to effectively deal with them—will you be able to begin to make sense of what might be on your horizon.

This exercise will be successful if, after reading this book, you are convinced that we are living in one of the most extraordinary periods of history, and that the experiences and tools that most of us have for dealing with incremental change will not work in this new context of explosive, exponential revolution. I hope you come away impressed that in order to navigate the rapids ahead, you will need to become proactive; simply dealing with events as they come along will guarantee failure, in most every area of life. We must learn how to think differently.

SYSTEMS-BASED PLANNING

This is a simple experiment in systems-based planning. It begins with an explanation, in the broadest terms, of how the system is defined. The fundamental nodes are:

- Information availability

- Social values

- Technology

- Global environment

Everything else is subsidiary to and derived from these three driving forces.

- What we know

- What we think about it

- What tools are available to us

- The influence of the (earth) systems that support human life

These form the underpinnings for everything else—economics, politics, energy, and all the rest.

We will explore these major components and a number of second-order ones as well so that you can begin to define the overall shape and texture of the system in your mind. Next we'll look at a number of examples that illustrate how these trends might interact, and then you will be on your way.

For no matter how you interpret what you are about to read, you will not see the world in the same way when you have finished.

And I hope that reading this book also changes what you do. For only if many of us do things much more differently than we have in the past, will humanity effectively deal with the ominous problems on our horizon.

Godspeed.

CHAPTER

1

A New Era

Requires

New Thinking

Where there is no vision, the people perish.
                                            —*Proverbs 29:18*

You are living in the period of time that will produce more change for humanity than any previous era in history. It is a time of extraordinary importance that will fundamentally reshape almost every aspect of your life during the next two decades. Wholesale change is taking place in almost every segment of your reality—and the pace will only increase in the coming years.

The trends are already in place. If you're an adult, during your lifetime science learned more about how nature works than was learned in the 5,000 years before you were born. Fifty years ago, astronomers could only identify two galaxies. Now we know there are more than 2 billion. Eighty percent of the scientists who have ever lived are alive today; and they (and every other segment of life) are producing extraordinary amounts of new knowledge. Some estimates say that the total amount of information in the world is now doubling every 18 months.

This explosion of information is changing who you are. You are a far different person today than you would have been had you lived, say, 200 years ago. If, this coming Sunday, you were to read the entire *New York Times,* you would absorb more information in that one reading than the average person absorbed in a lifetime in Thomas Jefferson's day. Over the next 20 years, the pace will only increase—because the forces that are driving this change are extraordinarily powerful, and exponential. *We must learn to operate differently.*

The coming two decades hold exceptional opportunity and hazard. As we will see, wonderful new technologies coupled with strange new scientific ideas could produce a renaissance in knowledge and human life that would dwarf any previous revolutions this planet has seen. At the same time, and for the first time, humans are now threatening the global system that produces the most basic requirements of life.

We will be able to take advantage of the opportunities and sidestep the minefields only if we:

■ understand, in broad terms, what this era is about,

■ learn how to think differently, and

■ become aware of the major forces that are driving the change.

THE FOUR HISTORICAL EPOCHS

So what's going on? Why all this change now? Has there been a time like this before?

Yes, in fact, there have been a number of times like this—transitions from one era to another. A look at the history of life on this planet is quite revealing. Figure 1-1 shows the period of the earliest known life. During those billions of years there were four major transformations or transitions. In the first case, there was a moment—about a billion years

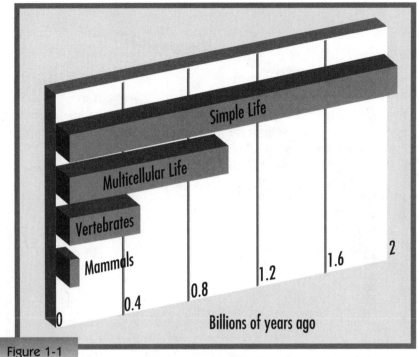

Figure 1-1 Mammals occupy the smallest portion of the early evolution of life on earth

ago—when, in an exclusively single-cell world, the first multiple-cell life evolved. This was followed, about 500 million years ago, by the first vertebrate beings. Some 50 million years ago mammals made their first appearance. Notice the length of each era compared to the previous one. A relationship of about ten to one is emerging. Earlier eras are about ten times longer than the ones that follow.

Not only is each succeeding era shorter, but it clearly represents a time with a much higher average level of information. Multiple-cell organisms are more complicated than single-cell ones, vertebrates are far more complex than their ancestors, and so on.

The progression continues, as Figure 1-2 shows, only in millions instead of billions of years. The first version of what ultimately became modern humans showed up about 5 million years ago, followed by *Homo sapiens* at 500,000 years ago. The hunter-gatherers began tilling the land some 50,000 years ago, beginning the age of agriculture. The ten to one relationship in time between eras continues, with

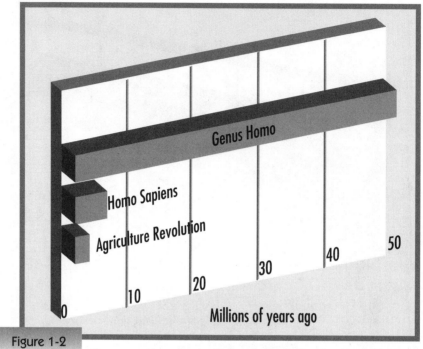

Figure 1-2
The genus *Homo* lived millions of years before it adopted an agricultural lifestyle

companion order-of-magnitude increases in the information content of the new period.

Five thousand years ago, the first humans moved into towns and cities, and only 500 years have passed since the dawn of the Industrial Revolution. Figure 1-3 shows the relationship of our present era, the Information Age (which started only about 25 years ago) to these earlier times.

These anthropological divisions have been paralleled by information technology inventions. In fact, it seems clear that information technology has had a great deal to do with the later epochs. The oldest discovered example of writing, scratches on an antler horn, has been dated to about 35,000 years ago, soon after *Homo sapiens* moved from hunting and gathering to farming. Five thousand years ago, when humans were moving into towns, the first writing system, cuneiform tablets, was invented to keep records of economic transactions. Table 1-1 shows that the printing press enabled the beginning of the Industrial Age a little over 500 years ago, and the microprocessor, the

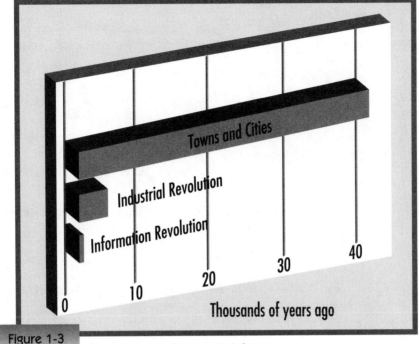

Figure 1-3
The Information Age is in its infancy

most powerful of all information technologies, initiated the Information Age less than 25 years ago.

Years Before 1994	Invention	Human Epoch
35,000	First notation	Hunter-gatherer
5,000	Writing system	Agricultural
540	Printing press	Industrial
23	Microprocessor	Information

TABLE 1-1. Information revolutions

THE INFORMATION AGE AND BEYOND

This regular relationship between the length of succeeding eras suggests that the Information Age may only be about 50 years long—and there is good evidence to confirm that that may well be the case. We may be halfway through the shortest and most information-

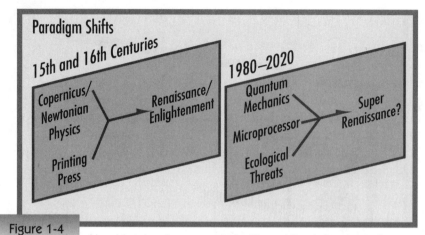

Figure 1-4 New ideas in science coupled with enabling infotech produce paradigm shifts

explosive era in human history, one that will end in about two decades. If we understand that this era may be only some 50 years long, and that each new era is characterized by a many-fold increase in available information over the past one, then the explosion in change—driven by increases in information—begins to make sense.

Look at it in another way. The last major shift began in the fifteenth century. Then, as can be seen in Figure 1-4, two powerful forces came together and produced the Renaissance and the Enlightenment—by far the brightest flowering of knowledge the world had ever seen.

In the fifteenth century, Johannes Gutenberg invented movable type, multiplying many times over the ability of humans to classify, duplicate, distribute, and communicate information. The printing press quickly spread each new scientific idea throughout the Western world, spurring additional new ideas from each person who received the information.

In the fifteenth, sixteenth, and seventeenth centuries, a series of revolutionary ideas in science—Copernicus' and Galileo's concepts of a planetary system and astronomy, and Newton's physics—completely devastated the existing explanations of physical reality. They redefined everything about life.

The Beginning of a New Era

Since then, new information technologies—the telegraph, telephone, television, and FAX machine—have had great impact. But for the last 500 years, another combination of a revolutionary scientific idea and an enabling information technology has not come along … until now. The revolutionary idea is quantum mechanics and the information technology is the microprocessor. Together they promise the kind of information explosion that characterized the Renaissance and Enlightenment—only this time it will be many times greater.

This time, though, it is not just a big idea and an enabling information technology coming together. There is an additional force: the influence of humans on the planet's systems that support life. Until the last few decades, humans have always been at the mercy of nature. The natural systems were so great, compared to the activities of people, that the effect of humans on the planet's life-sustaining capability was marginal, at best. Certainly, some places were polluted and despoiled, but the larger system was not threatened.

That has changed. Now, as you will see in the chapter on the environment, some of the industrial effects of humans are many times greater than those of nature, and there is good reason to be gravely concerned about the ultimate implications. If we are not careful, the new renaissance—and everything else—may die aborning.

So, as we navigate between two epochal global shifts, information technology, new science, and environmental problems are converging to produce an era that is moving so fast that few can understand it. But we must try, for if we can't make sense of the context in which we must live, we guarantee that every significant new event will be a surprise—and many of those surprises will be disasters.

LEARNING TO THINK DIFFERENTLY

An important part of making sense out of this period is learning to think differently. Throughout modern history, influenced by the power of the scientific method, we have broken big problems down into individual pieces and studied the parts independently. This linear thinking—taking one piece after another—has stood us in good stead in a number of areas. We have designed our academies around this approach: science, engineering, social science, fine arts, liberal arts, and

The Computer Is the Best Tool for Systems Thinking

In order to think systemically, one must "see" the system—either physically or mentally. The major nodes and linkages between nodes must be clear and logical.

The best tool for displaying and manipulating systems is the computer, which allows us to display a system and then observe it from any perspective. We can "navigate" the system, moving from one node to another, exploring the contents of the each node and the essence of the links between nodes.

Computer games like SimEarth, SimCIty, and SimAnt are also very effective tools for forcing us to confront the extraordinary complexity of complete systems. In these games the player is required to orchestrate the interactions of major systems that contribute to the well being of the earth, a city, and a colony of ants who are trying to get into a house from a backyard. As one parameter is changed, many others react—often in ways that were not predictable before the fact.

so on. Within each larger academic discipline, specialization has been rewarded—for example, within the field of science we have physics, chemistry, biology, and so on. Governments are similarly organized: commerce, defense, energy, state, and the like.

But specialization, particularly in this time of extraordinary complexity, interdependency, and high rate of change, has serious deficiencies. For one thing, specialists tend not to talk to each other; and when they do, they find it hard to communicate because they speak different languages. Also, being focused on a single issue by definition hides linkages to other aspects of the problem or system. Behavior that is found in a number of areas—say biology, economics, and political science—is not apparent to one who has his or her nose buried in a single discipline. And if there is anything that the new science of complexity and other recent findings suggest, it is that everything is connected to everything else. Everything is interdependent.

No longer is it adequate, for example, to struggle with an economic problem by looking only at economics. Changing domestic social values, advances in technology, political shifts, and pressures from the environment are also important players. The *system* must be examined. Linkages must be found and changing patterns and shapes identified. A new way of thinking—system thinking—must be developed that deals with the system as a whole, somehow building a set of mental images that reflect the multidimensional nature of the problem.

Entering Uncharted Waters

Designing a new way of thinking is not easy. Very few people have any idea how to do it, but there are some indicators of where to start. For example, one would never suggest that studying a single tropical plant by itself would be adequate to explain how it functions in the rain forest. No, the whole system that supports it, and to which it contributes, must be taken into consideration. Even then, because of the complexity of the rain forest, it would be foolish to suggest that harvesting and thereby eliminating one species from the system would have no significant impact on the rest of the system. The behavior of the system is far too involved for such simple, linear thinking.

Almost all other problems of any significance share the characteristics of a rain forest: many pieces working together in highly complex and dynamic ways that are not immediately apparent. The only way to understand the problem is to begin to understand the system.

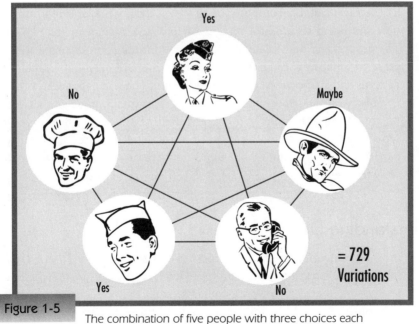

Figure 1-5

The combination of five people with three choices each produces hundreds of possible situations

Unfortunately, the very complexity of systems makes them hard to understand—so many things participating in so many activities. In even simple systems, the combination of possibilities of behavior become enormous. As Figure 1-5 shows, if five individuals each had a piece of a larger project, and each could make three different choices (yes, no, or maybe) in response to a particular issue, the "system" could behave in 729 different ways.

In a complex system, as in any significant aspect of life, the variables become almost incomprehensible and therefore cannot be dealt with in any logical way. We try things that we think will have a certain effect, and not only do we not get the desired behavior, but a number of other events happen that we didn't anticipate. The best example, perhaps, is the economy. Every economist seems to have a different idea about how it will behave, and most of them are wrong. It's simply too complex for linear, logical interpretation.

We Need a New Approach

What's the solution? We'll need to load the brain with as much information as possible about the components of the system, and then let the most capable computer of all, our minds, work on the information and begin to produce images of how the system might behave. The process and output are qualitative and intuitive, producing a strong sense of what might happen, or what appropriate behavior should be. Patterns and shapes and congruencies begin to become apparent.

This is not just speculation; specific group methodologies that play on this approach have had a great deal of success. They involve workshop sessions using psychological techniques that allow participants to systematically build new frameworks from which to view their worlds.

Understanding Driving Forces

It is not enough to try just to think systemically. If the right information is not available—or, more likely, it is incomplete—the final analysis, no matter how well one has thought, will be seriously flawed. You must start with a full deck. As we will see, there are so many extraordinarily important things happening in so many different disciplines, that it is imperative that we actively pursue trends outside of our small area of interest. If we do not, major events will be surprises and we won't have time to react to them.

Again, our society has a natural bias against casting a wide net. We'd rather focus on narrow specialties than consider information from diverse disciplines or sectors. That abbreviated perspective can be overcome by learning about the broad range of basic forces that are driving change. We must nose around in many different disciplines, attempting to identify those major issues that are likely to have a profound impact on the future.

We must boldly venture into the area of the generalist, attempting to learn some of the basics about the whole system. Those who effectively deal with this new renaissance will, of necessity, be renaissance people.

Significant change always starts at the edge. The first indications don't pop up in the middle of the status quo, but are generated by people who think differently. In our search for the early indicators of change—the seedlings of possible futures—we must necessarily wander throughout the sector edges. This uncertain, unstable landscape always has many risks and hazards that must be identified and avoided, but it is also home to the beginning of the future.

In the following pages we will map the edges, looking for precious stones. Do not be deterred by the rough exterior of some of what we find. Don't throw them out summarily; only the burnishing and polishing of time will yield the true nature of these trends—and for that we must be patient and observant.

You are now about to be exposed to trends in many different sectors of life. One by one they will give you some initial ideas of how they behave and how they might interact with other trends and forces. Each will give you a somewhat different perspective on the world arrayed in front of you. Inevitably, you will begin to build a new set of images about the future. Little by little, those images will change your life.

Let us start with the discipline that explains how everything is supposed to work: science.

CHAPTER 2

New Ideas

in Science

*It is the stars as not known to science that I would
know, the stars which the lonely traveler knows.*
—Henry David Thoreau

For the first time in some 500 years,
a scientific revolution has begun that
will fundamentally change the
world much as the Renaissance and
the Enlightenment did. A handful of
extraordinary new advances in
science are taking humans quickly
and deeply into areas that will have
profound implications for the
future. The process has already
begun that will change every aspect
of our lives.

THE LAST REVOLUTION

During the Middle Ages, physical reality—why things were, how they behaved, and so on—was explained in spiritual, mystical, and magical terms. Things happened because God willed them. There was no other reason. The church in Europe was there to explain God's interests and desires, and everything else was taken on faith. There were no laws of gravity, no chemistry (only alchemy), no physics or science as we now know it. The scriptures were the ultimate authority for science, and all of the stars and planets revolved around the earth.

It was Nicolaus Copernicus (1473–1543) who, near the middle of the sixteenth century, initiated the revolution that ultimately rocked the educated world. He suggested that the earth was spinning on its axis (that's why the sun and moon rose and set), and the earth and other planets really circled the sun.

The inventor of the astronomical telescope, Galileo Galilei (1564–1642), came along about a century later and observed the moons of Jupiter and the rings of Saturn, finally stripping the earth of any claim to being at the center of it all. His ideas were so menacing that the Church tried him and found him guilty of having "held and taught" the Copernican doctrine, forced him to recant his "past errors," and sentenced him to house arrest for the rest of his life.

Isaac Newton (1642–1727) was born in the year Galileo died. Newton developed the Law of Universal Gravitation and was the father of the physics that was practiced for the next 200 years.

These three men produced the framework for a new set of scientific ideas that, over a 200-year period, completely changed every aspect of the Western world. The Industrial Age that resulted would have been impossible for someone living in medieval Europe to even begin to imagine.

A NEW SCIENTIFIC REVOLUTION

Now, 250 years later, we are in the midst of another such revolution; but this one will be much greater and shorter than the last. A strange new understanding of physics anchors this upheaval: quantum mechanics. Beginning around the turn of this century with Max Planck's and Albert Einstein's ideas about the composition of light, and continuing with the contributions of Niels Bohr, Erwin Schrödinger,

Werner Heisenberg, and more lately David Bohm, a whole new way of explaining physical reality has come into being—one that flies in the face of the Newtonian physics on which the Industrial Age was built.

This new physics says that there is nothing solid in matter—no solid electrons, or protons, or subatomic particles. At the very bottom there are packets—chunks—of energy. It says that everything is connected to everything else, and that you can go forward and backward in time, because all time exists at the same time. Things can move faster than the speed of light—instantaneously, it seems. And in the end, the one thing that fundamentally shapes the packets of energy—that decides what appears to be real—is human consciousness.

Consciousness Is Causal

Quantum mechanics says that consciousness is causal. Your conscious mind determines everything you see, touch, feel, hear, smell, and taste. You, the observer, control the reality in which you live. As physicist Fred Alan Wolf has written in *Taking the Quantum Leap,* "Fundamentally, the observer creates reality by observing it. ... It is precisely how we observe that creates the reality we perceive. Change the how of it and you change the what of it."

Research has shown, for example, that as people with multiple personality disorder shift from personality to personality, their physiology similarly changes. Their mental state changes their physical state.

Think about that for a minute. If your mind really controls your reality and you are sick, poor, happy, or rich (you fill in the blank), whose fault is it? If you get in a car accident, why is it? If you get old and die, well, why do you get old and die? Why can't you fly—or transport yourself to another place at will?

This is weird, strange stuff. Although the concepts of quantum mechanics have been around for a while, the implications have not really worked their way into our daily lives until now. Some mainstream oncologists, for example, advise their patients to battle their cancer by meditating and building visual images of little soldiers in their bloodstream that search out and destroy the enemy cancer cells. Olympic athletes (and everyday ones, for that matter) go through exercises to visualize how they want to perform before they take to the field or court. Even corporate executives are meditating and visualizing.

It's just the beginning, but during the next two decades the implications of this hard-to-believe science will make significant inroads into the world's societies. Common understanding of these principles will probably be driven by some of the New Age and Eastern religious thinking that is growing on the fringe in Western societies—but that is how all major shifts like this take hold. New ideas—like the environmental movement—are first embraced by groups on the edges, and then they work themselves into the middle.

Like Newtonian physics before it, the implications of quantum mechanics will shake and redefine every aspect of life: how we perceive physical reality; how we deal with other humans; how families, businesses, governments, and schools operate; how we define and pursue security, happiness, God, and the other fundamentals of life.

UNDERSTANDING CHAOS

Newtonian physics says that there are two states of a system: stable and unstable (or chaotic). Most of the things you see, like buildings, trees, and coffee cups, are stable—they are not moving, and are unlikely to move unless an outside force pushes against them. This stability is the arena of classical physics. Stable systems are relatively easy to understand. There are physical laws that describe how they work. Because the situation is not changing, it can be clear what is happening.

Chaotic system behavior, by definition, has always been much more difficult to analyze and predict. Just think of the water running in a stream, smoke rising from a smokestack, or the movement of weather over the continent. For short distances or periods of time, one can anticipate what might happen; but the situation quickly becomes much more complicated when we consider larger units of measurement. In fact, until a few years ago, it was assumed that the behavior of complex dynamic systems was essentially impossible to understand.

That meant that huge areas of life—biological systems, ecological systems, economic systems, social systems—could never really be understood with the same precision as in physics. They were just too unpredictable.

The problem, 20 years ago, was mainly one of computing capacity. A complex system that was constantly changing involved a lot of mainframe and supercomputer time to plot its behavior. And because

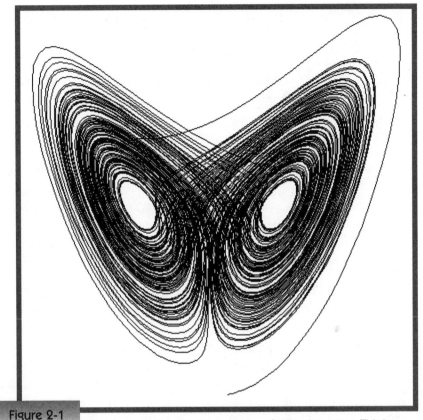

Figure 2-1   The Lorenz attractor: the behavior of a simple system. This is a plot of a system with three variables. Although not apparent in this illustration, it is three-dimensional. The behavior of the system is constantly being drawn toward the two "donut hole" attractors, never once repeating itself exactly.

the time on these machines was so expensive, and many scientists shared the same machine, researchers could not afford long runs. Edward Lorenz, for example, had to do 500 successive calculations in 1963 just to plot the first seven strands of his famous attractor, which is shown in Figure 2-1.

The New Ability to Understand the Behavior of Systems

Chaos theory (and its offspring, the science of complexity) is the study of the global nature of systems and how they emerge and adapt. Every

Complexity/Chaos Theory

The science of complexity and its famous sister, chaos theory, exist only because of the microprocessor. Before the advent of the small computer, trying to determine the behavior of a very complex system after millions of iterations of change was essentially impossible.

When scientists attempted to run some of these kinds of experiments on the new small, inexpensive computers that began to show up in the early 1980s, they discovered that if they pulsed systems enough times they could begin to see distinct patterns in this irregular, chaotic behavior.

The press heralded the new findings as being as important as quantum mechanics, for now there was a framework that could be used for analyzing complex dynamic systems. It was a science of *process*—dynamic behavior—rather than *state*, the domain of classical physics.

important problem of the future that deals with the universe that we see and touch on the human scale is about systems. Chaos makes strong claims about the universal behavior of complexity. It suggests that no matter what the medium—cars driving on an expressway, oil flowing in pipes, citizens voting in an election, the operation of the human brain—all systems obey its newly discovered laws. All whole systems behave in similar ways.

This new theoretical framework will have extraordinary implications for our future ability to understand the behavior of vast areas of human reality that in the past have been subject only to intelligent guesses. This will be particularly true as the computing power of microprocessors increases exponentially, providing tools that can easily crack social and organic codes that are opaque to today's technology.

The study of chaos theory spawned a beautiful by-product image, the fractal. Fractals, the graphic designs that are made by plotting the behavior of complex systems, are "pictures" of how dynamic systems behave within a given set of assumptions. Though derived from a simple mathematical relationship, the Mandelbrot set, shown in Figure 2-2, is the most complex object in mathematics. It includes every complex imaginary number that exists. As each segment of the boundary of the design is magnified, time after time, extraordinary additional detail is found, infinitely.

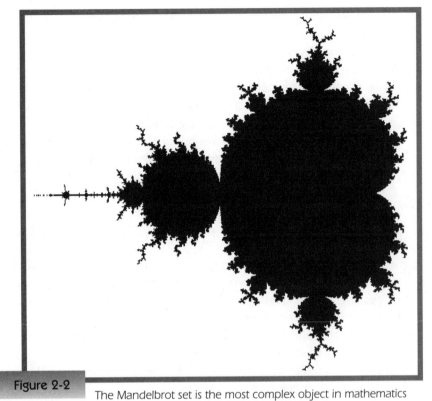

Figure 2-2 The Mandelbrot set is the most complex object in mathematics

INVENTING LIFE

One technology with immense implications for the future exists only because of the microprocessor. This is the discipline of computational biology and its principal derivative, artificial life (a-life). A-life is the study of relatively simple computer algorithms that, when turned loose in the memory of a computer, exhibit all of the characteristics of regular life. A single small organism (about 80 lines long) will self-replicate until there are many thousands living together. They examine themselves, destroy and consume other entities, creatively adapt to constantly changing situations, live off of other kinds of entities, and generally act as if they are alive. Common computer viruses are a simple form of a-life. As Steven Levy, author of *Artificial Life* says,

It is something quite different from genetic engineering, which uses fully evolved wet life as its starting point. The scientists of a-life are devising the means by which actual living systems can be generated, evolved, and observed. Theirs is an effort to engineer the course of evolution and extend the range of living systems on planet earth and beyond.

From this grand experiment, a more profound understanding of life itself, an ability to use its mechanisms to perform our work and, perhaps, the discovery of powerful laws of nature that govern not only biological systems but also any series of complex nonlinear self-organizing interactions may ultimately arise.

From *Artificial Life* by Steven Levy. © Pantheon Books.

Computer Code Adapts to Its Environment

The a-life routines are autonomous. Once they are turned on, they continue to adapt to the environment automatically until they are destroyed. Today, increasingly significant aspects of human existence are being defined in computer code. For researchers in this area, then, a-life appears to hold the answer to life itself, with all the potential opportunities and disasters that such knowledge would include. For example, some researchers envision sending molecular-sized machines to the moon, where the micromachines would replicate themselves and mine the surface for minerals, convert the minerals to metals, and configure the metal into certain products. Other researchers, however, fear that since the machines are on their own and can adapt and evolve independently, science-fiction-like scenarios might arise, in which "spores" of the machines send themselves off to other planets after they have ravaged the moon, or get loose on Earth and attack humans and all other organic life.

Much More Powerful Than "the Bomb"

Doyne Farmer, a leading scientist in this area says that understanding the powers of nature will be "very, very, very much more powerful than the discovery of the bomb, and it will have much wider consequences." He suggests, "By the middle of this century, mankind has acquired the power to extinguish life on earth. By the middle of the next century, he will be able to create it. Of the two it is hard to say which places the larger burden of responsibility on our shoulders."

How could the worst-case scenario occur? Some researchers suggest a horrifying example of a potentially destructive use of a-life techniques, "military applications ... from battlefield robots to satellite warfare." Since the federal government funds so much a-life research, this seems almost an inevitability. Farmer contended that if a-life came to realize its potential, those military uses would destroy even those who sought to utilize them. "Once self-reproducing war machines are in place, even if we should change our mind and establish a consensus, dismantling them may be impossible—they may be literally out of our control."

NEW SCIENCE

A small but growing group of researchers are looking into interesting areas on the fringes of conventional scientific knowledge. This new science, or frontier science, is unstructured, generally discounted by the current "experts," and very broad. But if these researchers make significant progress in the coming years, they will break open a whole new area of understanding that will upset much of existing science.

For instance, these thinkers are leading the attempt to bring the implications of quantum theory into practical use. If anything, they are characterized by their open-mindedness. This characteristic alone makes them worth noting, for many of the new ideas in science in the next 20 years are likely to come from them.

Although many ideas and areas of study are undertaken under this banner, three merit particular mention. These are consciousness research, bioelectromagnetics, and complementary medicine, the areas of study of the Center for Frontier Sciences, located at Temple University in Philadelphia.

Consciousness Research

Consciousness research involves inquiry into the nature of mind and its role in the physical and biological areas. In humans, different states of consciousness, beliefs, emotions, and intentionality have been shown to play active roles in bodily functions. Research on multiple personality disorder (MPD) indicates that the patient's physiology shifts measurably with each personality. These shifts include changes in allergy profiles, disease states, visual acuity, and EEG, to name a few. MPD research implies that the body/mind is a single indivisible unit.

Remote perception, the ability to view in one's mind accurate images of other locations separated from the observer by geography or time, has been demonstrated. Psychosomatic medicine and psychoneuroimmunology both show a distinct role of mind in health and disease. Biofeedback, hypnosis, the placebo effect, and autogenic training indicate that profound effects upon physiology can be generated by subtle mental shifts.

Dozens of studies have shown that the prayers and meditations of one person for another, often over long distances, correlate with a significant improvement of health and well being of the person being prayed for. Numerous investigations in consciousness research suggest the unity of mind and body, and the ability of mind to interact with matter in ways that transcend the limitations of ordinary space-time.

Bioelectromagnetics

The emerging area of bioelectromagnetics targets natural and artificial electromagnetic fields (EMFs) and their relation to life and health. Recent evidence shows a much greater sensitivity of life forms, especially developing ones, to low-level nonionizing EMFs than had been predicted from classical physics. Both positive and negative biological effects of such EMFs, ranging from extremely low frequency to the radio and microwave regions, have been documented for many different life forms. Effects range from those at the molecular and cellular levels to tissue, organ, systemic, and behavioral changes.

A related area of research indicates that EMFs generated within organisms, observed as coherent light emissions in the visible spectrum, are common to all life and may serve as informational signals governing life processes. Moreover, the well-known phenomenon of dowsing may also be related to EMF effects. Research on dowsing suggests that the biological response in the form of a spontaneous twitch of a muscle, observed as a jerk of a rod held in the hand as one is moving over a geological gradient, is due to variations in extremely low-intensity geophysical fields.

The increasing evidence from the wide range of research in bioelectromagnetics suggests a close connection with life and with fields that exist throughout the universe. It challenges the conventional discrete, biomolecular view of life, in which living functions may be reduced to a complex mix of biochemistry within the organism. Possibly, living systems may even be regarded as fundamentally electromagnetic in their nature.

Complementary Medicine

Complementary medicine focuses on the medical diagnostics and therapies that are part of subtle intervention. Some of these, such as acupuncture, homeopathy and infinitesimal drug doses, and the effects of healers are older systems of medicine that are not explained by the conventional biomedical model. Others, such as electro-acupuncture and various other electromagnetic methods, are relatively new.

Collectively, all of these have also been referred to as "energy medicine" or "soft medicine." Electro-acupuncture devices and other instruments that probe subtle measurements such as skin electrical conductivity are growing in usage. A steadily growing body of recent research documents the biological effects of extremely weak medicinal dilutions and homeopathic preparations. The health benefits of therapeutic touch, now used in hospitals worldwide, have been widely documented.

Evidence is mounting from many different avenues of research in complementary medicine that living systems are highly nonlinear and that subtle interventions in the form of very small stimuli can lead to significant beneficial effects without side effects. Such effects are not anticipated by the conventional biomedical model.

Enormous changes in science are only the beginning of our excursion. New technologies—the tools we build—are being created at unbelievable rates. Put on your seat belt and hold on, because you're in for the ride of your life.

CHAPTER

3

Extraordinary
Technology

Television? The word is half Latin and half Greek.
No good can come of it.
—C. P. Scott (1846–1932)

Technology, one of the principal driving forces of the future, is transforming our lives and shaping our future at rates unprecedented in history, with profound implications that we can't even begin to see or understand.

THE AGE OF THE MICROPROCESSOR

The rate of change is hard to comprehend. The total amount of information in the world is said to be doubling every 18 months or even less. In the last two decades, the update cycle for textbooks has shrunk from every five years to every one to three years. In some areas the growth of information is so rapid that by the time a book on the subject is published, it is obsolete. There are now 25 accredited physician specialties and 56 subspecialties. Thirty-five of the subspecialties were recognized in just the past five years. Additionally, 123 self-appointed medical boards certify physicians in areas ranging from addiction treatment to circus medicine.

At the center of this maelstrom, functioning much as the printing press did soon after its invention, is the microprocessor. In the same way that Gutenberg's movable type multiplied the spread of information during the Enlightenment, so the microprocessor-based computer is exponentially expanding the human ability to collect, analyze, manipulate, and communicate information.

Unlike the printing press, telephone, or any previous information technology, though, the microprocessor is fueling its own revolution. Printing presses, for example, did not directly produce more capable printing presses, but each new generation of computer chips is used to make more capable computer chips, compounding the rate of change.

Just as movable type and the printing press enabled the shift to the Industrial Age by greatly increasing the distribution of the ideas of Newton, Copernicus, and others, the microprocessor will be responsible for moving the concepts of Bohr, Einstein, and Heisenberg into the mainstream of society at a far more rapid rate. Even with books, information in the seventeenth century could take months or even years to become widely known; now the news of new scientific discoveries circles the globe in hours, if not minutes, after the event.

Geometric Growth in Proliferation and Capability

As we will see, the microprocessor is making everything in the developed world move faster. The metabolisms of societies are being speeded up by the exponential proliferation of devices that are also becoming more capable at equally exponential rates. We are actively exploring new disciplines and sciences that became feasible only in the

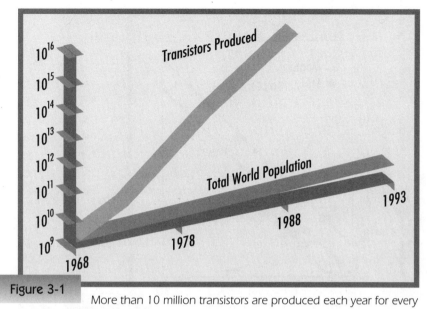

Figure 3-1 More than 10 million transistors are produced each year for every person on earth

last few years, with the advent of the iterative capabilities of the desktop computer.

The production of transistors, the most basic unit in the microprocessor, is increasing. As Figure 3-1 shows, the Advanced Research Projects Agency of the Department of Defense estimates that more than 10 million transistors are produced each year for every person on Earth … and the rate is growing exponentially.

Silicon-based transistors are being made smaller and smaller, so much so that 1991 industry estimates predicted somewhere between 100 million and 1 billion transistors would be crowded onto a single fingernail-sized chip by the end of the decade. The exponential increase can be seen in Figure 3-2. In a more recent announcement, IBM's Thomas J. Watson Research Center claimed to have developed the world's smallest transistor, an experimental metal-oxide semiconductor field-effect device with nanometric (billionth of a meter) dimensions. IBM's transistor will permit memory chip fabrication in the realm of 4 gigabits (billion bits) and beyond. Author George Gilder has written that by the end of the decade, the central processing units of 16 Cray YMP supercomputers, which now cost collectively some $320 million, will be manufacturable for under $100 on a single microchip that will contain about 1 billion transistors.

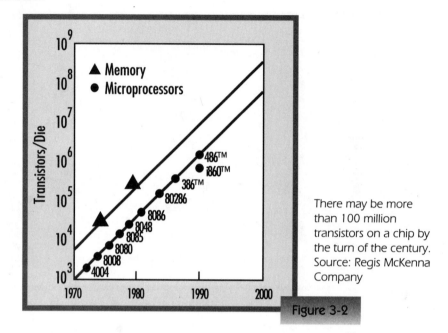

There may be more than 100 million transistors on a chip by the turn of the century. Source: Regis McKenna Company

Figure 3-2

Significant strides are also being made in a number of nonsilicon areas. For example, Tamarack Storage, a high-tech research company, has developed an intriguing holographic memory device. It quickly stores huge amounts of data three dimensionally in its array of crystals, by using two lasers that intersect at various angles within each crystal. The developers believe that the device could replace hard disk drives, and may be able to store more than 10 gigabytes of data in a crystal smaller than a sugar cube.

Japanese researchers are working on *optical* integrated circuits that will be 1000 times faster than silicon chips. Some projections suggest that they will be in the marketplace by the year 2000.

As the density increases, the cost comes down precipitously. Computing power is now increasing at a rate of 4,000 times per decade for a given unit of cost. That means a PC bought in the year 2000 will be 4,000 times more powerful than one purchased in 1990 for the same price. As shown in Figure 3-3, the rate of increase has stayed fairly constant since 1980. *Omni* magazine reported that home video games at the end of the decade will have power equivalent to the largest supercomputers made today. Carnegie Mellon's artificial intelligence pioneer Hans Moravec suggested in 1988 that single computers would bypass the raw computing capability of the human brain around 2010.

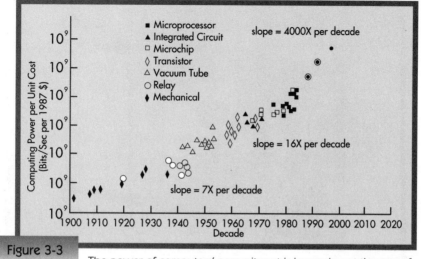

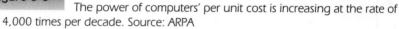

Figure 3-3 The power of computers' per unit cost is increasing at the rate of 4,000 times per decade. Source: ARPA

Others have suggested that it might be sooner than that. Nathan Myhrvold, planner for the software giant Microsoft, said that ten years from now video Christmas cards will be sent with special effects rivaling those in *Terminator 2*. You will be able to splice your kids' faces into TV shows.

The growth is astounding. It took a hundred years for the steam engine to make it to the marketplace. The microprocessor took only 20 years. As Figure 3-4 shows, even compared to more recent inventions like television, the rate of penetration of personal computers has been extraordinary: a million users in only three years. PCs have grown from almost nothing to over 60 million users in a decade.

Microprocessors are becoming a part of almost every aspect of life. Individual telephones have them, they are embedded in watches, they control washers, dryers, and ovens. The automobile industry is the largest customer of microchip manufacturers. The Toyota Camry is reported to have 64 microprocessors, controlling all systems from individual valves, engine ignition, and fuel mixture to heating and air-conditioning.

It is hard to imagine what the implications of this kind of growth and power might mean, for we are really only at the beginning of this revolution. In December 1991, for example, the *San Francisco Chronicle* reported on a major step toward building an artificial brain and other

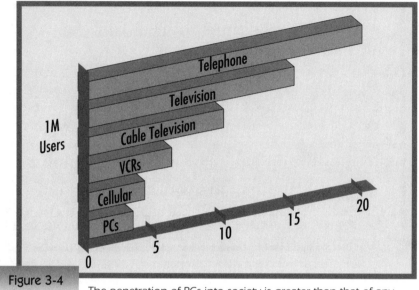

Figure 3-4

The penetration of PCs into society is greater than that of any other information technology. Source: Regis McKenna Company

"intelligent" machines. Scientists at the California Institute of Technology and at the University of Oxford created a silicon chip that behaves much like a human brain cell. The device, which they call a "silicon neuron," is explicitly modeled on the structure and internal workings of neurons in the cerebral cortex. It is unlike conventional computers because instead of working digitally, it operates in the analog mode, the same way a living brain works. Moreover, the device is so energy efficient that it uses only one ten-millionth as much power per operation as does a comparable digital chip. The feat—along with the earlier development of a "silicon retina" that works so much like a real eye that it is even fooled by the same optical illusions that trick humans—marks a significant advance in a field of computing that has long been overshadowed by digital machines.

So far, computers are still primarily used only to do more effectively what has been done by other means in the past. But when designers complete the transition into the new generation of devices that conceptually did not exist before the microchip, huge new increases in productivity and capability will be upon us. That will certainly happen before the end of the century.

COMMUNICATIONS NETWORKS: GIRDLING THE GLOBE

One of the most profound and far-reaching trends that underpins the rest of the technology revolution is the rapid interconnection of individual computers. Some have suggested that this global "nervous system" will be the dominant engine for economic growth in the twenty-first century. The world is being wired up: Global networks of millions of personal machines, eventually connected to each other by fiber-optic and satellite links, will eventually allow almost instantaneous communication to anyone else, anywhere else.

Local and Wide Area Networks

At the lowest level, as few as two computers can be connected to work together as a local area network (LAN). Thousands of businesses and other organizations have connected all of their PCs into LANs. This allows individual operators to easily send electronic mail (e-mail) to anyone else on the network, and everyone can share common databases, such as client records or manufacturing plans.

LANs are often connected together in wide area networks, where satellites or dedicated land lines provide the links. In this way a company with offices or factories in a number of locations can trade information between any computer, no matter where it is located, as though they were all hard-wired together in the same building.

Wireless Terminals

Wiring computers and peripherals into networks is a costly undertaking, particularly for business, when it must be redone every few years as technology becomes obsolete or the size or location of the company changes. There is therefore a growing trend toward wireless terminals—computers and other devices that can interface with other machines. This allows computers to be moved easily and, as long as they remain in proximity, continue to function in a larger network.

The first generation of this capability is on the market now for desktop PCs. Some small palmtop units can trade files between themselves when the units are pointed at each other. One columnist told of writing nine e-mail messages on her palmtop unit during a plane trip between Boston and New York, and sending them when she landed. "I think it could be the ultimate tool for mobile professionals. It could easily replace pagers and cellular phones." This trend is significant, for as electronics shrink they become more portable, and the need to constantly connect and disconnect from a local area network is troublesome.

Cellular Networks

One form of wireless communication, the cellular network, now covers this country and has arrived at most major cities in the world. It will only be a short time before one can be in constant cellular contact in any significantly populated American area. Almost anything that can function on a phone line, such as a computer or FAX can now access the cellular system and through that the larger global information network. The cellular system is so advanced and is spreading so rapidly (30 percent to 40 percent annually in the United States, as shown in Figure 3-5) that fiber-optic advocates, who once thought that fiber systems would ultimately be the major system for telephone traffic, now know that catching up and bypassing the advances that have been made by cellular operators is economically impossible.

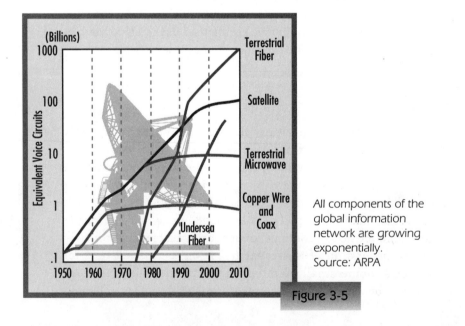

All components of the global information network are growing exponentially.
Source: ARPA

Figure 3-5

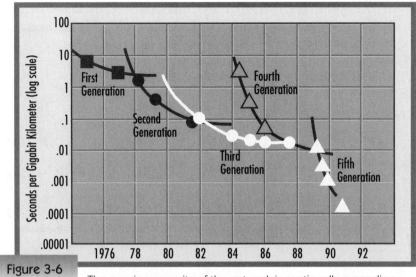

Figure 3-6

The carrying capacity of the network is continually expanding with increases in technology. The fifth generation of fiber optics is almost five orders of magnitude more capable than the first generation. Source: *Scientific American,* January 1992

Fiber-Optic Backbones

This rush to connect computers is obviously not limited to corporations and universities. Whole countries are wiring every home, business, and school in the nation. Japan expects to be completed by 2015. Turkey's system will move some remote locations from the medieval world to the Information Age almost overnight.

In the United States, the initial funding for the first of the latest generation networks that will be a part of a national telecommunications backbone was assured by passage of the Gore bill in December 1991. The prototype is the National Research and Education Network (NREN), which today operates at 45 million bits per second, a capacity that is also increasing geometrically, as shown in Figure 3-6. One study estimates that completion of a universal fiber network could boost U.S. annual productivity growth by 0.4 percent and add $321 billion to the nation's wealth over the next 16 years. The design for another section of this backbone, connecting 21 supercomputers from San Diego to Cornell, was recently announced by the National Science Foundation.

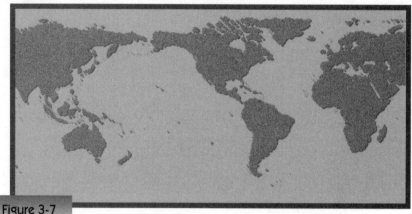

Figure 3-7

Undersea fiber-optic cables virtually connect the world

Undersea Fiber-Optic Cables

A fleet of almost three dozen cable-laying ships is laying undersea fiber-optic cables about as fast as it can, connecting continents and countries together. AT&T's TAT-9 cable, now in service under the Atlantic, can handle 80,000 transmissions at one time and has the capacity to carry in one day what the first cable, installed in 1956, carried in 20 years. Two additional AT&T transatlantic cables are planned, and a transpacific cable will soon increase this company's capacity to some 600,000 simultaneous calls when it begins service in 1995. Figure 3-7 illustrates the proliferation of undersea cables.

In total, by this means alone, there will be more than 1.1 million voice circuits between the United States and Europe by 1996, and 441,000 to Asia. (New techniques in data transmission that were widely deployed in 1993, like the so-called frame-relay format, will raise speeds of transmission nearly thirtyfold.)

Satellite Systems

A number of new communications satellite constellations will be an integral part of the global system. Private global satellite systems are scheduled to come on stream before the end of the decade. Large-scale low-earth-orbit (LEO) systems—like the 66-satellite Iridium system and the newly announced Teledesic 840-craft constellation—will provide telephone, video, and data communications to and from any place on Earth. Chapter 8 has more details on these systems.

The Internet

The growth of the Internet gives one a feel for the magnitude and significance of this evolving global system. Started by the Defense Department's Advanced Research Projects Agency, this "network of networks" connected only four host computer systems in 1968. By 1983, 200 agencies, schools, and corporate research labs were interconnected. In 1990 it was estimated that between 1991 and 1995 the number of international host systems would increase from 500,000 to 10 million. By 1993 the number was already close to 15 million.

In 1993 the "net," as shown in Figure 3-8, was growing at the rate of over 25 percent per *month*. At that rate (which of course cannot continue), every person in the world would be connected by 1997. John Quarterman, a "cyberspace cartographer," said recently that the Internet was "growing so quickly that within five years its theoretical

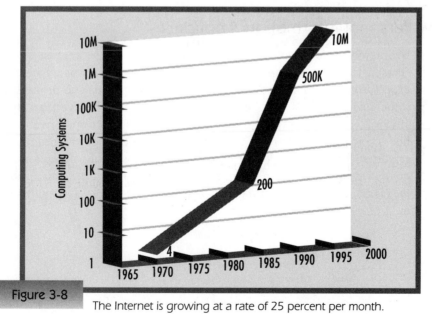

Figure 3-8

The Internet is growing at a rate of 25 percent per month.

Source: ARPA

population will exceed that of any country save China or India." Vinton Cerf, a codesigner of the Internet and now president of the nonprofit Internet Society, predicts there will be 100 million U.S. Internet users by the end of the decade. (That is about 40 percent of the present population.)

In addition to network growth, the capability of the Internet is increasing because of higher transmission speeds (now gigabits per minute), and the reach down to the grassroots (schools, small businesses, libraries, state and local government). Transmissions of packets of information swelled from 50 million a month in 1988 to more than 20 billion a month in 1992.

Already one can interchange mail, documents, books, pictures and photographs, voice and music, video and television images and programs, and films on the Internet. Huge databases located at universities, government agencies, and research institutes are, in many cases, accessible to anyone at no cost. Users can access over a thousand universities with databases of computer programs and other information.

On large commercial service networks like CompuServe (which is connected into the Internet), one can pay bills, shop at thousands of stores, make reservations and buy airplane tickets, monitor the stock market, and research large databases of newspapers, magazines, and encyclopedias, all from a home computer.

New Personal Information Appliances

Ultimately, this space-land-undersea network will be accessed by "personal information appliances," which will include all of what we expect from television, radio, FAX machines, computers, and probably some devices that haven't been thought of yet. Some believe that "By 2015 or so, our planet will be enshrouded in a delicate spiderweb of fiber-optic cable and circled by a galaxy of artificial communications satellites. Either network will be capable of transmitting symphony-quality sounds and video images of astounding clarity to wall-sized panels no thicker than picture frames, mounted in homes and exurban mini-office clusters."

INFORMATION IS THE CAPITAL COMMODITY

We are quickly moving toward the time when anyone can get any kind of information to almost anyone else, anytime. We are also increasingly moving information instead of people. And we're essentially doing it instantly.

Acting much like a body's nervous system, this global network will pulse with data and will be the prime conduit for the capital commodity of the coming age: information. It will allow new ideas to sweep the globe and give extraordinary access to information to those who are connected. As Alvin Toffler suggests, the very concept of power is shifting from being defined by money to being information-based. This, by the way, is exacerbating one of the major problems of the coming decades, the increasing disparity between the have and have-not nations. Toffler, referring to the effect that information technology will have on the tempo of human activity, calls them the fast and slow societies.

Toffler and Japanese futurist Taichi Sakaiya speak of future economies being "knowledge-based." As information becomes more important in the relative success of an individual or group, the most significant resource then becomes the base of knowledge that has been acquired about the particular subject or project. No longer are natural resources, labor pools, and the other traditional metrics of power and wealth as applicable as is the knowledge base that can be drawn on.

The global information network (which is far more refined in the United States than in any other region), is the perfect tool that will allow the sophisticated knowledge worker to mine the databases and knowledgebases of a huge number of sources.

In an age defined by interdependency, this globe-girdling network will also facilitate the interchange of information between and among disciplines, something that has significantly held up the pace of discovery and enlightenment for most of history. On the other hand, when information is the key commodity and the world is wired, then governments may lose their ability to track and tax the transfer of that key commodity across their borders.

ARTIFICIAL INTELLIGENCE

The microprocessor is the keystone for a great number of other technologies. One area that has been under development for some time and that promises significant benefits in the near future is artificial intelligence, or AI. AI is about designing computer programs that think for themselves—that have an aspect of autonomous human logic.

Expert Systems

Expert systems, programs that mimic the decision-making process of an expert in a particular discipline, are the best-known version of this set of computer applications. An expert system might be written to stand in for an insurance application analyst, for example. It would go through the step-by-step process of evaluating each of the processes that a human analyst goes through to determine the quality of an application for insurance. Many thousands of expert systems have been written, each for a specific task.

More generally, AI applications do things like monitoring the usage of long-distance telephone or credit card accounts for anomalous activity. If, for months or years, your telephone credit card bill has averaged $50 a month, and suddenly a series of lengthy international calls pushes your bill up to $200 in a week, an AI program will probably spot the change immediately and flag a human to look into whether your card has been stolen. Similar programs operate large machines, monitor complex systems, and analyze stock market behavior.

Rule-Based

Most AI programs are rule-based—the rules for each and every decision the program might make have been written in computer code and are part of the program. The problem with this approach is that the program knows nothing that it hasn't been told. If a particular rule or situation has not been accurately anticipated and translated into computer code, the application will not respond "correctly."

Put another way, computers do not have common sense. Unless it has been explicitly told in advance, a software program does not know, for example, that when a closet door is opened, the Pacific Ocean will not be lapping over the threshold. It also does not know how people think and how governments and interest groups might react to given situations. Where system relationships are relatively mechanical, well understood, and predictable, AI has worked rather well. But when a domain of interest begins to include those areas dominated by human decisions, values, and interests, then the software comes up short.

This huge body of information, which most of us take for granted, has been assumed to be an impassable roadblock to building causal systems intelligent enough to tackle some of the major problems that humankind routinely faces. It now appears that obstruction may be about to be removed.

CYC: A HUGE BREAKTHROUGH

In the early 1980s, the Microelectronics and Computing Corporation (MCC) in Austin, Texas, a consortium of U.S. computer companies, banded together to attempt to build a sixth-generation computer. One of their major projects, Cyc (from enCYClopedia), centered in their artificial intelligence lab, became an attempt to overcome this common-sense problem with symbolic processing.

Writing Down All Common Sense

Headed by Dr. Douglas Lenat, Cyc is, simply stated, a heroic attempt to identify the component parts of the common understanding of human beings and to enter them, rule by rule, into a knowledgebase. As Lenat puts it:

> Perhaps the hardest truth to face, one that AI has been trying to wriggle out of for 34 years, is that there is probably no elegant, effortless way to obtain this immense knowledge base. Rather, the bulk of the effort must (at least initially) be manual entry of assertion after assertion.

> Half a decade ago, we introduced our research plans for Cyc, a decade-long, two person-century effort we had recently begun at MCC to manually construct such a knowledge base.

The details of their work are interesting:

The bulk of the effort is currently devoted to identifying, formalizing, and entering microtheories of various topics (such as shopping, containers, emotions, etc.). We follow a process that begins with a statement, in English, of the microtheory. On the way to our goal, we identify and make precise those Cyc concepts necessary to state the knowledge in axiomatic form. To test that adequately, stories that deal with the topic are represented in Cyc; we then pose questions that any reader ought to be able to answer after having read the story.

...The aim is that one day Cyc ought to contain enough common sense knowledge to support natural language understanding capabilities that enable it to read through and assimilate any encyclopedia article, that is, to be able to answer the sorts of questions that you and I could after having just read any article, questions that neither you nor I nor Cyc could be expected to answer beforehand.

Cyc Will Assimilate Information on Its Own

Doug Lenat and his friends are building the basis for HAL, the computer in the movie *2001*. In the next couple of years, they expect to have entered enough basic information into Cyc that it can begin to assimilate information on its own—it already understands about 75 percent of a *USA Today*-type article. Online texts will be piped into the system and the role of humans in the project would "transition from the brain surgeons to tutors, answering Cyc's questions about the difficult sentences and passages." The system would learn as fast as information could be fed to it.

Cyc Will Be Packaged with PCs

All of the MCC corporations that are participants in the Cyc project are individually designing applications that will use Cyc's abilities. Lenat believes that because Apple Computer, Inc. is involved, it is likely that by 1996 Apple computers will come bundled with a CD-ROM Cyc disk that represents the common sense of a human. Digital Equipment Corporation is building a Cyc-based application whose job it is to ask questions about a potential Digital customer and come up with the right size computer for them. This would involve an internal Cyc intellectual process that, given that the basic business unit in a hotel is a room and at a car rental agency a car, would be able to use relatively deep understanding of what goes on at each place to decide that for a hospital, which is a new potential customer, the right business unit is a bed, not a room.

The Cyc team is working on an initial product, a smart spreadsheet application. Because it is intelligent, it will understand what the numbers in each spreadsheet cell stand for. It will also know what is reasonable in most situations, and will highlight those cells that end up with illogical data.

Cyc is obviously important. It should be able to mimic different human cultures, responding as they might from varying philosophical and religious bases. It is far enough along that its inventors believe that by 1995 it should be able to deal concurrently and in real time in dynamic, technical, and conceptual situations with many humans—and probably teach them something in the process.

PARALLEL PROCESSING

Some of the shortcomings of traditional rule-based systems have been sidestepped by parallel processing machines and their associated software. Parallel processors utilize many, in some cases thousands, of parallel-configured microprocessors, which function together roughly like a human brain. Each processor is like a neuron, connected to many other neurons, hence they are often called neural networks. Like a brain, parallel processing systems can *learn*—determine new information on their own—by analyzing inputs and making independent deductions about relative importance and significance.

AI has great potential for automating many activities that are expensive, dangerous, or time consuming. So far, the great claims that have been made for the future of AI have not come to fruition; but it seems likely that with the combination of some of the new developments mentioned here, along with significant advances in microprocessor power, the next two decades will see a significant expansion, both in quantity and quality, of artificial intelligence applications.

At this time, however, there is one major stumbling block: Parallel processors cannot effectively deal with complex problems involving hundreds of inputs. Although parallel processors have made significant contributions in the areas of signal processing, forecasting, and pattern recognition, because of the intrinsic bounds of the most commonly used architecture, such systems reach their limit of effectiveness with problems that have more than about 300 inputs or components. Above that level they run into a "brick wall," and effectiveness is reduced to very low levels. This is a problem because most issues of major significance involve many more than 300 components.

HOLOGRAPHIC NEURAL TECHNOLOGY

Enter Holographic Neural Technology (HNet) developed by the AND Corporation in Hamilton, Ontario. This new approach to neural networks effectively eliminates the brick wall and increases the productivity of neural net systems by orders of magnitude.

Computer software is almost exclusively written in real numbers (0,1,2,3). HNet is written in complex numbers (real and imaginary). The basic equations are variations of those that describe holographic principles, as well as of those from quantum theory. This approach allows information to be superimposed or enfolded by a convolution of complex vectors. Very large numbers of patterns can be overlaid onto a single neuron cell. Unlike the usual methodology, which may require many thousands of learning cycles to reach a level of effectiveness, HNet systems reportedly require only one to three (at the most) passes to map the desired information. Projects that take a hour and a half to run on a very large conventional neural array can be completed within 1/40 of a second using HNet. HNet capability increases with an increase in the number of inputs to the neuron cell, and a single cell can accommodate 64,000 inputs.

HNet Could Make Voice Recognition Affordable

Consider the application of this technology to voice recognition, as an example. Any given word can be vocalized in a wide number of tones and inflections, over different durations. HNet is capable of explicitly mapping a virtually unlimited variety of vocal intonations onto the same storage set and differentiating between this class and a very large set of alternate structures. This suggests a capability for voice recognition systems operating at a complexity far beyond that currently achievable. There is a distinct opportunity to create real-time speaker-independent and continuous voice recognition systems. Very few neurons (four to six cells) are required to accurately identify spoken words from a large vocabulary after only a single exposure to each word. Large training sets may be employed to allow the system to recognize virtually any form or utterance of the word.

HNet is a pattern recognition system. Many, many things in life are patterns of one type or another. Most of what we see, think, and analyze are combinations of generally understood components arrayed in different configurations. Behavior is defined in patterns. Different cultures behave in varying patterns. Trends are patterns. With development, this could be an enabling technology with immense possibilities.

VIRTUAL REALITY: CHANGING WHAT IS REAL

We define reality by our senses. What we see, hear, feel, smell, and taste is the sum of our experience. By saturating the sight and sound senses, a good movie can "transport" a viewer to a different place and time. In much the same way, modern computers can synthetically produce video, audio, and kinesthetic inputs that generate for the participating subject a "virtual reality."

Howard Rheingold, author of *Virtual Reality,* describes the process as being a new technology that creates the illusion of being immersed in an artificial world, or of being present in a remote location in the physical world. To enter virtual reality (VR), a person puts on a head-mounted display (HMD) that looks like a scuba mask. A pair of tiny television tubes, special optics and wide-angle lenses, and a device that tracks the position of the user's head are mounted in the HMD so that when it is worn, the normal view of the outside world is completely blocked: In place of the physical world, the user sees a stereographic, three-dimensional computer graphics depiction of a world model that exists only in a computer. The person is immersed in the artificial world and is able to navigate within that world and to manipulate objects in it.

VR Will Revolutionize Many Areas of Life

Virtual reality, another profound technology based on the microprocessor, enables us to move information rather than people. Because of this it is already beginning to revolutionize many areas of life. Doctors located in the United States have done operations on patients halfway around the world using VR. In their "eyephones" they saw the world exactly as it was at the other location and picked up and used instruments by remote control.

Research scientists are also using VR in interesting ways. Rheingold talks of "grabbing" and moving two molecules at one university installation. He could "feel" when the two otherwise invisible particles were bumped into each other, and could see and feel the difference when he configured them in different ways.

The military has built a huge system, called SimNet, which allows participants scattered around the world to simultaneously visit the same virtual battlefield in whatever type of airplane, tank, or other equipment they use. Ships in the Pacific can have real-time radar displays that look like the "battlefield" located in North Carolina. Army tankers in trainers in Fort Knox, Kentucky, look out of their sights and see the same location—only from each of their individual perspectives. Air Force pilots in California can "fly" missions in support of the other participants from their trainers at the same time.

The SimNet team (from the Simulation Lab, at the Institute for Defense in Alexandria, Virginia) has built a database of one of the major battles of Desert Storm, and is able to replay that engagement varying almost every possible aspect: time of day, number of enemy tanks, location of enemy and friendly installations, view of the battlefield from any location in the area, and so on. Trainees can rerun the battle, trying different tactics and observing the change in results.

Virtual reality's biggest short-term commercial potential lies in the entertainment area. VR arcade games are already in many malls, and Sega, a major electronic game manufacturer, has introduced a home VR game.

The Virtual Office

Steve Pruitt and Tom Barett, in *Cyberspace, First Steps,* give a practical example of how VR might be used. They draw the mental picture of the Corporate Virtual Workspace (CVW) of the near future. "Austin," a software engineer, gets up in the morning, goes to his study, and dons his customized computer clothing. He logs in to the fiber-optic network via his home reality engine, and in doing so connects his Personal Virtual Workspace (PVW) with his employer's CVW.

> As he steps into the CVW, he enters a vast network of interconnected hallways in a bustling virtual corporation. He enters the CVW via his office, number 16 on the red hallway... . Even though Austin's PVW appears to his colleagues as just another office along the red hallway, he has organized *his* perception of it much differently. He perceives it as a control center at the confluence of several hallways. Upon entering his PVW, Austin can look out the window and down about 30 feet to view three hallways converging below him.

The red hallway contains offices and conference rooms for software engineers from all over the world who are involved in the CVW. The blue hallway is reserved for client offices (PVWs). The third, green, hallway supports a collection of resource centers. Vast collections of trade journals and technical publications are available in different resource centers that are organized around particular subject areas.

In much the same way that he would in a present-day office building, Austin interfaces with his colleagues and clients by walking down the hall and entering offices, does research using huge knowledgebases, and tests his products—all without leaving his study at home.

VR holds the promise of revolutionizing business, education (for history, go back and walk through ancient Rome), travel (preview your trip by visiting your destination first virtually), and even common conversations (talk with relatives in a different state as if you were in their home).

Jaron Lanier, the premier philosopher of virtual reality, believes strongly that VR is to the Information Age what the telephone was to the Industrial Age. The first phase of this trend, telecommuting, is already in place. Many people now work at home, and stay in touch via e-mail, FAX, and telephone.

VIRTUAL PROTOTYPING

One of the major problems in designing vehicles, particularly high-speed aircraft, is anticipating how the device will actually react with the external atmosphere when it is built. The amount of drag and stability that a vehicle ultimately exhibits is a function of a very complex interaction between the surface of the body and the air or water that it is driven through.

The equations that describe fluid flow (the so-called Navier-Stokes equations) are theoretically capable of exactly defining the flow down to the smallest turbulent eddy. The problem is that they are so complex—perhaps even the *most* complex relationships, in the case of hypersonic flight—that it has been impossible in the past to produce more than general approximations by mathematical means. The accepted solution has been to build scale models of the vehicle, put them in a wind tunnel or test tank, and then measure the forces on the model as air or water passes by.

This type of testing is representative of the basic approach people have had to take in many different areas. If the problem is too complex to model mathematically, one has to go out and test a model and note the results. This is about to change.

The power of specialized computers is becoming so great that engineers will soon be able to directly model 80 percent of the fluid flow across a complex shape, and approximate less than 20 percent of the energy contained in the very small eddy currents. In theory, this would allow ships, aircraft, cars, and trains (and anything else that flows through a fluid) to be completely designed with computers and not have to be physically tested. Shapes could be quickly adjusted to optimum, and a wide variety of external conditions could be virtually simulated. This direct solution of turbulence would allow virtual prototyping: A device could be built completely in a computer, and its characteristics would almost exactly be known before one piece of metal was cut or machined.

What might the implications of this capability be in other areas, such as social science or biology? Might we soon be able to anticipate the behavior of complex relationships that we have always left to fate?

BIOTECHNOLOGY: SHAPING ORGANIC LIFE

Biotechnology—using technology to manipulate and take advantage of the genetic structure of plants, animals, and humans—is another revolutionary technology. Biotech is very broad. It includes fish farming, forestry, production of enzymes for laundry detergents, and genetic engineering of bacteria to clean up oil spills, kill insect larvae, or produce insulin. Biogeneticists are even working on designing better food and animals. It is therefore difficult to construct generalizations about the discipline. Companies in the United States, Europe, and Japan, for example, are producing products in the areas of health care and pharmaceuticals, agriculture, chemicals, energy, and bioremediation.

Health Care

At this time, most biotech products are primarily in the health care area. Although the pace has slowed considerably since then, a venture fund report on the biotech industry in 1992 suggested that "Never have so many revolutionary therapies come into the marketplace in so short a time. More products were approved in 1991 than in any of the previous eight years. More potential products are awaiting approval than at any time in the industry's history." Some three dozen genetically engineered pharmaceuticals are now on the market, designed to treat everything from leukemia, diabetes, hepatitis, and hemophilia to AIDS. Still a couple of years away in preclinical stages of development are start-ups focused on neurobiologicals, treatments for Alzheimer's disease, Parkinson's disease, brain and spinal injuries, migraine headaches, schizophrenia, and anxiety.

Some of the advances in this area are a direct result of developments in computer technology. Computer modeling allows scientists to design specific molecules to interact with cellular receptors to block or enhance the desired cellular activity. Increasingly sophisticated computer models of human and animal systems, coupled with the mapping of the human genome, are also hastening the day when animals will not be used in testing these new chemicals.

Agriculture

Biotech is both producing pharmaceuticals *for* plants and manufacturing pharmaceuticals *from* plants. A number of genetically engineered seed stocks have been developed for corn and sunflowers that offer much better resistance to pests and disease and that produce products with enhanced natural characteristics. The first gene-spliced tomato made an ill-fated run at the supermarket shelves in 1993, but the final chapter in that story has not yet been written. Calgene Fresh, Inc. designed a tomato that resists softening and will also have an extended shelf life, but even with federal government approval, a spate of negative press (and a boycott by major chefs) delayed the scheduled introduction.

There is a lot of biotech activity taking place in the tomato patch. Firms in the United States and Europe are working on other gene-spliced varieties. Some tomatoes have been manufactured that will grow in one-half salt water. Richard Carlson and Bruce Goldman, in their book, *2020 Visions, Long View of a Changing World,* catalog the huge industrial potential for biologically altered organisms:

> Genetically engineered microorganisms already concentrate ore and clean up toxic-waste spills. Many chemical processes today involve high temperatures, high pressures, imperfect catalysts, and toxic by-products and are, therefore, energy-inefficient and hazardous. For thousands of years, "yeasts of burden" have been put to work in the brewing and baking industries. Thirty years from now, noiseless assembly lines of yeast or bacterial cultures—each batch genetically altered to contain a particular ultra-efficient enzyme catalyzing one step of a chemical process—will produce bulk chemicals of exquisite purity; additional genetically engineered microorganisms will gobble up any toxic wastes produced. Scientists will design new enzymes by computer, then build them from scratch in the laboratory and insert them into microbes that will do their bidding.

> © 1990. Reprinted with permission from The Stanford Alumni Association.

At Louisiana State University, write John Naisbitt and Patricia Aburdene in *Megatrends 2000,* biochemists are working on engineering potatoes, rice, and cassava that will have the protein value of meat. They mention a company in New Jersey that uses genetic selection to grow strains of popcorn that have their own butterlike flavor. At Cornell University scientists are breeding apples that will not turn brown when cut up and exposed to air. The Japanese have developed a seedless watermelon. Pest- and frost-resistant fertilizers are on the market. Genetically engineered seeds for alfalfa plants that have more protein, require less fertilizer, and grow faster were tested in 1989.

In January 1988, on a farm in Wheelock, Texas, seven genetically identical purebred calves were produced from genetically engineered embryos. In theory, thousands of identical animals could be produced through cloning.

Genetically altered cows in England are presently being used to produce drugs in their milk, thereby replacing whole pharmaceuticals factories. Continuing the process, the cows give birth to calves that also produce the desired medicines. Sheep produce a blood-clotting chemical in their milk that is used to treat hemophiliacs. Mice have produced a blood clot-dissolving substance that is used to treat human heart attacks. The same chemical is being derived from a herd of altered goats. As few as 300 goats could provide the world's requirements for this medicine.

ESA Agenetics, an agricultural biology firm, is using plant tissue culture to develop a commercial production capability for taxol, a scarce compound derived from the Pacific yew tree, which shows promise as a treatment for ovarian cancer. Technology columnist Michael Schrage believes that the $20 billion global market in conventional chemical pesticides needs rethinking. "Ecologists, entomologists, and agribusiness folks are growing more enthusiastic about the potential of biopesticides—targeted technologies designed around biological principles, as opposed to the traditional chemical weapons of mass destruction."

The Human Genome Project

The best-known biotechnology project is the $3 billion, 15-year global attempt to map the human genome—the entire human genetic code. The objective is to determine the location, identification, and function of each of the 50,000 to 100,000 genes that go into making a human being. Rapid progress is being made in the United States, and major efforts are underway in Europe, Japan, and the former Soviet Union.

Researchers will concentrate first on specific areas that they believe are responsible for such diseases as cystic fibrosis, muscular dystrophy, Huntington's disease, Alzheimer's disease, and manic depressive disease. With such genetic libraries available, the greatest initial impact will be on detection, diagnosis, screening, and genetic counseling rather than on therapy.

Principal Benefits

Biotechnology brings with it a host of benefits. Perhaps the most significant will be the greater understanding of the role of genes in illness, and the ability to compensate for them. There will be a great increase in the number of recognized disorders. Biotech includes the most fruitful area of research for understanding the nervous system, molecular neurobiology. Huge health benefits have also attended classical genetic methods, with the production of the organism that produces penicillin, for example, increasing more than 100 times in the past several decades.

Biotech may also have some unanticipated social and economic benefits. Some plants like tobacco, for example, which currently have a rather negative reputation, are ideal vehicles for gene-splicing and the production of valuable pharmaceuticals. If crops like tobacco (and coca) suddenly became more valuable as breeding stock for medicines than for smoking, the result could be a dramatic change in the economic and geopolitical realities for significant regions of the world.

Ethical Issues

As with other emerging technologies, many people have legitimate concerns that biotechnology is "messing with nature." Critics have developed rather frightening (though others say far-fetched) scenarios about new gene-altered organisms running amok. There seem to be two major areas of concern: understanding and controlling the research that is being done, and dealing equitably with the knowledge that is produced.

Controlling Research

There are potential problems associated with the control and direction of biotechnology research. The root problem, say critics like Michael Fox in his book *Superpigs and Wondercorn,* is not so much with the technology itself as with our worldview. "I am not in principle opposed to biotechnology. However, I am opposed to those who seek to use it only for profit regardless of ethical, social, environmental, and animal-welfare concerns." In reaction to the news about the gene-spliced tomatoes that were tried in supermarkets last year, Greg Goldin, in the August 21, 1992 edition of *LA Weekly,* points out that the tomato's selling point is its improved taste, a byproduct of biotechnology being used to fix a human-created problem. Store-bought tomatoes are tasteless because they are harvested green to allow growers to ship the vegetables across the country without spoiling. "Presumably, the tomato will taste better because they will stay on the vine approximately three to five days longer than a conventional tomato," Goldin writes. But why should people in the Midwest and East depend on huge tomato farms in California and Mexico in the first place, when the crop can be grown locally by smaller growers? It is our industrialized system of farming that needs to be changed, not the genetic blueprints of our food, argues Goldin.

Concern of Technologists

Others have questions as well. A British survey reported in *New Scientist,* on August 29, 1992, found that environmentally concerned technologists are even more suspicious of biotechnology applications than the general public. The *New York Times* reported that more than a thousand of America's most respected chefs have promised not to serve genetically altered foods in their restaurants, and have called on the FDA to strictly regulate the foods. There have been problems. In one case, 31 people died and 1,500 contracted a potentially fatal blood disease after ingesting a genetically engineered batch of L-tryptophan, a dietary supplement.

Genetic code changes naturally, though slowly, in nature. Scientists point out that these are often genetic anomalies, and so the distinction between natural and unnatural is not clear. There also appears to be a natural limit on how far organisms can be altered. Experts say that radically different varieties are impossible. So far, the major concerns about runaway organisms have been unfounded, and there is already a rapidly growing collection of products in the marketplace to evaluate.

Dealing with the New Knowledge

With knowledge comes power, and biotech is about to generate an explosion of knowledge about human beings. Tests will soon enable us to know in our youth whether we are carrying genes that will predispose us to disease in our later years, and whether we can pass on these genes to our children. This ability will lead to a subtle but important change in perception. Science will begin to relate mental differences and health problems with molecular differences in brain and genetic abnormalities. No longer will it be random fate that deals some a bad hand of personal cards, it will be the result of "who they are." When the direct link between one's genetic code and one's personal characterists is established, knowledge about a person's particular code will become extraordinarily powerful.

For example, think of how people relate to each other based on their perception of each other's intelligence. Might a person's personal genetic map take on a similar role as an arbiter of social value? How will employers and insurers use this information?

Perhaps, as Theodore Friedmann suggests in *The Genetic Revolution,* there is little conceptually new here—the same issues exist with medical information. But the magnitude of the problem and its potential for abuse is much greater. As he says:

> We shall come to understand which genes are responsible for defects in development and metabolism, tumor development, aging, neuropsychiatric disorders, and many other illnesses. As a result, we shall be capable of undertaking screening and detection programs for many disorders, which often lack effective therapy. We shall also be able to use genetic tests to identify individuals for medico-legal and forensic purposes. These applications raise troublesome questions, however, regarding the involuntary application of predictive genetic techniques in other areas, such as employment and medical or life insurance settings, where the rights of individuals, employers, and insurance companies will inevitably clash.

Some therefore argue that personal genetic information should be kept confidential. Nevertheless, a recent survey indicated that the majority of Americans believe that personal genetic information should be publicly available.

Ultimately, of course, there are the *Brave New World* considerations. Should we (governments?) "engineer" humans not only to eliminate disease, but also to enhance other characteristics (big, dumb guys for laborers, for example). Those days appear to be more than two decades distant, but we are not currently without problems. Arthur L. Caplan, director of the University of Minnesota's Center for Biomedical Ethics, recently said, "Just the Human Genome Project alone is the Full Employment Act for bioethicists." Those bioethicists and many new ones who will follow them will have their plates full for years.

COMPUTATIONAL CHEMISTRY/MATERIALS SCIENCE

Paulina Borsook, writing in the *Whole Earth Review,* in Fall 1992, said,

> Computational chemists are on the verge of being able to create, on demand, materials that have specific properties, whether of flexibility, durability or the ability to turn an alluring shade of lavender when the late-afternoon light strikes them at a certain angle.

> Dirac, one of the fathers of quantum mechanics, said in 1929 that "The underlying physical laws necessary ... for a large part of physics and the whole of chemistry are completely known, and the difficulty is only that the exact applications of laws lead to equations much too complicated to be solvable." No chemist has had the time or the means to perform the calculations, so no chemical engineer has been able to use the solutions to build new materials. It is turning out that advances in computer hardware and software may prove Dirac wrong: Supercomputers and new ways to use them may finally be able to solve the equations that explain and describe the material universe.

Along with nanotechnology, computational chemistry is fundamentally changing the relationship of humans to materials. Throughout history designers have built things with the materials that were available. While new materials, such as plastics, certainly were invented over time, those new compositions were often, if not always, the result of trial and error and broad experimentation. Sometimes even mistakes yielded unintended materials with practical value.

As Borsook said, computers are changing all that. Today a designer working on a bridge looks up the characteristics of the materials that are available, and computes how much of it is required to handle the loads that are anticipated. We are approaching the time when the designer of a bridge may compute the characteristics of the structural material required to meet her needs (flexibility, abrasion resistance, color, strength) and then order the mill to manufacture the material in the configurations she desires.

Computational chemists are beginning to be able to do the calculations that explain the most basic properties of materials and then should be able to translate that information into practical use. "In

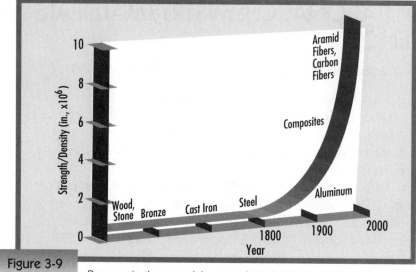

Figure 3-9 Progress in the materials strength-to-density ratio of materials is increasing exponentially. Source: National Academy Press

theory," Borsook says, "it is possible to apply the equations to understand precisely how it is that a piece of wood is brown and hard. Once that mathematical solution is understood, it should be a matter of engineering to create other substances that are equally brown and hard." The computers required for this breakthrough are very large, but with the rate at which computing power is increasing, this capability should soon become more common.

Recent Progress

Progress in materials design is greatly advancing both in conventional materials science terms and in molecular design, as illustrated in Figure 3-9. Richard Carlson and Bruce Goldman summarize some of the progress:

■ *Catalysts* accelerate chemical reactions. Almost all the major catalysts were discovered by accident; we did not know why they worked. Now we design them. A catalyst that could efficiently make methanol from natural gas would revolutionize the energy sector.

■ *Alloys* are combinations of metallic compounds. Alloys lighter than aluminum and stronger than steel are under development.

■ *Plastics* are hydrocarbon materials; some of the best new plastics are derived from wood, not oil.

■ *Composites* such as wood are the key to the superiority of biological materials. New artificial composites outclass all other materials in strength per pound.

■ *Ceramics* were the first human-created materials (pottery), products of an art that changed very little for thousands of years. A moldable ceramic that could safely substitute for steel in automobile engines would double fuel efficiency. We are now designing ceramics that are perfect electrical conductors. Commercial microelectronics devices employing ceramic superconductors are just beginning to show up. A University of Houston team has devised a continuous process for fashioning rods of ceramic superconducting material—a step toward the production of practical superconducting electric power cables and electromagnets.

One of the advantages of these new materials is that they will last longer. Because of increased use of ceramics and plastics, one estimate says that the average life of cars will increase from 10 years to 20 years by the year 2000.

Futurist Jerome Glenn has written that 40 percent of all engineering research in the 1980s was in materials science.

New materials are being developed, such as metal that dissolves in water, alloys of metal and plastic, and materials that seem invisible (clear like glass but will not reflect light from the surface like glass).

Other new materials will include those that form with light, such as methyl methacrylate. When this plastic powder is sprayed in an area that has lasers shot through, it will form small plastic filaments to make a three-dimensional object. The object will dissolve by altering the light wave pattern and form a new shape. Improved materials will be forged by containerless melting, called "acoustic levitation," which is created by 160-decibel sound waves. The waves suspend materials in furnaces for cleaner melting to produce improved fiber optics and lenses.

EMERGING TECHNOLOGIES

A number of scientific endeavors appear close to breakthroughs. With the amount of effort that is being given to each—and with the advances being made in computational capability—it is not far-fetched

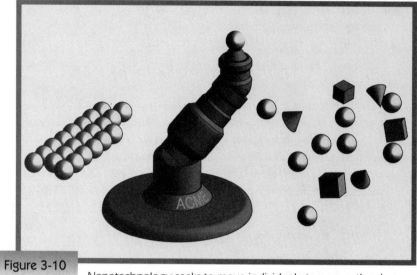

Figure 3-10   Nanotechnology seeks to move individual atoms exactly where they are needed, at blinding speeds

to believe that we will see significant developments within the next two decades. In each case, the implications would make major changes in the way we live.

Molecular Nanotechnology

Throughout history, most everything that has been manufactured by humans was built from the top down: A larger piece of material was shaped into something smaller. Regardless of the material, and except in some esoteric chemical processes, this has been the universal approach. Now, however, this is about to change, and the implications will be immense.

Molecular nanotechnology is the process of building things from the bottom up. As illustrated in Figure 3-10, nanotech starts with individual atoms and uses molecular-sized machines to put them together in predetermined configurations. It is a "revolution times a revolution," and will mean thorough and inexpensive control of the structure of matter. As Eric Drexler, who coined the term nanotechnology, says, "Twentieth-century technology is headed for the junk heap."

Nanotechnology has profound applications virtually everywhere—including energy, environment, communications, space development, construction and housing, food, population, defense, transportation, and health, to name a few. As Dr. Drexler has written in *Nanosystems—Molecular Machinery, Manufacturing, and Computation,*

> Molecular manufacturing will be able to make almost anything with little labor, land, or maintenance, with high productivity, and with modest requirements for materials and energy. Its products will themselves be extremely productive, as energy producers, as materials collectors, and as manufacturing equipment. There has never been a technology with this combination of characteristics, so historical analogies must be used with care. Perhaps the best analogy is this: Molecular manufacturing will do for matter processing what the computer has [and will] do for information processing.

Nanomachines would be machines—shafts, bearings, cams, articulated arms, pumps, and so on—put together in combinations that function like small factories. Drexler's computations suggest that a mature molecular manufacturing capability will be able to make products for about the cost of the raw materials alone. This doesn't take into account the front-end design cost, but in any case, things will be much cheaper. Furthermore, products will be typically 80 times more durable and stronger, since they can be made of diamond as easily as of any other material. These characteristics suggest, for example, that solar cells can be made efficient, as cheap as newspaper, and as tough as asphalt—tough enough to use for resurfacing roads—collecting energy without displacing any more grass and trees.

Minuscule devices smaller than red blood cells could cruise the bloodstream searching for fat deposits and infectious organisms. When they found them they would destroy them. Medical devices built to the size of bacteria and viruses, using artificial intelligence from tiny computers, could continuously monitor and repair the operation of every cell in the body. Cells that "sagged" from their original configuration could be fixed, thereby slowing aging.

Pocket supercomputers could become commonplace. Using nanoprocessors almost too small to see, they would have millions of times the computing capability of the largest supercomputer today. One estimate suggests that components of molecular size could make a single desktop computer of the future more powerful than all the computers in existence today combined. If clusters of a few atoms could be the elements of an information code, every book, magazine, pamphlet, and newspaper ever printed, complete with graphics, could be stored in a volume the size of a credit card.

Major increases in communications capacity could be had with data-cables that included "amplifiers, nanocomputers, switching nodes, and everything else needed, and were loaded with software that 'knows' how to act to transmit data reliably."

Agriculture can become much more efficient as plants are grown in greenhouses, produced by molecular manufacturing. Nanomachines could eliminate pests and automate the growing process.

In terms of transportation, underground tunnels for high-speed trains could be bored cheaply and lined with very durable materials. They could probably be made less expensively than roads. Energy would be much cheaper and not fossil-based.

Molecular nanotechnology would establish conclusively the definition of power in terms of information, as Alvin Toffler suggested. Individuals would have the ability to have an extraordinary influence on humankind—with no resource other than a computer and the knowledge of how to use it effectively. In one Drexler scenario, Singapore becomes a global military power because two smart researchers with computers and nanomanufacturing capability design a nanomachine that threatens everyone else.

The first usable products from molecular manufacturing should be available by 2002, followed quickly by further rapid development. In addition to all of the obvious advantages of being able to manufacture consumer items inexpensively, in time, molecular nanotechnology could conceivably eliminate the world's problems of food, energy, environmental pollution, and waste.

Cold Fusion

Room-temperature fusion research, effectively dismissed by the U.S. scientific community, is alive and well in Japan and India. Cold fusion is the process that researchers believe takes place when an electric current is sent into palladium and platinum electrodes that are immersed in a jar of heavy water, rich in deuterium. The experimental results sometimes suggest that lots of energy is released in the process.

If that is true, it could lead to the development of a virtually unlimited supply of inexpensive energy.

The idea was largely deprecated, especially in the United States, when the experiments of Drs. Pons and Fleischmann, who claimed to have discovered cold fusion, could not be replicated by other researchers. But in 1989 Japanese scientists, intrigued with the concept, invited Stanley Pons and Martin Fleischmann to Japan to discuss their work. Since then, Japanese experimenters have apparently replicated Pons's and Fleischmann's findings, producing up to 70 percent more energy in heat than was put into the system in electricity.

The *Wall Street Journal* reported that five to six labs in the United States, India, and Japan have conducted experiments that produced as much as three to four times more excess heat than the input power, although researchers are questioning whether it is "cold fusion" they are seeing, or another phenomenon.

Twenty or so university groups are pursuing cold fusion in Japan, mostly on a financial shoestring. But now Japan's Ministry of International Trade and Industry (MITI) has decided to fund some of the research. If this effort produces more concrete results, it could open a whole new avenue of potential future energy sources and would shift the focus of a good deal of energy research.

Condensed Charge Technology

Condensed charge technology (CCT) produces small, tightly bound, dense clusters of electronic charge (balls of lightning) of enormous power relative to their small size. The underlying phenomena are ubiquitous: spark/arcs of almost any kind—lightning, for example, or even the familiar blue "pop" one gets from static buildup when one walks across a carpet on a dry day and then touches a metal object. In its uncontrolled state, such "spark," large and small, is destructive and disruptive, and so scientists and engineers have traditionally labored to eliminate it completely from all electronic systems. Thus the most important point about CCT—and that which distinguishes it from any other electronics technology—is that ways have been discovered to integrate spark, or more accurately micro-arc discharges, into, not out of, a system, thereby taking advantage of the many beneficial properties inherent to the phenomenon. It can then be made, controlled, and used on command.

The developers of CCT at the Institute for Advanced Research in Austin, Texas, say that a number of applications could be in the prototype stage within a year or two:

- 60 to 90+ GHz radars the size of a credit card and made largely out of plastic could be used for automobile and aviation applications

- Tiny, throwaway X-ray devices that can be made small enough to be put inside of a hypodermic needle, for medical, lithography, and inspection

- Super-quick computers and switching devices with subnanosecond speeds

- Extremely high-frequency communications—90 GHz is very easy

- Small, stand-alone energy conversion/storage devices; zero-point energy generators take energy out of vacuums

- Deep space propulsion—taking energy out of the vacuum of space and therefore eliminating the need for carrying fuel

- Very high-resolution, full-color flat panel displays with higher resolution and far less cost than HDTV

HOLOGRAPHY

Although to date it has primarily been used for novel and small security applications (like credit cards), holography shows the possibility of significant development in the next two decades. The real breakthrough will come when full-color, three-dimensional projection becomes possible. Large-scale (about 2-foot-square) flat holograms in full color are now displayed at MIT's media lab. Media lab leaders believe that holographic color projection may be ten years away.

If holographic information can be digitized and therefore transmitted (assuming adequate bandwidth) to remote locations, a whole new era will open up. "Picturephones" may project the person on the other end of the line into the middle of your room as a "light sculpture." Conference calls would take on a new meaning in this context, and could well threaten the growth and function of airlines and other transportation.

ROBOTICS

Although robotics have a well-established position in Japanese industry, it has not, so far, turned out to be what many prognosticators thought it would. Businesses in the United States and Europe have not embraced industrial robots at nearly the rate of the Japanese, and other, more consumer-oriented versions are very much in the development phase. Even so, industry sources believe that the use of robots to make clothes will be commonplace by the turn of the century.

This general trend is likely to change, perhaps dramatically, in the next two decades. Robots are, in one sense, collections of other more basic technologies: sensors, controlling and analysis software, pattern recognition capabilities, and so on. Most all of these other technologies will make significant strides in capability, size, power requirements, and other design characteristics, and the synergy of the combination of these other advances should accrue directly to robotics.

BIOELECTRONIC DEVICES

Jerome Glenn, in his book, *Future Mind,* says that according to Dr. William Dobelle of the Institute for Artificial Organs in New York City, "By the turn of the century, every major organ except the brain and central nervous system will have artificial replacements." The Japanese government believes these advances will come between 2000 and 2010.

A strategic component of this trend is the nerve chip, which is being developed by scientists at Stanford University Medical Center with support from the Veterans Administration. It is an electronic interface for individual nerve cells to communicate with a computer. This human-machine linkage will be used to program and control artificial hands, regenerate damaged nerves, and enhance human capability in many other ways.

If artificial eyes convert video to nerve signals, won't it be possible to use the same technique to superimpose computer-generated information in front of one's field of view?

Combinations Produce Synergy

The above trends, as profound and interesting as they are, tell only half the story. When one considers what might happen when different technology disciplines intersect, often a synergy can be seen that spurs on development in all fields and produces synthetic products that are much more powerful than a single technology might produce. Here are just a few possible combinations:

A-Life, Molecular Design, and Nanotechnology

Consider, for example, the interaction between artificial life, computational chemistry, and nanotechnology. One can easily see these disciplines becoming married together at the point where molecular design determines the molecular characteristics required for a particular device or organism, nanotechnology provides the design of the nanomachine needed to configure the structure, and artificial life brings the control software routines that allow the nano-assemblers to operate autonomously. This, of course, is the breeding ground for both the best- and worst-case scenarios having to do with nanotechnology and a-life.

Advanced Pattern Recognition and Shrinking Electronics

Early versions of pattern recognition, of the kind that will become refined with holographic neural technology, are already making themselves known. There are reports that automatic translation of text messages sent on overseas telephone lines will soon be common. An American would send data in English and would receive the Japanese response to the message in English. Similarly, the Japanese speaker would send and receive in Japanese. This capability will surely expand, in time, to include voice communications.

Soon after that, industry observers believe that electronics will become small enough, and pattern-recognition efficient enough, that people may carry a card-deck-sized unit (in a shirt pocket, perhaps) that, through an ear plug, would provide automatic translation of voices in the vicinity. These translation devices could have a profound effect on geopolitics and social attitudes. Military special operating forces predict such devices by 2000 (see Appendix B).

The foremost restriction on communication, and therefore on understanding and relationships between two cultures, is language. When one can communicate openly with others, a much greater amount of knowledge and understanding immediately becomes likely. Technology of this kind would begin to eliminate one of the major barriers to integration and cooperation. It is hard to overestimate what the significance of this might be.

Virtual Reality and Computational Science

The day may soon come when molecular designers manipulate molecules by "reaching out and grabbing them" with virtual reality equipment. Combinations could be tried and then easily reconfigured at will.

Virtual Reality and Global Networks

This is the *Neuromancer* combination. In his book by that title, William Gibson told of a world where information thieves "jack-in" to "cyber-space" and find themselves virtually navigating throughout the communication networks of the globe. Different databases "look" different, security systems appear forbidding, and large visual avenues connect the various peripherals. This is not too far-fetched. People are already working on pieces of what might ultimately amount to this capability.

Artificial Life, Cyc, and the Internet

One of the most interesting ideas cruising around the Internet is that of "knowbots," or knowledge-robots. These software entities would be designed to operate like a very sophisticated research assistant. You would tell your knowbot what information you were looking for, and then send it off into cyberspace. The knowbot would be intelligent, and have Cyc-supplied common sense—it would learn and make decisions as it navigated from database to database trying to find the basic requested information, and making excursions to chase down sources mentioned in footnotes. After its foray, a completed digest would be deposited back at your doorstep.

One wonders what might result from the merger of knowbots and a-life. What if knowbots were really autonomous? What if they developed a mind or interests of their own? What if a knowbot decided that it was interested in power or money?

Advanced Pattern Recognition and Computers

One of the most intriguing coming capabilities of powerful pattern recognition software is word recognition. As mentioned, large machines are already being readied to do translation. A more common use will be to interface with computers and ultimately with other "appliances."

The *Wall Street Journal* reports that IBM has been working to develop a voice-activated computer for more than 20 years and has now begun to sell its first product. It has a vocabulary of only 20,000 words and sells for about $10,000. Other manufacturers have systems in use with vocabularies of up to 50,000 words. The new Lexus has a car phone that can be activated by voice. Just tell it which of the preset numbers to dial and it does so automatically.

It seems clear that with advanced pattern recognition capability we will soon be able to easily and fully communicate verbally with common computers. Close behind that should be voice recognition systems for homes to control heat, lighting, and other appliances. Most anything that requires a manual input of settings is a candidate for vocal control.

Communications Networks, Condensed Charge Technology, and Cyc

When Cyc brings common sense to computer systems, those capabilities will very soon find themselves in America's living rooms. Televisions (or "personal information appliances," as they will probably be known) will become intelligent and interactive, learning individual preferences and adjusting to different viewers. This kind of capability coupled with large, quarter-inch thick, flat screen monitors will give viewers a "window" into cyberspace. An extraordinary selection of topics will be available, spanning the areas of entertainment, education, shopping, business, and communication. The trends are already in place: 500-channel television will be in homes when this book goes to press; hang-on-the-wall gas-plasma color monitors are available in Japan now.

Intelligent Cars

Three new technologies are being brought together for the car of the future, with some expected to be ready in five years. In 1993, *The New York Times* summarized some developments.

■■ *Vision enhancement*—An infrared camera near the rearview mirror would allow the driver to "see" in the dark or through fog or snow. A heads-up display, similar to those used in tanks and warplanes, is being developed to allow the image to appear on the windshield in front of the driver.

■■ *Autonomous Cruise Control*—Using a radar signal reflected off the car in front, a computer calculates the time distance, based on speed, between the two cars and adjusts the throttle and the brakes to maintain a specified margin.

■■ *Collision Avoidance*—Using a combination of sensors, radar, and video cameras, an on-board computer will determine key aspects of the car's environment. For example, it would warn the driver of traffic over three lanes, or of obstacles, or if it senses that the car is going off the road. In the future it may have the capacity to adjust the steering of the vehicle.

Business Systems

To see where the rest of the world will be in five or ten years, look at where the leading edge is today. In business technology integration, USAA, the giant insurance company that services military officers and their families, is at the forefront. *Fortune* summarized their operation in 1993.

USAA's system employees scan all incoming mail that contains more than a check into their computer network—nearly 14 million pieces a year. When a customer buys insurance on jewelry, say, which takes effect 24 hours after the postmark on the appraisal mailed to USAA, he can telephone a service rep and get an instant answer to the question, "Did my appraisal come, and can my wife wear her necklace to the theater tonight?"

When a customer calls to say she has had an accident, the system will digitize and store her phone call and scan the photos and the reports from doctors, lawyers, and appraisers that she sends in. The company is also working with IBM to develop a multimedia system. In a lawsuit, for example, it would allow a USAA employee to hold a conference call with a lawyer in Miami and a doctor in Fort Lauderdale, in which all participants can hear the recording of the original telephone accident report and view on their screens documents, X-rays of injuries, and color videos of damage to the car.

WHAT IS TECHNOLOGY DOING TO US?

When we think about the magnitude and rate of change of technology that we are experiencing we need to ask, What is this technology doing to us? What are we becoming? Technology does not just change the way we do things. It changes the way those who use it see and understand themselves and the world in which they live. A philosophy comes bundled with every new technology; when one is embraced, the other is there as well. We need only consider how cars, telephones, television, and airplanes have changed our perspectives of ourselves, our relationships to others around us, and our understanding of the world, to know that this is true. The example of the role of television in society is most illuminating.

Television: The Most Powerful Mind Tool

Recently, the Canadian Innu Indian tribe, which had been moved in 1967 against their will to an isolated island, was successful in getting the government to move them back to the mainland, where they could resume their traditional caribou hunting. All adults in the tribe were unemployed, and their living conditions were so poor that 25 people committed suicide last year, out of a total population of about 500. Television, which allowed them to see how their lives compared with those who were better off, eventually mobilized them. They made a videotape of their situation, highlighting Innu youth sniffing gasoline and talking about suicide, and gave it to the Canadian Broadcasting Corporation. The outpouring of concern from Canadian viewers forced the government to agree to move them back to the mainland. Television made them aware of their condition, and television made others aware of it.

In India, Star TV, the new Asian satellite television programming service, has been in service only since September 1992. Already, however, it has been cited as the chief inspiration for major changes in Indian culture, such as fashion and popular music, and has increased the demand for brand-name products. It has also engendered vigorous new calls to liberate the Indian economy from once-dominant state control. For viewers from Burma to Beijing, this window on the West (MTV, BBC, American sitcoms, soap operas, and so on) is providing a bewildering taste of commercials and unfiltered news. *Santa Barbara* is the highest rated show on Indian television. Tom Hunter, vice president for international programming at MTV, said, "India is the most enthusiastic audience we have."

As Van Wishard observed in *The American Future,*

> Television is the most effective instrument ever invented for influencing the minds of masses of people. (It took 40 years for *Gone with the Wind* to sell 21 million copies. But, in one night, 55 million people watched the movie version.) As *The Wall Street Journal* noted, "TV has become more significant than any other single factor in shaping the way most of us view our world … more than religion or politics."

Some argue that television may become the most important force for globalization, the major driver that integrates Europe culturally and linguistically.

What Will Computers Mean for the Future?

In light of the experience with television, one wonders what the impact will be of computers, biotech, virtual reality, and some of the other technologies we have discussed here. This is far more powerful technology than the world has ever experienced before—with profound capabilities for both good and bad.

We are entering a super renaissance—a time when we are changing life, creating life, linking people together much closer and faster, changing the meaning of reality, time, space, and location. We are about to design and manipulate matter, and are on the edge of tapping the greatest energy source in the universe. What will this all mean to us as human beings? These are perhaps the most important questions that we should be asking about this new age of information and technology.

TECHNOLOGY TRENDS AND DRIVING FORCES

Throughout this brief excursion through the breeding ground of technology, a number of trends and forces have become apparent. Take a good look at them, for they will shape the way humans interact with and adapt to the extraordinary world that is emerging.

- *Speed.* Everything is going faster, so speed is increasingly being used to measure value.

- *Trend toward light.* Light is the fastest communications medium with the greatest capacity to carry information. There is a clear trend toward using light and optics in information technology.

- *Information.* Information, in the form of knowledge, is what allows speed. Information is the capital commodity of the future.

- *Going to digital.* Information in all forms is being converted into digital forms so that it all can be transmitted through the same cables, fibers, frequencies, and equipment.

- *Global connectivity.* Everything is being connected to everything else. In time, almost every home, office, school, and government agency in the developed world will be connected in a huge information system by way of every computer and telephone.

- *Global accessibility.* There will be no place on the surface of the earth where one can't access the whole network.

- *Moving information instead of people.* Information technology is making it more advantageous—in almost every situation—to move information rather than people.

- *Power migrating toward individuals.* Individual people will increasingly be able to access, analyze, and manipulate information (the source of wealth and power) without the need for larger organizations like corporations and governments.

- *Systems thinking.* All things of importance are coming to be understood as systems; in most cases, they are highly complex, dynamic sets of sometimes widely dispersed components. In science, particularly, there is a move toward the integration of disciplines. In manufacturing, there is a move toward concurrent engineering.

- *Organic models.* Large systems increasingly are seen to mirror and behave like organic models.

- *Increasing complexity.* Manufactured systems are becoming more complex and faster.

- *Increasing vulnerability.* The more complex a system becomes, the more likely the chance of system failure. There are unknown secondary effects and particularly vulnerable nodes.

▪ *Qualitative becoming more important than quantitative.* Software, intuition, speed, and quality are areas that are pregnant with opportunity.

▪ *New structures and organizations.* All structures and organizations (business, government, education) will reconfigure to adapt to the faster, more interconnected world and to the more powerful and enabled individual.

▪ *New info-criminals.* There will be a significant increase in information crime, more viruses, and a growing international information criminal element.

▪ *Unpredictability.* Technology is a huge effort with lots of people in an extremely complex context where there are fundamental changes in the underlying principles. We almost certainly will not anticipate some of the significant changes that will certainly occur.

▪ *Punctuated change.* One or more of the reality-exploding nascent technologies will come to fruition soon and send shock waves throughout the global system.

▪ *Isolated perspective.* Most of the population of the world will not participate in this revolution. The implications of that are profound.

Although great good has obviously come from our use of technology—and extraordinary benefits loom on the horizon—humans have not always used our tools in the best way for our planet. Next, we'll see how that technology can be applied to perhaps the most important problem of our age: the decreasing quality of the environment that supports life on this planet.

CHAPTER

4

Environmental Alert!

For better or worse, the nineties will be a decisive decade for the planet and its inhabitants.

—Lester Brown

For the first time in history, the influence of human beings on this planet has become so great the we appear to be threatening the most fundamental systems that sustain human life. A variety of ominous signs have recently been observed. Are these "miner's canaries" warnings to us that something very serious is afoot?

■ The beds of sea grass, vital nurseries for many marine species, are getting smaller in many coastal areas. The cycles of algae plagues, which kill much sea life, are becoming more intense.

■ There has been a 50 percent drop in the sperm count of men worldwide since 1944.

■ In Greek waters, biologists are seeking the reason for the large-scale death of sea sponges. In France, scientists are puzzled about an affliction that has caused sea urchins to lose their spikes.

■ The atmospheric level of heat-trapping carbon dioxide is now 26 percent higher than the preindustrial concentration, and continues to rise.

■ A virus killed 18,000 seals in the North Sea in 1988, while another strain caused a major epidemic among dolphins in the western Mediterranean in 1990. "Now we have it in the eastern Mediterranean," said Seamus Kennedy of the British Government Veterinary Sciences Laboratories in Belfast. "We have gone back over the literature for more than a hundred years and we found nothing like it, no other cluster of virulent epidemics like we have now."

■ The earth's surface was warmer in 1990 than in any year since recordkeeping began in the mid-nineteenth century; six of the seven warmest years on record have occurred since 1980.

■ All around the world, species of frogs and toads that have existed for 200 million years are simultaneously dying, without any clear indication why. "Frogs are in essence a messenger," says David B. Wake, director of the Museum of Vertebrate Zoology at the University of California. "This is about biodiversity and disintegration, the destruction of our total environment." A new university study suggests that part of the problem may be increased ultraviolet radiation from the thinning ozone layer.

■ Every fall millions of reddish-brown and black Monarch butterflies move southward across the United States to Mexico, where they spend the winter. But in 1993 some of the normally crowded migration routes were nearly empty. There is a 90 percent decline of the creatures in the eastern United States.

■ The North Atlantic has become much rougher over the last 30 years, scientists say and, surprisingly, gustier winds are not to blame. Average waves were about 30 percent higher in the mid-1980s than during the 1960s. Recent studies indicate that waves were nearly 50 percent higher at the end of the 1980s than they were 30 years ago. The cause is puzzling. Wind affects waves, but average wind speeds in the North Atlantic have not increased.

■ The number and intensity of earthquakes in California is increasing. The average size has increased six times in the past decade, much greater than in previous decades.

These indicators, and many more, suggest that humans are doing things to the earth that have consequences that we don't understand. Ultimately, they could be disastrous.

IT'S A PROBLEM OF NUMBERS AND TECHNOLOGY

The problem is one of both numbers and technology. Human beings produce waste. Today, the amount of waste we produce is so great that it has the distinct possibility of changing the behavior of the earth's ecological system.

In theory, the planet could well sustain the growth in population that we are experiencing if we didn't produce so much waste—waste that we dump into the larger environment. On one hand, those of us in developed countries, particularly in the United States, live personal lifestyles that are relative orgies of waste. In 1990, for example, the average North American produced 1,518 pounds of municipal solid waste per year, compared to 722 pounds produced by the average western European.

On the other hand, much of our technology for producing energy, products, and food generate by-products that at some time in the process are perceived to have no obvious value and are discarded. Ninety-eight percent of the materials used in U.S. manufacturing do not go into the end product, but are part of packaging, transportation, and so on. Eighty percent of all products are thrown away after one use. Our commercial, governmental, and educational processes are also intrinsically wasteful systems. If we were dealing with small numbers of people, the effect wouldn't be as significant; but both the population and the scale of industrialism are growing exponentially.

For the first time, the effect of humans has become so great that our presence may be changing the way the global system operates. Consider, for example, that the global industrial system is steadily growing larger in comparison with the natural environment. The

Global Business Network's Hardin Tibbs has shown that the amount of human-generated waste is reaching damaging levels, regardless of whether or not it is composed of traditional pollutants. The industrial flows of nitrogen and sulfur are equivalent to or greater than the natural flows; for metals such as lead, cadmium, zinc, arsenic, mercury, nickel, and vanadium, industrial flows (as shown in Table 4-1) are as much as double the natural flows, and for lead, 12 times greater.

Metals	Artificial	Natural	Ratio
Lead	332	28	11.9
Zinc	132	45	2.9
Copper	35	6.1	5.7
Arsenic	19	12	1.6
Antimony	3.5	2.6	1.3
Cadmium	7.6	1.4	5.4

Table 4-1. 1990 worldwide emissions to atmosphere (thousands of tons)

Source: J.O., Nriagu, "Global Metal Pollution," *Environment* 32(7): 7–32

Presently we have serious, but fuzzy indicators of stress on the system. The most worrisome concern is the possibility that we are seeing the initial indications—the first weak signals—that the system, in response to this extraordinary increase in pollution, is about to shift to a different operating state, a state that may not support life as we know it.

This is not just idle speculation. Recent research on ice core conductivity data from the cap ice in Greenland shows that throughout the planet's history the Earth experienced climate shifts between glacial conditions and warmer weather in just a year or two. Climate experts now must strive to explain the causes of such abrupt changes. The new findings raise questions about whether global warming from greenhouse gas pollution could soon knock the climate into a new pattern. "The lesson to me would be that the atmospheric system clearly has inherent instabilities, and it can clearly change in extremely short times. It ought to add just one more note of caution to proceed slowly," says Gifford Miller, a geologist with the University of Colorado at Boulder.

Perhaps one of the most basic problems is that we don't value waste. The mechanisms that we use to keep score don't include pollutants in the cost of what we do. The big question is whether new ideas about this problem will be embraced soon enough.

There are both encouraging and discouraging signs. According to a 22-nation poll by the Gallup organization, environmental damage, once dismissed as a concern of the rich, is now widely recognized as a threat to human health. Protecting the environment has joined problems of economic livelihood, crime, and violence as major concerns around the world. On the other hand, there are also indicators that people are becoming bored with activists harping about pollution, and are beginning to discount some of the more startling trends.

Let us look at the effect of humans on the environment, starting with the most serious, intractable long-range problems, and working our way through solvable but politically difficult issues, to overlooked major issues, and finally to important but lesser issues.

LONG-RANGE PROBLEMS

The really big problems are those with a global scope that require global intervention, are poorly understood, or involve our favorite addictions (like cars, political power, money, or seaside resorts). Let's take a look at three: the atmosphere, the loss of coastal wetlands, and the loss of rainforests.

The Atmosphere: The Air We Breathe

The "atmosphere problem" has two related but different aspects: one, the depletion of upper atmosphere ozone, which shields the earth from ultraviolet radiation that can kill the organic life that produces food and oxygen; and two, increases in carbon dioxide and other "greenhouse gasses," which keep heat from radiating back into space, thereby causing the earth to heat up.

The Hole in the Ozone

At the simplest level, life survives on Earth because it is shielded from the sun's deadly ultraviolet rays by the ozone layer, located 30 miles above the planet's surface. Ozone is an unstable molecule, consisting of three oxygen atoms, which absorbs ultraviolet (UV) light. The ultraviolet light that penetrates the ozone layer is enough to cause sunburn, cataracts, and skin cancer in humans and animals.

Moreover, it appears that a rather small additional decrease in the thickness of the ozone layer might produce major ecological disruptions. The problems would start in the oceans. Already, in some regions of the world, seasonal variations show a 7 percent to 8 percent thinning of the ozone layer. When it reaches an estimated 11 percent to 12 percent, some scientists believe the plankton in the oceans would begin to die. Phytoplankton, the microscopic plants and animals that drift with the currents of the oceans, are the base of the oceanic food chain. They also produce oxygen—40 percent to 50 percent of the planet's atmospheric oxygen, and the free oxygen in the ocean that is necessary for fish to live. As the plankton began to die, so would the fish that depend on them. Since 70 percent of the food protein eaten by humans living on the Pacific Rim comes from the sea, it is clear that even in its early stages, this is a potential catastrophe.

The large "hole" in the ozone that opens up seasonally over Antarctica appears to be getting larger in each succeeding year. People in Patagonia, for example, have been advised by the Argentine Health Ministry to stay indoors as much as possible during September and October. In Queensland, in northeastern Australia, more than 75 percent of citizens who have reached the age of 65 have some form of skin cancer, and children are required by law to wear large hats and neck scarves to and from school for protection against ultraviolet radiation. At the Royal Society for the Prevention of Cruelty to Animals in Sydney, about 500 cases of feline skin cancer are turning up each year now—a few years ago there were almost none. Although the thinning has been greatest near the geographic poles, there is reason to believe that this protective layer is also thinning in the mid-latitudes.

We don't know for certain what is causing the atmospheric ozone depletion. A great number of researchers suspect that a major culprit is the use of chlorofluorocarbon (CFC) substances. CFC gases are used in refrigeration and fire extinguishers, and at one time were the most common spray-can propellants. Alarm over the potential effects of CFCs on the ozone layer has precipitated a global commitment to eliminate their use by the year 2000. Recent reports estimate that after that date there will be a significant decrease in CFCs in the atmosphere and that their effect, if any, on the ozone layer will similarly decrease (over many decades) toward normal levels.

The case, however, is not that clear. There are great disparities in the amount of UV light that reaches different regions of the world. The closer to the equator you live, the more natural UV radiation you receive. Some places get significantly more than others, with no apparent effect on plants, animals, and humans. Sometimes UV levels fluctuate wildly on time scales that range from minutes to years.

But if CFCs are the culprits, then we may be living with them for a long time. They do not cause damage until years after they have been released in the lower atmosphere. Even if the use of these chemicals were completely stopped today, yesterday's releases would still be causing damage for almost a decade. Clearly, the degradation may increase before the situation begins to get better.

The problems of the Australians and Argentinians may seem far removed from those in North America, but they're not. The protective ozone shield in heavily populated latitudes of the northern hemisphere is thinning twice as fast as scientists thought just a few years ago. And scientists have recorded higher levels of ozone-depleting chlorine over northern New England and Canada than they have ever recorded over Antarctica or anywhere else.

Even though there is some question about what really is causing the thinning of the ozone layer, author Frederik Phol's prudent admonition seems reasonable: "If the consensus of most scientists is wrong, and there is, after all, no danger to the ozone layer, then doing what the consensus suggests will unnecessarily cost us all some money and inconvenience. But if the scientists are right and we do nothing, it will cost us a great deal more money, a great deal more inconvenience, and a very great deal of suffering and human lives."

Global Warming: The Greenhouse Effect

The other major atmospheric issue is global warming. It is probably the least understood, perhaps the most intractable, and potentially the most disturbing of the environmental climate problems.

A report published in late 1990 by the Intergovernmental Panel on Climate Change (IPCC) warned that global warming could soon force temperatures higher than they have been in hundreds of thousands of years. The report, prepared by 170 scientists from all over the world, concluded that if the world's economies follow a "business as usual" scenario, increases in carbon dioxide and other trace gasses in the atmosphere will cause the earth's average temperature to rise by about 5 degrees Fahrenheit before the end of the century.

When most of us see a quote like this, we don't know how to interpret it. To understand it better, we should ask three questions: What is it? Is it happening? What are the consequences?

What is it? The greenhouse effect refers to the way the greenhouse gases (CO_2, chlorofluorocarbons, methane, and nitrogen oxides) trap heat from the surface of the earth by preventing it from radiating back into space—just as closing the windows heats the interior of a car on a sunny winter day. Without the greenhouse effect, the average temperature of the planet would be below freezing.

Is it happening? Evidence is beginning to show that it is. We know that the earth's surface was warmer in 1990 than in any year since recordkeeping began in the mid-nineteenth century; six of the seven warmest years on record have occurred since 1980; and the atmospheric level of heat-trapping carbon dioxide is now 26 percent higher than the preindustrial concentration, and continuing to climb.

What are the consequences? Initially, a warming climate may not seem like a problem. It would make the climate in New England like the climate of New Jersey, and it would extend the growing season for the Scandinavian countries and Russia. However, there are some associated issues.

The first issue is the rise in sea level. As the temperature rises, more of the polar ice could melt, raising the level of the sea. Scientists predict different increases, from a few inches to as much as 50 feet, depending on the model used. George Denton and Terry Hughs, of the University of Maine at Orono, suggest that if the temperature rises sufficiently to melt the Ross ice shelf, much of the West Antarctic ice sheet (which is grounded below sea level) may break off from its moorings, become unstable, and raise the sea level as much as 6 meters (approximately 18 feet)—considerably more than would be predicted on the basis of temperature alone. The loss of the reflective properties of the ice sheet would raise the temperature even more, which would melt more ice, thus generating a positive feedback condition.

According to Harold Borns, glaciologist and scientist with the West Antarctic Initiative on Ice Sheet Stability, research conducted during the 1992 field season may indicate that the West Antarctic ice sheet may already be becoming unstable, as isolated streams of ice are moving with great speed through the ice sheet.

Yet another issue is the stability of climate during times of change. From research into other times of climate change, such as the Little Ice Age, scientists at the University of Maine's Quaternary Studies Institute have suggested that although average temperature may rise, the rise may not be smooth. In one year the growing season may be longer than the mean annual growing season, only to be followed by a year in which it may be considerably shorter. This climatic instability would be a major problem for large-scale agriculture, which relies on regular growing length. We can breed a plant to accommodate cold or heat, but not both.

The lack of reflectivity of the ice raises another major issue: The earth may not be able to continue to dissipate energy as effectively as it has in the past. Some scientists now believe that heat and other energy reflected and generated by the planet have in the past been rather easily transmitted away from the surface through the layer of atmosphere that surrounds it. With increasing greenhouse gases reducing the ability of the earth to radiate energy, a number of other phenomena are taking over to allow the escape of this energy. Increased numbers of hurricanes, earthquakes, and volcanoes, they believe, could well be providing new paths for release now that the efficiency of conventional radiation paths is decreasing. The rising level of wind speeds accompanying some recent major weather events is believed to be a direct result of this insulative factor, which has increased the slope of the gradient between high- and low-pressure atmospheric systems.

The most important problem associated with the greenhouse effect is that we don't know how to proceed, and we may not have time to do what is needed. There are some nascent proposals for collecting large amounts of CO_2—large-scale ocean farming of kelp, for example—but these are years away from being effectively evaluated and implemented. Scientific research based on observed trends and their complex interactions is slow. By the time we have sufficient evidence to be sure about our observations, it may be far too late to do anything about it.

Loss of Coastal Wetlands

The intractability of the problem of disappearing wetlands is due to the combined effects of global warming, political pressure, and real estate development. Coastal wetlands are a productive and dynamic environment, critical to both ocean life and waterfowl. When sea levels are constant, wetlands extend themselves by capturing silt. They grow on one side, extending out into the water, and retreat on the other, as marsh slowly becomes dry land. If the sea level rises, the process reverses; marsh is lost to the sea, but reclaimed from once-dry land. Rivers bring fresh water and silt, and replenish the barrier beaches that protect the marshes. Beaches are unstable land forms of sand that are changed constantly by the action of wind and waves. They guard the Atlantic and Gulf Coasts and are flooded several times a century.

Now we have dammed the rivers, cutting the flow of silt and sand, and we have also heated the atmosphere, raising the sea level. The result has been accelerated flooding and loss of both barrier beaches and coastal marshes. Louisiana alone is already losing 30,000 acres of coastal marsh per year.

A sensible policy would be to abandon the barrier-beaches to the sea as the water level rises and to let them recreate themselves inland. Money should be spent on resettlement and issues of greater environmental priority. Fighting the sea is hopeless and impossibly expensive. The current federal flood insurance guarantee program alone would suffer losses of hundreds of billions of dollars to sea-level rise. Here is one of many examples where economics and the environment are allied against traditional politics.

Loss of Rainforests

An even more urgent problem, which owes its intractability to its global nature and to the poverty and politics of the third world, is the loss of rainforests. The United Nations Food and Agriculture Organization report of September 1991 showed that the world's tropical forests are being cut down at a rate 40 percent faster today than they were ten years ago. In 1990 approximately 42 million acres of tropical forest were cleared, an area about the size of Washington state. This is more than an acre every second—much of it cleared and burned by poor people desperate for land and food. Rainforest loss

▬ contributes to greenhouse warming

▬ destroys the cleansing ability of the atmosphere

▬ threatens wildlife

▬ creates new semi-deserts

▬ increases large-scale flooding

Tree burning accounts for about 30 percent of worldwide total CO_2 emissions. Brazil, whose annual rainforest losses run to between 12.5

million and 20.5 million acres, released as much carbon into the atmosphere by burning trees as the United States did burning fossil fuels.

The problem centers around poverty and politics. The governments of Latin America and Indonesia are faced with overpopulation and political turmoil in the cities, and are using their rainforest frontiers as an escape valve. These policies produce short-term economic benefits from logging (timber is one of the few raw materials that has risen in price) and immediate—and generally unsustainable—increases in agricultural output.

Forest destruction is being financed, directly or indirectly, by loans from the World Bank as well as private U.S., Japanese, and European lenders. Happily, U.S. political pressure is already reducing World Bank loans for environmentally destructive projects. However, even with these efforts, significant further loss of rainforest is inevitable.

SOLVABLE BUT POLITICALLY DIFFICULT ISSUES

Some issues are easier to solve technologically, but political realities make solutions much more difficult. Three of these problems are acid rain, disappearing habitat, and drinking water.

Acid Rain Kills Trees and Fish

Rainfall is naturally acidic, but its acidity is increased by the burning of fuel containing sulfur (mostly from coal), which produces sulfur dioxide, and by high-temperature combustion (car and truck exhaust), which creates nitrogen oxides. Lakes and trees are the primary victims of acid rain. In lakes it kills off algae, the bottom of the aquatic food chain. This results in the death of fish, many invertebrates, and fish eaters, such as loons. You can tell where acid rain has affected lakes—they are crystal clear and sterile. Acidic mists also kill high-altitude coniferous forests in both the United States and Europe.

The obstacles to reducing acid rain are mostly political. In the United States, the automobile industry and high-sulphur coal interests in the East and economically weak Midwest oppose strict sulfur standards. Old (pre-1975) power plants are allowed to operate with few controls, while new power plants (not just those causing the damage) are required to install expensive control technology. Thus dirtier, older plants are kept in operation well past the time when they should have been retired.

Rapidly Disappearing Habitat

In addition to the problems of loss of marshes and coastal wetlands, and clear-cutting and burning of rainforests, we are losing a wide variety of plant and animal life. This is due primarily to destruction of habitat.

Species Are Disappearing

Biologist E. O. Wilson estimates that people have recently begun to extinguish other creatures at a rate thousands of times the natural rate. We already know the value of many of these species. Less well known, and reason for serious concern, is the role that many of these disappearing creatures play in the larger environmental system within which we live. For example:

- Venom from a viper that lives in the rainforest is important to the manufacture of the preferred prescription drug for high blood pressure, capoten.

- Waterfowl populations in the United States have dropped by 30 percent since 1970. Songbird populations are suffering sharp declines or local extinctions, and mallard and pintail duck populations are down 50 percent since the 1950s.

- The White House Council on Environmental Quality estimates that 30 percent of the continent's freshwater fish are threatened with extinction.

- Fish and shellfish catches in the Southeast have dropped 42 percent since 1982.

The Rape of the Oceans

Commercial ocean fishing is raping the seas. Worldwide, 13 of the 17 principal fishing zones are depleted or in steep decline. As the global population has exploded, fishing has tried to keep up with the demand, growing by more than 50 percent in one generation. But this pressure could not be maintained, and now precipitous drops in catches mean that almost all of some species have been caught and many others may

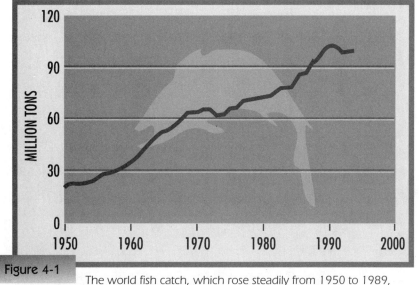

Figure 4-1 The world fish catch, which rose steadily from 1950 to 1989, began to fall in 1990. Source: FAO

have been mortally wounded. "Tuna are doomed," explains one fisherman, quoted in the *Wall Street Journal.* "They're too valuable to live." Figure 4-1 shows the beginning of the drop.

Fifteen years ago, foreign high-technology fish factories (ships that catch and process on board) were working off our coasts, destroying our fisheries. The United States declared a 200-mile limit of national jurisdiction to hold off foreign fleets.

U.S. fishermen, encouraged by the government and the 200-mile limit, invested in high technology. They built bigger ships equipped with sonar and electronic fish finders, electric harpoons, and spotter planes for giant tuna. This started an addictive cycle: The more technology the fishermen bought, the more fish they had to catch; the more fish they caught, the fewer fish there were, which in turn increased the reliance on high technology.

Since the beginning of the 200-mile limit, U.S. fish stocks have declined. In the Atlantic 9 of 12 of the valuable ground fish stocks are decimated. The haddock catch is reduced to a fifth of what it was. Cod, flounder, tuna, Atlantic salmon, and swordfish stocks are depleted. Oyster and clam catches are both down by half. Where fishermen once brought back 50,000 pounds of fish from a three-day trip, now the best

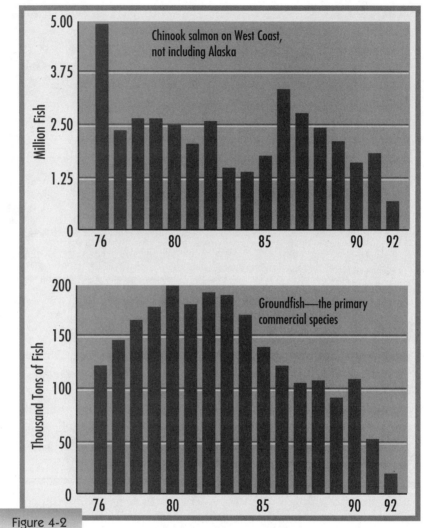

Figure 4-2

U.S. chinook salmon and groundfish catches have dropped precipitously since 1976. Source: National Marine Fisheries Service

outfitted and most expensive boats work twice as long to bring back less than half as much. The cost to New England has been 14,000 jobs. Salmon stocks of Washington, Oregon, and California are almost nonexistent (as shown in Figure 4-2), and for the first time there may be no ocean salmon fishing on the West Coast in 1994.

Woods Hole Oceanographic Institute scientists predict that the response to this trend will be growing near-term legislation of fishing stock in order to sustain these natural resources. Already the New England Fishery Management Council is considering drastic conservation measures that would essentially cut the catches in half over the next five to seven years in order to give the stocks a chance to rebuild.

But a number of issues contribute to this problem, not just overfishing. Therefore it's questionable whether aquatic populations can be effectively replenished any time soon. In part, it's a system problem. Some endangered species we can save, and we're trying. But when we look at species loss on a case-by-case basis, we may win the battle and lose the war, for most species loss is due to habitat destruction. If we exhaust our energy in saving a few species and fail to halt the destruction of the oceans, coastal wetlands, and forests, humans and all species will suffer the consequences. We need to see the problem of species loss as an indicator of the global problems of habitat and climate change and attack it at that level.

Problems with Drinking Water

Most of the water on Earth is not drinkable: 97 percent is seawater, 2 percent is locked in ice caps and glaciers, and a large portion of the remaining 1 percent lies too far underground to reach. Of the tiny sliver that remains (see Figure 4-3), human populations—from the slums of South America to the overburdened farms of China—are outstripping the limited stock of fresh water throughout the third world.

In the past we have been distracted by issues of security and economics; now the ecological crises we have ignored may threaten as strongly as any enemy. For example:

▪ Water could be the first resource that puts a limit on human population and economic growth. According to the United Nations, 40,000 children die every day, many of them the victims of the water crisis.

▪ Countries are already prepared to go to war over oil; in the near future, water could be the catalyst for armed conflict.

Rain is the primary source of fresh water. A reduction of precipitation often results in serious droughts, as 80 arid and semi-arid countries with 40 percent of the world's population know well. Although global circulation models generally predict that precipitation will gradually increase between 4 and 12 percent if carbon levels in the atmosphere

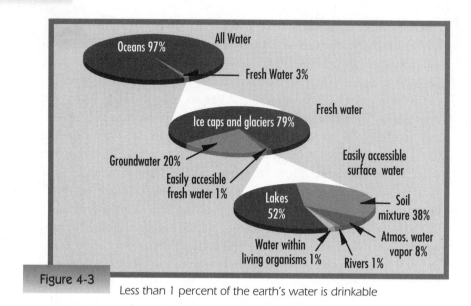

Figure 4-3

Less than 1 percent of the earth's water is drinkable

double (12 to 36 percent in higher latitudes), clean water for drinking may still be a problem due to industrial pollution.

Sandra Postel of the Worldwatch Institute summarized the situation in *Last Oasis: Facing Water Scarcity:*

> There is a large unmet demand for household water. Nearly one out of every three people in the developing world—some 1.2 billion people in all—do not have access to a safe and reliable supply for their daily needs. Often they resort to shallow wells or stagnant pools that are easily contaminated with human and animal waste. As a result, waterborne diseases account for an estimated 80 percent of all illnesses in developing countries. And women and children walk several kilometers each day just to collect enough water for drinking, cooking, and cleaning.
>
> [Considering rainwater,] nine out of 14 countries in the Middle East already face water-scarce conditions, making it the most concentrated region of water scarcity in the world. [This forces reliance on desalination of sea water and the mining of transnational aquifers, which is often unsustainable. Transnational rivers also then become a drinking water supply source, with all of their historical problems of controversy and violent conflict.] Populations in six of [these countries] are projected to double within 25 years, and so a rapid tightening of

supplies is inevitable. With virtually all Middle East rivers being shared by several nations, tensions over water rights are a potent political force throughout the region, and could ignite during this decade.

The arid kingdom of Saudi Arabia, which pumps 75 percent of its water from fossil groundwater, represents one of the most egregious cases of unsustainable water use in the world today. A major push by the Saudi government to raise food self-sufficiency largely explains the escalation in groundwater pumping. The Libyans are also linking their economic fate to a nonrenewable water supply. Engineers project that the wells will run dry within 40 to 60 years.

In and around Beijing, water tables have been dropping 1 to 2 meters a year, and a third of its wells have reportedly gone dry. About a hundred Chinese cities and towns, mostly in the northern and coastal regions, have suffered shortages in recent years. This North China Plain area, with a population of 200 million, will have 6 percent less water than needed by 2000. The daily shortfall in Beijing alone will be 66 percent of that city's current consumption. The Chinese government is aware of these figures, and is thinking about a massive project to divert the waters of the Yangtze River near Shanghai a total distance of 1,190 kilometers overland to Beijing, to compensate for increased water needs.

The litany of problem areas is long:

- At least 8,000 Indian villages have no local water supply at all. Their residents must hike long distances to the nearest well or river.

- In Russia, the mismanagement of land around the Aral Sea has cut it off from its sources of water, causing the volume of the once giant lake to shrink by two-thirds in 30 years. Now storms of salt and pesticides swirl up from the receding shoreline, contaminating the land and afflicting millions of Usbeks with gastritis, typhoid, and throat cancer.

- In the Western United States, four years of drought in the late 1980s and early 1990s left municipalities and agricultural interests tussling over diminishing water stocks.

- In Mexico, as many as 30 million people do not have safe drinking water. A government report there asserts that "water will be a limiting factor for the country's future development." The demands of Mexico City's 20 million people are causing the level of their main aquifer to drop as much as 3.4 meters (11 feet) annually.

Mohammed El-Ashry of the World Resources Institute estimates that around the world 65 percent to 70 percent of the water people use is lost to evaporation, leaks, and other inefficiencies. Additionally, in the developing world, over 95 percent of the urban sewage is discharged directly into surface waters without treatment, increasing the likelihood that what water there is, will be polluted.

The scarcity of fresh water for agriculture makes famines more likely every year. Because of the dependence of many countries on U.S. food exports, a two-year drought in the U.S. breadbasket could rapidly lead to a global food calamity.

The Middle East Situation Is Critical

Decades of overpumping have caused seawater to invade Israel's coastal aquifer, a key source of fresh water. Some 20 percent of the aquifer is now contaminated by salts or by nitrates from urban and agricultural pollution, and water officials predict that a fifth of the coastal wells may need to be closed over the next few years. This degradation of the coastal aquifer greatly deepens Israeli dependence on the reserve underlying the West Bank.

Competition for water is especially fierce between Israel and Jordan, which must share the Jordan River basin. Many towns in Jordan receive water only two times a week, and the country must double its supply within 20 years just to keep up with population growth.

Israel is far from secure, despite its formidable conservation technologies. An expected 750,000 Palestinians in the Gaza Strip face what Zemah Ishai, Israel's water commissioner, calls a "catastrophe" because of overpumping and contamination of groundwater.

It's particularly tough in Egypt, where the population of 55 million is growing by 1 million every nine months. Egypt already imports 65 percent of its food, and the situation could grow far worse. The flow of the Nile, Egypt's only major water supply, will be reduced in coming years as upstream neighbors Ethiopia and Sudan divert more of the river's waters. Egypt's only practical course is to brake population growth and reduce the enormous amount of water wasted through inefficient irrigation techniques.

A War Over Water?

In the near future, water could be the catalyst for armed conflict. Israel and Jordan, Egypt and Ethiopia, and India and Bangladesh are but a few of the neighboring nations at odds over rivers and lakes.

Thomas Naff, Middle East water analyst at the University of Pennsylvania, has said, "It is water, in the final analysis, that will determine the future of the Occupied Territories, and by extension, the issue of conflict or peace in the region."

History shows that environmental destruction can have far-reaching consequences. The salinization of irrigated land led to the fall of Mesopotamia and Babylon, and perhaps even the Mayan civilization of Central America. Similar pressures are at work today. Sandra Postel estimates that 60 million hectares (nearly 150 million acres) of irrigated land worldwide have already been damaged by salt buildup.

Even the United States Has Water Problems

Water problems, deforestation, climate change, and desertification work together to produce the most pressing situations in other parts of the world. However, in the United States, the water shortage is the result of bad economic policy rather than a serious environmental problem. In the American West, shortages exist because water is underpriced. Generally city dwellers pay over $100 per acre foot (enough water for the average family for a year). Farmers may pay as little as $10 dollars per acre foot (less than the cost of storing and delivering their water).

The result, according to the Global Tomorrow Coalition, is that the water available to each American will drop by 50 percent between 1975 and 2000. U.S. consumption increased from 89 billion gallons per day in 1980 to more than 100 billion in 1988.

Much of the United States depends on groundwater, which initially comes from rain and snow, for its agricultural, industrial, and drinking water supplies; but major U.S. groundwater supplies are being unsustainably "mined." Groundwater is being removed faster than it is replenished in 35 states, including the rapidly growing states of California, Arizona, and Florida. In Florida, for instance, as coastal aquifers are drawn down, ocean saltwater is increasingly seeping into freshwater supplies, making it undrinkable.

Meanwhile, the aquifers of the high plains are being depleted so fast that farming communities from Nebraska through Texas are facing the prospect of not having enough water to continue farming operations. The Ogallala aquifer is a vast reservoir that supplies Nebraska, Kansas, and parts of Colorado, New Mexico, Oklahoma, and Texas with most of their water. Since the end of World War II, irrigation systems pumping water up from the Ogallala have turned the Dust Bowl of the

1930s into a farming center that grows much of the nation's corn, wheat, sorghum, and cotton—crops worth much more than $20 billion a year in all. Thirty years ago the Ogallala contained roughly as much water as Lake Huron. But far more water is drained from the aquifer every year than rainfall restores, and today the supply is drying up. In parts of Texas, New Mexico, and even Kansas, the water table has dropped more than a hundred feet since the mid-1950s.

Farmers in the region are already working to cut back their water consumption. Some have stopped growing corn, which requires a huge supply of water, and have begun growing cotton, wheat, and sorghum, which do not. Many have turned to irrigation methods that conserve water, and they have flattened their fields so that desperately needed moisture does not run off. But in the end, these techniques can only slow the depletion of the Ogallala, not stop it. By 2000 many Great Plains farmers will have had to go back to dry-land farming, working harder to produce smaller crops. If the present trend continues, by 2020 the six states that depend on the Ogallala will have lost more than 5 million acres of irrigated farmland, an area the size of Massachusetts.

The U.S. problem is not just with groundwater sources. California gets most of its water for drinking and agriculture from snow melt from the Sierra Nevada mountains. As a result of increased population growth in Southern California, and a four-year drought in the late 1980s and early 1990s, the water supply system became overtaxed and began to drain the Northern California lakes and rivers that supplied the Los Angeles area. Tension between urban and rural interests built, and new legislation and policies were enacted that fundamentally changed the historical relationship of Californians and water.

Some observers see a new age dawning in the American West. Under inexorable urban, political, and environmental pressures, water—the lifeblood of this arid region—has slowly begun to flow away from farms and ranches and toward the big cities. Farmers are now encouraged to sell their water to the cities, and new legislation would reserve large amounts of water to repair environmental damage in California. New laws substantially raise the rates paid by farmers, encourage water conservation, and end the practice of renewing water contracts for 40 years at fixed rates.

OVERLOOKED MAJOR ISSUES

We have overlooked some major issues capable of causing serious problems worldwide. These include desertification, rapidly changing weather patterns, natural disasters, and the behavior of our oceans.

Desertification

The destruction of rainforests often produces desertification—humankind's oldest and least publicized environmental problem. This is a serious but little understood issue.

■ More of the world's productivity has been destroyed by deforestation, overgrazing, irrigation, and plowing fragile soils than by all other forms of pollution combined.

■ A combination of complex causes, ecological, economic, demographic, and political, has caused the growth of deserts.

■ It is a slow process that takes place over decades as salts poison the soil, wind blows it away, and erosion cuts the land.

The natural systems that maintain water supplies are being disrupted by humans. Vegetation traps water, reducing runoff and replenishing groundwater supplies. Deforestation can reduce the amount of rainfall. The process is circular. Usually, as much as half the moisture from rain settles on trees and quickly evaporates into the sky, to precipitate again in a continuous cycle (see Figure 4-4). Throughout the world, tree cutting has led to floods, mud slides, soil erosion during the rainy seasons, and water shortages during dry periods.

In drier regions, shrubs help maintain rainfall. Once groundcover is stripped, the land hardens and less moisture evaporates into the air. At the same time, the naked soil reflects more sunlight, triggering atmospheric circulation processes that reduce rainfall by drawing drier air into the area. The result of these processes is desertification, a gradual conversion of forests into marginal land and marginal land into wasteland. This is taking place at an unprecedented rate as the world becomes overpopulated and poverty-stricken people clear land for homes, farms, and fuel.

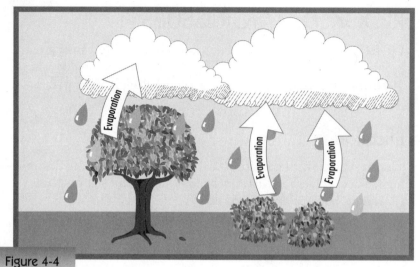

Figure 4-4

Trees and vegetation recycle rain to make more rain

Rapidly Changing Weather Patterns

The issues addressed thus far add up to an increasing likelihood of climatic instability. According to Irving Mintzer of the Stockholm Environmental Institute:

> Global warming due to the greenhouse effect will have many important consequences for natural ecosystems and for human societies ... many scientists now believe that, if current trends continue, one of the important potential impacts of rapid global warming is a further increase in the frequency, duration, and severity of extreme weather events. If such changes occur, most of the negative impacts will be felt in developing countries.

As you can see quite graphically in Figures 4-5, 4-6, and 4-7, the incidence of major weather events has been growing exponentially since the beginning of the century. Other sources suggest that some of these trends will increase in frequency and magnitude in the coming years. There will be more and larger floods, for example, because people are growing in numbers, deforestation is increasing, unsuitable farming is being done on steep slopes, and so on. When these activities diminish the soil's ability to hold rainfall or snow melt, runoff occurs much more suddenly, resulting in floods.

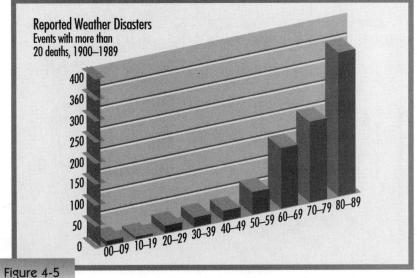

Figure 4-5

The number of major weather disasters has increased exponentially in this century. Source: USAID/OFDA

The stability of our climate is the product of the interaction of many parts of a complex system that humans are increasingly influencing. Figure 4-8 shows graphically how:

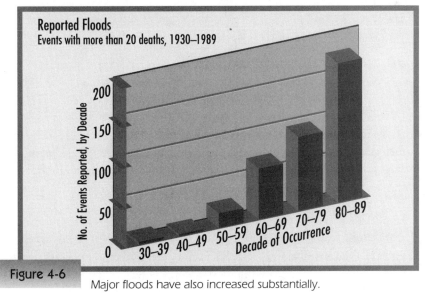

Figure 4-6

Major floods have also increased substantially. Source: USAID/OFDA

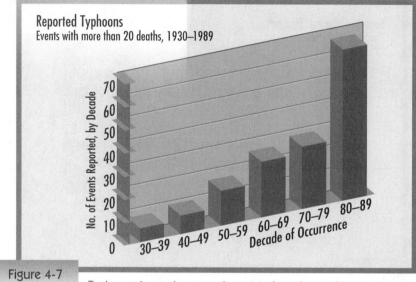

Reported Typhoons
Events with more than 20 deaths, 1930–1989

No. of Events Reported, by Decade

70
60
50
40
30
20
10
0

30–39 40–49 50–59 60–69 70–79 80–89
Decade of Occurrence

Figure 4-7

Typhoons have also caused more serious destruction.
Source: USAID/OFDA

Loss of rainforests removes the means of cleaning the atmosphere of greenhouse gases.

Tree burning and exhaust fumes add to greenhouse gases.

Greenhouse gases and a loss of upper-atmosphere ozone may cause global climate change.

Times of climate change are likely to be times of major differences in temperatures and growing-season lengths on a year-to-year basis.

Loss of wetlands, rainforests, and desertification all lead to loss of recycled moisture.

Atmospheric moisture moderates climate. Humid climates have warmer winters and cooler summers.

Loss of moisture contributes to water shortages, which contribute to loss of moisture in a negative feedback loop.

The combination of these effects may be devastating for world weather patterns. The following examples may be harbingers of things to come. Already the patterns are being studied by an increasing number of researchers.

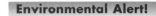

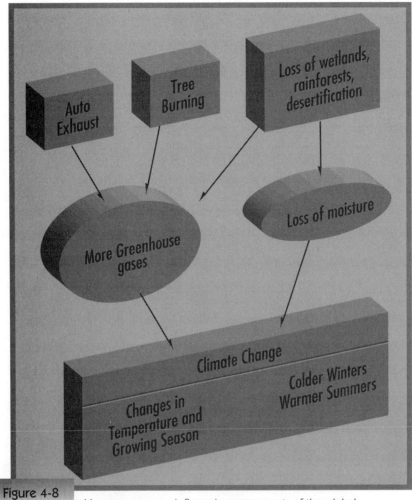

Figure 4-8 Humans are now influencing many parts of the global climate system

More Hurricanes

In 1992 the *San Francisco Chronicle* asked the question: Was Hurricane Andrew a freak, or a preview of things to come? Many scientists had been saying that recent storms prove that global warming is changing the world's climate. Why had the previous three years seen two major hurricanes—Andrew in 1992, and Hurricane Hugo, which leveled parts of South Carolina in 1989, which were rated 5 and 4 respectively on the 5-point scale that measures storm intensity? And what about

Gilbert, which ravaged Jamaica and Mexico's Yucatan peninsula in 1988 and was rated a 5? Is there a pattern here?

One predicted consequence of the greenhouse effect is that we will have more severe storms. If the climatologists' computer models are right, a hurricane that would otherwise have rated a 3 would be energized to an Andrew-size 5. "[We could see] a 50 percent increase in the destructive potential" of the most powerful tropical storms, says meteorologist Kerry Emanuel of the Massachusetts Institute of Technology.

Robert Sheets, who directs the National Hurricane Center of the U.S. Weather Service in Coral Gables, Florida, is reported to have said that some meteorologists contend that global warming could set off atmospheric changes producing far more powerful storms, packing winds up to 225 miles per hour. "We've been in a real lull in hurricane activity," he said. "The indications are we are going to return to more hurricane activity within the next decade—maybe next year, maybe the year after."

William M. Gray, of Colorado State University, thinks that the frequency of severe hurricanes in the United States is linked to the amount of rain in the western Sahel region of Africa, just below the Sahara. He believes that an extended drought is likely to end there within the next few years, concluding the long lull in major hurricane activity here. Between 1947 and 1969, a rainy period in the Sahel, 13 hurricanes with winds of more than 110 miles an hour struck the U.S.

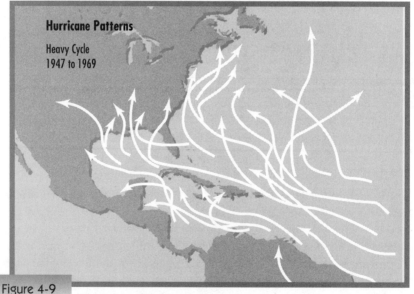

Hurricane Patterns

Heavy Cycle
1947 to 1969

Figure 4-9

There have been huge changes in the cycles of hurricanes

east coast, as shown in Figure 4-9. From 1970 through 1987, a dry period, only one such storm hit. This is not only distressing for the safety of coastal communities, it is also expensive.

It appears the problem is even more complex than that: El Nino, the Pacific Ocean weather phenomenon, apparently influences Atlantic Ocean hurricanes. In any case, there is good reason to cast a weather eye to changes in both the East and the West.

At a recent insurance industry conference, James Gustafson, executive vice president of General Reinsurance Corporation, was cautious in his predictions, but said that hurricane Andrew taught important lessons and raised disturbing questions for the future. He noted that all of the industry's ten worst catastrophe losses have occurred since 1988, and that even adjusting for inflation, their severity and frequency have increased dramatically in recent years. While claiming no expertise in climatology, Mr. Gustafson said, insurers need to consider the possibility that more violent and frequent storms are here to stay.

Structures such as homes and sea walls are built to withstand storms of a certain severity. If they are battered by stronger winds, they are simply going to be destroyed. And if insurers write their actuarial tables based on a Hugo or an Andrew occurring only once a century, they may be seriously underestimating the odds on disaster.

Natural Disasters Bring Increasingly Greater Destruction

Others have noted that the toll inflicted by hurricanes, floods, earthquakes, and other "acts of God" has climbed steadily for more than 20 years. "At any moment, we could be hit with an event causing thousands of deaths and economic damages as high as $100 billion—unless we are better prepared," said Stephen Rattien, who oversees disaster research at the National Academy of Sciences. That event—a major quake on the Hayward Fault east of San Francisco, for instance—would produce casualties at levels usually associated with third world disasters. It could overwhelm the insurance industry, topple banks, and send shock waves throughout the economy.

The infrastructure supplying water to Southern California is most vulnerable. The Los Angeles/San Diego area gets roughly half of its water from a single canal system, the California Aqueduct, which carries water from the Sacramento River Delta 800 kilometers (500 miles) south to Los Angeles. Mark Reisner, author of *Cadillac Desert,* an examination of Western water, notes that the delta is sinking by as much as 7.6 centimeters (3 inches) a year, leaving the area, much of it already below sea level, ever more vulnerable to sea-water intrusion. A major earthquake on the nearby Hayward Fault could destroy the levees that protect this crucial water supply. "It's a fragile, fragile system," says Reisner, "ludicrously so since 19 million people depend on it."

Understanding the Behavior of the Ocean

The world's weather is largely determined by the ocean. So vast is the world ocean that one of its regions, the Pacific Ocean, is 25 percent larger than all of the land surface of the world combined. When we consider the earth as a system, this huge mass of water clearly plays a major role in the transfer of energy across and through the surface of the planet.

For most of history, humankind has understood little about the operation of the ocean. Today, however, giant steps are being taken that, within the next two decades, will open up many of the secrets of how the ocean functions and what its contributions to weather and other phenomena really are.

A number of new sources are producing a huge amount of new information about the sea. Remote-sensing satellites launched in 1992 carry radar to measure ocean currents, waves, wind stress, and ice cover. Undersea data on salinity, plankton, temperature, and currents is being gathered by ships systematically towing instruments repeatedly over large expanses of ocean. One interesting, though perhaps not surprising, thing that has been learned through these techniques is that there are a huge number of undersea storms swirling around deep in the seas of the southern hemisphere.

New computer analysis capability is allowing researchers to begin to model the behavior of the oceans, although present capacity does not begin to show a comprehensive picture. That may be changing. A new generation of unmanned robots is being designed that, by 1998, will autonomously cruise the oceans to gather data. Hundreds of these robots will be deployed at less than one-tenth the cost of doing it by ship. They will survey oceans from the bottom to the surface, contributing data to a master model of the whole system.

For the shallow water areas, the Army Corps of Engineers is developing a system called SHOALS (Scanning Hydrographic Operational Airborne LIDAR Survey). This surveyor allows a helicopter to sweep an area with a laser system and collect bathymetric ocean-bottom information from a large number of floating "pellets" that give it a horizontal accuracy of less than 20 feet and a vertical accuracy of less than 1 foot. The position of each sensor is established by using the Global Positioning System (GPS).

The combination of all of these sources should soon make it possible to design an operational system for monitoring the global ocean in much the same way the atmospheric weather is monitored now. This Global Ocean Observing System could be working as soon as 2015.

IMPORTANT BUT LESSER ISSUES

Finally, let's look at some issues that are less catastrophic, but still troubling. These issues are toxic waste, garbage, and lower atmosphere ozone.

Toxic Waste

Toxic waste contributes to the global problem of environmental degradation and climate change, not to mention its potential direct effects on humans. Our oceans, soils, and atmosphere are remarkable systems; they have amazing buffering qualities. We can pour seemingly endless quantities of stuff into them and the natural buffers return the systems to normal. However, it is likely that these are "threshold systems." A threshold system implies that the system as a whole has at least two stable states. Up to a certain point, it seems to remain unchanged regardless of what is done to it; and then, suddenly, a very small additional change knocks the system into another stable state.

When we begin to pump huge quantities of toxic waste into the system, we seriously risk influencing a state change. And we *are* pumping huge quantities of toxins into the system. The United States alone produces about 4 billion pounds per year, more than 15 times the estimates of the runner-up, the former Soviet states. Not all of these substances, of course, go directly into our air, water, or ground; but ultimately, there is no alternative for many of them.

U.S. Military a Major Polluter

Although our industrial process is a major polluter, it is not the only villain. In fact, it is not the largest culprit. The military is.

Officials have identified 10,924 hazardous hot spots at 1,877 U.S. military installations—and the Pentagon is responding. At a time of shrinking defense budgets, environmental cleanup is the fastest-growing category of military expenditure—up 18 percent, from $2.9 billion in 1992 to $3.4 billion in 1993 funding. The task is so overwhelming that accurate cost projections are almost impossible to make. Some analysts put the figure at $20 billion over the next 30 years, not including overseas bases or the nuclear facilities run by the Department of Energy. The Department of Energy alone may have to spend as much as $300 billion, to clean up toxic materials at 45 of its facilities. The Pentagon's inspector general has said the cleanup bill might go as high as $120 billion—about what America spent on the Apollo space program in today's dollars. Another $1.8 billion per year will go to fund programs designed to prevent further contamination. Thus the secondary "story" on toxic waste is the cost of the cleanup.

But the good news is that many are working on the problem and have managed to make some progress. In 1982 American factories were turning out some 77 billion pounds of toxic waste every year. Since then, the amount going into landfills has been cut by 65 percent. By 2000 we should be detoxifying 90 percent of our waste, which will bring us equal to industrialized West Germany today. This is not enough—today Holland and Denmark destroy or recycle *all* their toxic waste.

Radioactive Waste

Chemical, industrial, and toxic waste can be recycled. But 50 years after the beginning of the atomic age, we still don't have a long-term plan for the disposition of more than 15,000 metric tons of spent nuclear fuel from the nation's 106 operating nuclear power plants, which will have grown to nearly 50,000 tons by the year 2000, as shown in Figure 4-10. The material is no longer useful, yet it will remain dangerously radioactive for the next 10,000 years.

The facts are riveting:

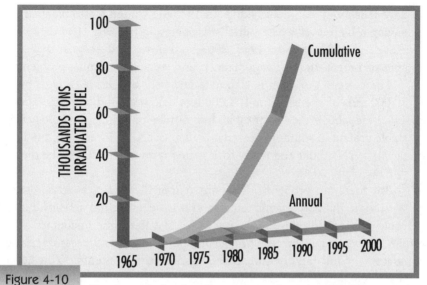

Figure 4-10 The amount of radioactive waste generated worldwide grew to enormous proportions in 1990. Source: Worldwatch Institute, Pacific Northwest Laboratory

- Civilian nuclear power has produced roughly 95 percent of the radioactivity emanating from waste in the world.

- In 1990, the world's 424 commercial nuclear reactors created some 9,500 tons of irradiated fuel, bringing the total accumulation of used fuel to 84,000 tons—twice as much as in 1985.

- The United States houses a quarter of this, with a radioactivity of more than 20 billion curies. (The bombs dropped on Hiroshima and Nagasaki released an estimated 1 million curies.)

- Within eight years the global figure could pass 190,000 tons. The cumulative output of irradiated fuel from nuclear plants is now 20 times what it was in 1970.

- Total waste generation from all the nuclear reactors now operating or under construction worldwide will exceed 450,000 tons before the plants have all closed down in the middle of the next century, projects the U.N. International Atomic Energy Agency (IAEA).

Attempts to deal with this growing waste have been failures. At best, short-term storage is waiting for long-term answers; at worst, there are many unmitigated disasters.

All the countries using nuclear power are pursuing geologic burial as the solution to their waste; yet, by their own timelines, most programs have fallen way behind schedule. In 1975 the United States planned on having a high-level waste burial site operating by 1985. The date was moved to 1989, then to 1998, 2003, and now 2010—a goal that still appears unrealistic. Germany, France, and Japan have similar problems.

The current U.S. plan is elaborate and very expensive. It is to bury 70,000 tons of spent fuel rods 1,000 feet below ground level and about 1,000 feet above the water table, in a 6-mile-long ridge of geologically stable ground in southern Nevada. If all goes according to plan, the first facility will be built and ready for the first radwaste in 2003. The dump will be full by 2030.

But there are problems. The site, Yucca Mountain, is crisscrossed with more than 30 seismic faults, and it is believed that an earthquake could dramatically raise the water table. If water came in contact with the buried waste, the resulting steam explosions could burst open the containers and rapidly spread their radioactive contents. "You flood that thing and you could blow the top off the mountain. At the very least, the radioactive material would go into the groundwater and spread to Death Valley, where there are hot springs all over the place," says University of Colorado geophysicist Charles Archambeau. And so scientists and policymakers continue to look for ways to deal with this growing, ominous issue.

The worst U.S. pollution has taken place at processing and weapons manufacturing plants. The problems at sites in Washington, South Carolina, and Colorado are illustrative.

Hanford Plant, Hanford, Washington: High-level liquid and semisolid wastes containing radiation and chemicals are stored in 177 underground tanks. Some 66 of 149 older tanks have been found to be leakers or potential leakers. Many have been found empty. Potentially explosive hydrogen gas generated in some tanks is a major concern. Two hundred square miles of groundwater are contaminated. The Department of Energy (DOE) admitted in 1990 that airborne releases of iodine 131 from Hanford in the 1940s were large enough to cause health risks to nearby residents.

Some of Hanford's problems come from dumping highly radioactive liquids into unlined trenches or pits. Some of the leaking waste has ended up in the Columbia River, contaminating shellfish hundreds of kilometers away in the Pacific Ocean.

Savannah River, Aiken, South Carolina: Aging production reactors were shut down in 1988 for safety reasons. The DOE is pumping industrial solvents out of an aquifer beneath the site. Ten of 51 large steel tanks containing high-level nuclear wastes have developed leaks. Tank and transfer pipe leaks have contaminated thousands of cubic feet of soil. Groundwater is contaminated with tritium, and potentially cancer-causing industrial solvents have seeped into the Tuscaloosa Aquifer.

Rocky Flats, suburbs of Denver, Colorado: Contaminated groundwater from Rocky Flats may affect drinking water supplies in the Denver suburbs. A series of accidents, spills, and fires at the facility, beginning in the 1950s, has contaminated the area with plutonium and other hazardous elements.

Russia and Eastern Europe

In most places toxic and radioactive waste is an "important, but lesser issue," but not in the former Soviet Union and Eastern Europe. There, it is a problem of the highest order. The pictures painted by *The New York Times, Time* magazine, and Murray Feshbach and Alfred Friendly, Jr., in their book *Ecocide in the USSR,* is the same: inadequate policies implemented poorly. This is a natural consequence of an informationally closed society that manifests itself on two levels; the government, or policy level, and the level of the individual. On the policy level, the leaders of the USSR had to prove the superiority of the Communist state. It was mandated that all sectors of society (including science) serve the needs of production and that there be no bad news—a policy that has had pernicious consequences.

Because the state was the major manufacturer, it could use and waste resources without paying economic or ecological costs. Furthermore, there were no checks from other sectors of the society, and early warning signs were regarded as bad news and thus covered up. Now, with the end of the cold war, we are seeing a horror story of ecological contamination and destruction. The map in Figure 4-11 tells the horrible story.

■ The Chernobyl meltdown released heavy isotopes of plutonium and uranium in 1986. There are 19 similar reactors still running in the former Soviet Union.

■ In Chelyabinsk, the Techa River is contaminated by the explosion of a tank containing radioactive waste from a weapons plant in 1957.

■ In the Barents Sea, a nuclear submarine, complete with reactor and torpedoes, sank; and nearly 165,000 cubic meters of liquid waste were dumped there between 1961 and 1990.

Figure 4-11 The former Soviet Union is littered with extremely serious toxic waste problems.

In Novaya Zemlya, a nuclear dump containing up to 17,000 barrels of solid radioactive waste, at least eight submarine reactors and three reactors from an ice breaker were dumped between 1964 and 1990.

Weapons builders sent nuclear waste into Lake Karachav, which has become "the most polluted spot on the planet." It is so radioactive that standing at its shore for an hour would be lethal.

616 radioactive sites have been discovered inside Moscow since 1982.

Seventy percent of Chernobyl's radioactive fallout remains in Byelorus. Half of its territory was covered with fallout. About 20 percent of the farming land has been withdrawn from production, and more than 40 percent of the forests have been contaminated.

The problems are not just with radioactive materials.

In Byelorus, 92 million cubic meters of liquid manure from 261 meat-producing complexes are discharged into the republic's rivers and lakes each year. Ecological degradation is expected to increase threefold by 1995. Of the 214 biological water treatment installations, 149 (70 percent) are either out of order or were never put into operation. The total chemical pollution and the complete failure of underground sources for drinking water is expected in ten years.

▓▓ Air pollution levels in every major industrial city exceed former Soviet norms, sometimes by a factor of 50.

The only good sign in this bleak picture is that the Russian people have become ecologically active. There are strong bases of popular concern. A spring 1990 poll in Moscow and its suburbs found 98 percent of those questioned more worried about pollution than about rising crime, the threat of AIDS, international conflict, or even the reality of food and consumer goods shortages.

The U.S. Garbage Problem

Against the problem in the former Soviet Union, the garbage problem in the United States seems small in comparison. All we need to do is to stop waste and to start recycling; and yet the very magnitude of the problem makes cleanup difficult. A short list gives a feel for the problem. Every year we throw away:

▓▓ 16 billion disposable diapers

▓▓ 2 billion razors and razor blades

▓▓ 220 million tires

▓▓ More glass and aluminum than existed in the entire world prior to World War II

▓▓ 160 million tons of garbage—twice as much per person than any other industrialized nation

And then, of course, there is sewage. According to the Scripps Institution of Oceanography's Scott Jenkins, "Almost every city has grown faster than its sewer system has grown, and so almost every city is in the situation where the sewer system is overburdened." Boston's sewage system, currently in the process of an expensive overhaul and modernization, has pumps so old that they will be exhibited in the Smithsonian.

Lower-Atmosphere Ozone

High-altitude ozone is not the only problem. There's also the increase in low-altitude ozone. The action of ultraviolet light initiates chemical reactions between hydrocarbons and nitrogen oxides to produce ozone smog. The thinning of the upper atmosphere layer means there is more ultraviolet light, and therefore more smog.

The problem in some major cities is severe. There is an often cited story about a flight of sparrows making their way across Mexico City. They fell out of the air, one by one, killed by the toxicity of the atmosphere. The pollution of urban air costs many billions of dollars in health care (to say nothing about personal suffering), and causes significant erosion and damage to buildings and other structures. In the Los Angeles basin, there are now thousands and thousands of children who by the age of 10 have permanently impaired respiratory systems because of the atmosphere they breathe.

But smog is increasingly a problem in less populated areas as well. In the tropics, the intense radiation of the sun quickens the production of ozone and can make pollution more dangerous than in cooler regions. A vast pool of ozone and smog is concentrating over fires raging across fields and grassland of Brazil and the savannas of southern Africa that is comparable to the pollution over industrial regions in Europe, Asia, and the United States.

During the burning season, a thick pall of smog, produced by vegetation fires and aggravated by other exhaust, hangs over central Brazil and large parts of South Africa. Doctors in both areas report that at this time of the year people suffer many more respiratory problems than at other times. For example, according to a *New York Times* report in October 1992, in an area just north of Brasilia, almost every pollution monitoring instrument went off scale. Air conditions at 11,000 feet were approaching a Stage 2 smog alert in Los Angeles. In a Stage 2 alert, on a three-stage scale, children and the elderly are advised to stay indoors. On the ground it must have been close to deadly.

SOLUTIONS AND STRATEGIES

Throughout this book we will talk about the link between ecological, social, economic, and political problems. We have mentioned the difficulty in dealing with problems that are global in scope, and we have outlined the systemic problems of thresholds, positive feedback, and system instability. These issues argue for the need to see the world and our role in it in a much different way. We must understand that environmental issues are *security* issues, as much so as the threat of a terrorist with a missile or bomb. Once we understand that, we will think of these problem in a completely different light. We will treat the threat to our environment as a threat.

As Sandra Postel has suggested, eliminating these threats to our future will require a fundamental restructuring of many elements of society. We will have to do things differently. Among other things, we must

- reduce our use of energy—in the North by something like 80 percent

- shift from fossil fuels to efficient, solar-based energy systems or to zero-point energy

- develop new transportation networks and city designs that lessen automobile use

- work for the redistribution of land and wealth so that the poor can make a positive contribution to these problems

- push for equality between the sexes in all cultures

- effect a rapid transition to smaller families

- reduce the consumption of resources by the rich to make room for higher living standards for the poor

We must change the incentives. Our present economic incentives are all wrong. Productivity is measured in dollars. The world in which we are living is nothing more than the result of humans working the present system to their advantage. The present system values money—and little else.

We desperately need a system that is built on human values and those things that maintain the environment that supports us. We must change the definition of productivity away from dollars, to energy and waste. It will require us to rethink our basic values and vision of progress.

Worldwatch Institute's Lester Brown said in 1992, "Put simply, the global economy is rigged against both poverty alleviation and environmental protection. Treating the earth's ecological ills as separate from issues of debt, trade, inequality, and consumption is like trying to treat heart disease without addressing a patient's obesity and high-cholesterol diet: There is no chance of lasting success."

But, we may well ask, is this possible? Can we do anything to halt the destruction of our environment? The answer is yes. And many people are trying. In her book *Paradigms in Progress,* Hazel Henderson has proposed a new economic system that encompasses these ideas. Michael Rothschild, in his *Bionomics,* has proposed a new framework for an economy that mirrors biological systems. Paul Hawken eloquently deals with the underlying problems in his *The Ecology of Commerce*. Hardin Tibbs is developing his *Industrial Ecology*. But be warned: What is proposed, in all cases, is radical surgery.

Building a working biosystem is not just theoretically possible, it's been done. A Swiss agronomist, working by himself in Kenya, has created a successfully operating ecosystem on some of the most difficult terrain imaginable, abandoned limestone quarries. Starting with nothing but fossil coral rubble, he began his reconstruction by looking for an appropriate tree. He knew the species had to withstand heat, drought, sun, and wind and be able to provide its own nourishment from the atmosphere. He found six trees that would thrive, the best being the casuarina tree.

He planted many of them, and as they became established he introduced millipedes to help turn the tree litter into soil. Insects were required to pollinate the trees and other plants. A fish farming operation was started in some of the quarry ponds, and that drew birds—now 130 species in all. He worked slowly, step by step, and today there is a fully functioning mixed-use forest. Rainwater has returned and other trees have been planted. People are now employed to tend and extend the forest, with wages that are paid with money from forest products. There is even a lake with a hippopotamus and fish.

IMPLICATIONS FOR THE FUTURE

World population is growing by 92 million people annually, roughly equal to adding another Mexico each year; 88 million of these people live in the developing world. To many in the third world, the vision of the wealthiest nations asking them to conserve their forests seems incredibly imperialist. To motivate them, we will have to make it worth their while. And that means that we may have to consume less energy, have less of the world's wealth, and help others to conserve their environments in spite of the grinding poverty in which they live. This will necessitate thinking beyond our borders and our generation, as well as investing in resources.

There appear to be two paths that humankind can take relative to the most serious problems of the spoiling of our environment. Absent any extraordinary reason to do otherwise, it seems likely that there will be a relatively slow increase in awareness of the seriousness of the problem by a growing number of people. The profound changes that are needed to seriously offset the growing trends will be perceived by enough powerful people to be expensive and hard to accomplish that progress and change will be evolutionary, and therefore ineffective in holding back the ultimate disaster.

On the other hand, the possibility exists that some significant event will capture the attention of a large portion of the earth's population and leadership and convince them that a serious change in direction is required to maintain the system that supports human life on the earth. A clear change in the earth's weather patterns, or a rapid increase in natural disasters, might be enough to provide a shift in direction.

The key to dealing with this problem lies in a fundamental change of perspective. Then Senator Al Gore characterized this mindset well in his book *Earth in the Balance:*

> I have come to believe that we must take bold and unequivocal action: We must make the rescue of the environment the central organizing principle for civilization. Whether we realize it or not, we are now engaged in an epic battle to right the balance of our earth, and the tide of this battle will turn only when the majority of people in the world become sufficiently aroused by a shared sense of urgent danger to join an all-out effort.

We must not wait until it is too late.

We are greatly hindered in what we can ultimately do if the population of the world continues to climb as it has. Billions of new, poor people will be flooding onto the world stage. This is another major piece of the system that we must understand.

CHAPTER

5

Exploding

Population

In the physical world, one cannot increase the size or quantity of anything without changing its quality.
—*Paul Valéry*

Until recently, the number of humans inhabiting the earth was never a problem or an issue. The planet's capacity to support human life was a given—some places were relatively crowded, but those were local problems. As Figure 5-1 shows, that perspective was accurate until about World War II. Suddenly, the rate of the world's population growth (the difference between births and deaths) began to accelerate at unheard-of levels. From the beginning of history, the rate had almost always been less than 1 percent. But in a span of only 40 years, it rocketed to almost three times that.

The growth rate peaked about 1968 and is estimated to be heading down toward zero in the year 2100. The "baby boom" of the United States was a precursor to a global boom—and we are going to be living with the consequences of it for many decades to come.

A GLOBAL EXPLOSION

World population passed the 5 billion mark during 1987, and is now growing by about 1.6 percent a year. We lived through a high point that will probably never be duplicated.

Annual increases in the absolute size of world population have also been growing for more than two centuries; since the end of World War II, they have reached numbers that are enormous by historical standards. In the ten years from 1975 to 1985, world population grew by about 760 million, a number equal to the estimated total world population in 1750. Since 1990 the annual addition to the population has averaged about 90 million people; and that is estimated to reach a peak of some 95 million a year, on average, between 1995 and 2000. By 2005 there should be 6.7 billion humans in this global community. If the trend continues, that will grow to 10.7 billion by 2030. As Figure 5-2 clearly shows, even though the annual growth rate of world population is now declining, the numbers added each year are likely to

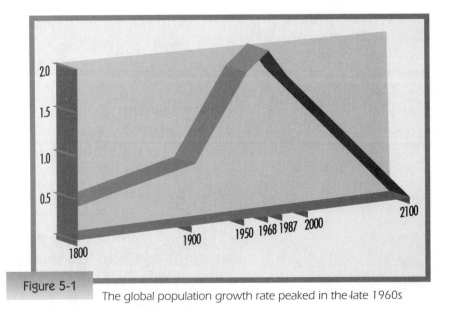

Figure 5-1

The global population growth rate peaked in the late 1960s

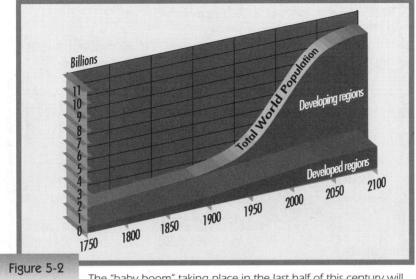

Figure 5-2 The "baby boom" taking place in the last half of this century will more than double the population of the planet. Source: UN

increase for at least another decade, because the size of the base population to which this growth rate applies has become so large.

Population Growth Is Greatest in Africa, Asia, and Latin America

Of the projected 3.4 billion addition to world population between 1985 and 2025, 3.1 billion, or 93 percent, will occur in Africa, Asia, and Latin America, giving these regions 83 percent of the world's total population, and reducing that of North America, Europe, the former USSR, Japan, and Oceania from 24 percent in 1985 to just 17 percent in 2025. The largest absolute increase, 1.7 billion, is projected for Asia, again reflecting its large population base. These relationships can be seen in Figure 5-3, which shows the doubling rate for a selected group of developed and developing countries.

All other things being equal, by about 2035 India will pass China as the world's most populous nation. Relative growth in Africa and Latin America is projected to top the world average by a large margin. Africa is projected to add 1.1 billion people, reaching 1.6 billion in 2025, tripling the 555 million of 1985. By 2035 the population of Brazil plus

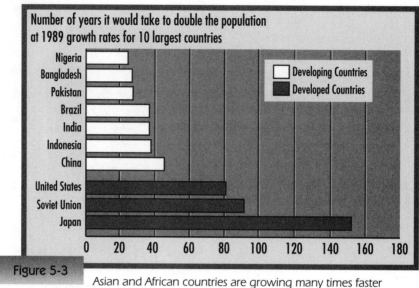

Number of years it would take to double the population at 1989 growth rates for 10 largest countries

Figure 5-3

Asian and African countries are growing many times faster than developed countries. Source: U.S. Bureau of Census, Center for International Research

Argentina will almost equal that of the United States—whose population density would increase by about 20 percent. Latin America's will be 779 million in 2025, close to double 1985's 405 million. The worst-case developing countries are doubling every 20 to 30 years. Some specific examples of population growth are shown in Table 5-1.

Jacques-Yves Cousteau has put it in personal terms.

> During my lifetime—82 years only—the world population has more than tripled. If nothing drastic is done, in another 80 years, 2070, the population will triple again, reaching the absurd figure of 16 billion human beings. Every six months, the equivalent of France (50 million) is added. Every 10 years, there is a new China born in the poorest regions of our earth.

Cousteau allows that the real number may end up being closer to 12 billion, but he has made his point.

A word of caution about both the magnitudes and regional distribution of population in projections to 2025: Because of its currently high birth rates and declining death rates, Africa has the *demographic* potential to grow as projected, rivaling the growth of Asia and

Latin America over the last three decades. But there is no guarantee that Africa has the political, social, and economic base to support such increases.

	1950	1990	1995	2025
AFRICA	222.0	642.0	747.0	1597.0
Somalia	2.4	7.5	8.4	18.7
Zaire	12.2	35.6	41.8	99.4
Egypt	20.3	52.4	58.4	90.4
Nigeria	32.1	96.2	111.3	216.9
NORTH & CENTRAL AMERICA	220.0	427.0	453.0	596.0
United States	152.0	249.0	258.0	300.0
Mexico	28.0	88.6	98.0	150.0
Canada	13.7	26.5	28.1	34.2
SOUTH AMERICA	111.6	297.0	326.0	494.0
Brazil	53.4	150.0	165.0	245.0
Argentina	17.1	32.3	34.2	45.5
ASIA	1337.0	3117.0	3413.0	4912.0
Bangladesh	41.8	115.6	132.2	234.9
India	357.0	853.0	946.0	1442.0
China	554.0	1139.0	1222.0	1512.0
Japan	83.6	123.4	125.9	127.5
EUROPE	392.0	498.0	504.0	515.0
France	41.8	51.6	57.1	60.3
Italy	47.1	51.6	57.1	52.9
U.K.	50.6	57.2	57.8	59.6
Germany	68.4	77.6	77.3	70.9
Spain	28.0	39.0	40.0	42.0
WORLD	2516.0	5292.0	5770.0	8504.0

Table 5-1. Specific examples of population growth (population = millions)

Source: World Bank, *World Resources 1992–1993*

We Are Producing Many More Poor People

The problem with population growth of this kind is that countries that don't have an effective infrastructure to deal with it bear the brunt of the explosion. This inverse relationship results in the most pressure being concentrated in the places most likely to fail. Some parts of the world have too many people in relation to available local resources, such as potable water and arable land. In other parts of the world, too many resources are consumed too fast by too few.

Growing Urban Centers

As the world population doubles, urban population triples as people move to cities looking for work and food. Latin America is an example of what is happening across the world in areas of high growth.

Latin America is the most urbanized part of the underdeveloped world. In 1950, only 42 percent of Latin Americans were city dwellers; today almost 73 percent live in cities, according to the United Nations. This compares with 34 percent in Africa and 33 percent in Asia. Despite oppressive poverty, Peruvians seeking a better life, for example, have been fleeing the countryside for Lima at the rate of more than a thousand a day and building settlements that seem like a never-ending expanse of small straw huts next to a noisy highway. The trend has created megacities throughout the continent, as shown in Table 5-2.

Country	Population	City	Population
Argentina	32 million	Buenos Aires	12 million
Chile	13 million	Santiago	5 million
Peru	22 million	Lima	7 million
Mexico	90 million	Mexico City	20 million

Table 5-2. Populations of Latin American megacities

The equation is similar in many countries: The major city attracts one-quarter to one-third of the country's population, with many living in squalid slums or shantytowns encircling the affluent inner city. Experts say that by the year 2010, Rio de Janeiro and São Paulo will be one continuous megalopolis 350 miles long with almost 40 million people.

The relationships between the developed world and lesser-developed countries can be seen in the population densities of major cities, as shown in Figure 5-4. New York, for example, has a density of 10,000 people per square mile; in Tokyo, it is 22,000 per square mile. In Bombay, 150,000 souls are crowded into the average square mile.

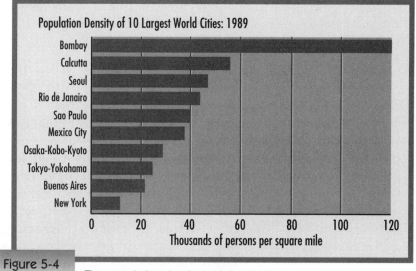

Population Density of 10 Largest World Cities: 1989

Bombay	
Calcutta	
Seoul	
Rio de Janairo	
Sao Paulo	
Mexico City	
Osaka-Kobo-Kyoto	
Tokyo-Yokohama	
Buenos Aires	
New York	

0   20   40   60   80   100   120

Thousands of persons per square mile

Figure 5-4
The population density is highest in the poorest cities. Source:
U.S. Bureau of Census, Center for International Research

The Poor Will Know That They Are Poor

The Population Reference Bureau's Barbara Torrey has suggested that one important result of urbanization is the impact of images from CNN and other video sources. CNN will hit these people. In the past, transnational communications were concentrated between certain developed countries and were almost exclusively audio. In the last decade, that has changed. With the advent of satellite repeaters and networks like CNN, live images from the developed world are now beamed around the world and available for reception almost everywhere. In cities, instead of a few people being exposed to TV, almost everyone will be.

But TV does not only reach those in urban areas. A Coast Guard commander tells of riding in a dugout canoe to a small jungle village in the Philippines that had no land access. There, he saw perched on a stand in the middle of the collection of thatched huts, a communal television, connected to a satellite dish. Each night the villagers gathered around to watch MTV, beamed from the United States.

For the first time in history, the poor are beginning to understand how relatively poor they are compared to the rich nations. They see, in detail, how the rest of the world lives and feel their increasing disenfranchisement. The "ideas" of the industrial world will also accompany the quality-of-life images, and will threaten the familiar and comfortable concepts that have been the basis for life for those who have been relatively isolated.

Environmental Implications

On a global scale, a world population of this size is primarily an environmental and food problem. Urban consumption in energy and transportation is much different than in rural areas. As we have seen, providing new infrastructure and products for economic development (at least as it has been done in the past) produces large amounts of land, water, and air pollution. Increased energy production and physical infrastructure development required to support burgeoning populations, combined with traditional industrial process waste, have become such a problem that a new concept of national development is required—one that is more environmentally benign.

Population growth is not the sole culprit in environmental degradation, but it is a driver. Other factors, including poor land management, poverty, and inappropriate technologies, also contribute to the problem.

Feeding the Multitudes

With so many new mouths to feed, the requirement for food is predictably crucial. As much food will have to be grown worldwide in the next 40 years as has been grown in the last 14,000. Even so, barring any technological breakthroughs, the gap between population growth and food production will widen. Although efforts are underway in some places to protect soil, conserve water, and restore the productivity of degraded land, nevertheless an estimated 24 billion tons of topsoil wash or blow off the land each year. Thus every year the world's farmers must try to feed 93 million more people with 24 billion fewer tons of topsoil.

"But doing everything feasible on the food side of the food/population equation is not enough," warns Worldwatch's Lester Brown. Something must be done to reduce the number of hungry people. Even then, concludes the final report of the 71st American Assembly on International Population Policy, "Reduction of fertility in and of itself will not cause hungry poor nations to become rich. But it can provide time and relieve pressure on societies to direct resources toward satisfying the minimum needs of rapidly growing economically dependent populations." It is a systems problem, and all parts of the system must be addressed.

The Global Teenager

The rate of population growth has been so great that the major proportion of the globe's denizens for the next two decades will be poor young people. By sometime in the mid-1990s, over half the humans on earth will be under the age of 20, and their plight will be worse than those of today. The *Whole Earth Review* in Winter 1989 summarized the situation eloquently:

> The natural condition of youth is to hope and aspire, to find a worthy task and master it, to locate oneself in a community and give one's best to advance it. To have faith, once again, and in this way to strengthen an identity. But how can faith, especially the new and often frail faith of the young, withstand the iron hammer of the economy, reducing whole nations to rubble or forging others into pavilions of luxury?
>
> The young are signed up for the most intensive course, a crash course. Just coming on the labor market, heads stuffed with images of affluence, they find out quickly enough their value to society. They are the most unemployed class in the world, also the worst paid and least protected. They are offered the most boring, filthy, dangerous and demeaning jobs available. In the language of one of those UN reports: "The key words in the experience of young people in the coming decade are going to be: 'scarcity,' 'unemployment,' 'underemployment,' 'ill-employment,' 'anxiety,' 'defensiveness,' 'pragmatism,' and even 'substance' and 'survival' itself."

Later in the same issue, Kevin Kelly observed that adding to this tempest is the curious phenomenon called "high adolescent density," the observation that when the number of youths in a society overshadows the number of mature adults, younger people have no role models except peers. "Call it the *Lord of the Flies* syndrome. Anything can happen, and whatever does happen forms the psychological basis for the rest of that generation's life. In the long run, the most important thing about global teenagers is that, like the baby boom in America, their character will be the main event of world culture long after they outgrow pimples."

Immigration Pressures

As people increasingly crowd into places with limited capabilities to support them, they will move on, not only within their country but to other countries. We only have to look at our own hemisphere—Mexico and Haiti come to mind—to know that this is true. It is an even more acute problem in Africa and Southeast Asia, not to mention Central Europe.

In light of the huge increases in population that the world will experience in the next two decades, it is becoming clear that international migration is likely to be one of the major challenges to the global economic system in the 1990s. Bailey Morris, writing in *Economic Insights,* suggests that not since the turn of the century, the last great migration period from 1900 to 1910, have so many people been on the move. "According to recent estimates, more than 80 million people currently live outside their country of citizenship. For the first time in memory, all of the major OECD countries are net immigration nations, a trend that is expected to continue through the decade. Thus, the great migrations of the 1990s promise to be an international issue equal in importance to the environment, trade and the search for sustained global growth."

Both Europe and the United States have concerns about significant increases in immigration. As shown in Figure 5-5, the Western Europeans are watching Eastern Europe, Turkey, and North Africa. The major U.S. assault is from Mexico and Central America.

The world's labor force is projected to increase by almost 800 million by 2010, and 93 percent of these additional workers are expected to be in developing countries. Where will they go for jobs? That is at the root of deep fears in the industrial world—that North America and Western Europe will be swamped by migrant workers seeking jobs and higher wages. The trends, as shown in Figure 5-6, are not good. The number of legal and illegal migrant workers, today some 25 million to 30 million, has been rising despite some government interventions. An additional 16 million refugees are waiting in countries like Thailand until they can find other places to go, and about 2 million immigrants are admitted legally, half of them into the United States.

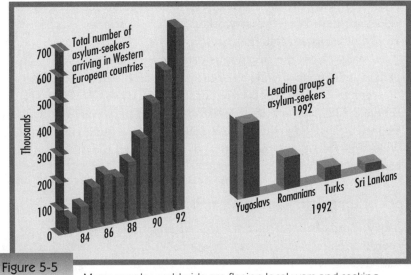

Figure 5-5

Many people worldwide are fleeing local wars and seeking asylum in Western Europe. Source: Intergovernmental consultations on asylum, refugee and migration policies in Europe, North America, and Australia

Two of the biggest problems in regulating immigration, Morris says, are its close links to issues of national sovereignty and the desire of most governments to sweep the problem under the rug. Official reactions, therefore, are often in response to crisis: half-starved Haitians

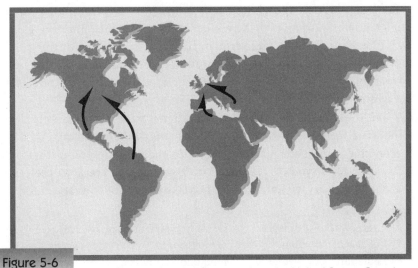

Figure 5-6

The major immigration flows are into the United States, Canada, and Western Europe

in fishing boats off the coast of Florida; Albanian refugees in Italy; Pakistanis and other "guest workers" who are stranded in post-Gulf War Middle Eastern countries.

In many places the situation is becoming desperate. Robert Kaplan, perhaps more than anyone else of late, has chronicled the rapid erosion of order in Africa and other regions. In his *Atlantic Monthly* piece in February 1994, he suggests that "Africa may be as relevant to the future character of world politics as the Balkans were a hundred years ago," when "the threat was the collapse of empires and the birth of nations based solely on tribe."

A Lack of Long-Term Government Planning and Policy

Bailey Morris believes that the lack of long-term planning and policy coordination rests in large part on the belief of governments that rather than dealing with the larger system, they can turn immigration on and off like a faucet. But this will not be the case in the coming decades, if the policies of the past are any indication of future decisions. "Demand-pull immigration has given way to dramatic supply-push."

Industrial countries often discuss immigration in crisis terms because they are being overrun by migrant workers, the same group that they used to recruit. Until fairly recently, all of the industrial countries needed outside workers to do their low-paying jobs, and they developed immigration policies with incentives for such groups. In the 1950s and 1960s, the United States and Western Europe recruited migrant workers to fill what were believed to be short-term labor gaps.

The switch from demand-pull recruitment to supply-push migration is now evident everywhere, and helps to explain the scramble to find trade and aid strategies that encourage potential migrants to stay at home.

But the solution does not lie in traditional trade and aid approaches; industrial countries will have to make *structural* adjustments to their economies and labor markets to reduce the demand-pull factors that attract migrant workers. Taking a cue from Philip L. Martin, a professor at the University of California at Davis, the developed world must do three things:

1. Acknowledge that there is no simple or single cure for the immigration dilemma; not a new development program, not a new immigration category, not a new type of regional economic block. It must be considered as a system.

2. Look harder internally for the reasons—the motivations—why immigrants come.

3. Recognize the critical links of the system: Immigration patterns and policies promise to join trade and finance as major forces in the international economic system.

THE UNITED STATES IS UNDERGOING SIGNIFICANT CHANGE

Although it will continue to grow, because of the much greater population increases in other areas of the world, the United States is becoming a relatively smaller piece of a growing pie. An increase in births among American women, coupled with massive immigration, will add more people to the nation's population over the 1990s than at any time since the baby-boom decade of the 1950s, says the Census Bureau. By the middle of the next century, the U.S. population is expected to grow by about 50 percent from its 1993 level of 255 million. The population density will, of course, increase—up about 20 percent by 2025—which probably translates into a fifth more people in our cities.

More People of More Cultures

Most of the growth will be from minority groups, which means that America will become a much more polyglot nation. New population projections (see Figure 5-7) also underscore the nation's rapidly changing ethnic profile: By the middle of the next century, virtually half of the population will be made up of African-Americans, Hispanics, Asians, and Native Americans, and our current terminology of "majority" and "minority" will become meaningless. The Census Bureau projects that the number of Hispanics will surpass African-Americans in two to three decades. And by the middle of the next century, Hispanics will nearly quadruple to 81 million, or more than a fifth of the population.

Rand Corporation demographer Peter Morrison projects that by the year 2000, today's politically salient minority groups—African-Americans, Hispanics, and Asians—will make up a slightly larger share of the total U.S. population than they do today. African-Americans will

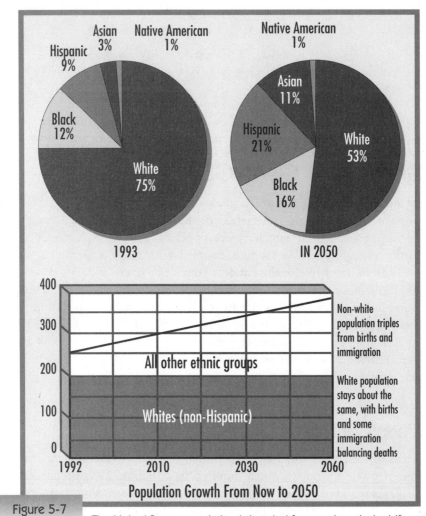

Figure 5-7

The United States population is headed for a major ethnic shift.

Source: U.S. Census Bureau

increase from 12.3 percent of the population in 1989 to 13.1 percent in the year 2000; Hispanics, currently 8 percent, will grow to 9.4 percent. Other races, primarily Asians, will increase from 3.4 percent to 4.3 percent.

Local and Regional Clustering

Far more important than these national shares, Morrison suggests, are the distinctive regional and local patterns of population distribution. Hispanics and Asians are highly clustered in a few regions of the country. In 1989, 73 percent of all Hispanics lived in California, Texas, New York, and Florida; in 1980, 49 percent of all Asian-Americans lived in California and Hawaii. In California, for example, one of every four cities above 50,000 in population has no racial or ethnic majority of any kind.

Minorities are clustering in regional areas, upsetting historical racial mixtures. Already, one in four Californians is Hispanic; nearly 4 million Hispanics live in Los Angeles County alone. Counting illegal aliens, they make up almost half the population. Two million more live in the neighboring counties of Orange, San Diego, Riverside, and San Bernardino. These figures will quickly grow. By the year 2010, Southern California will have become a Hispanic subcontinent— demographically, culturally and economically distinct from the rest of America.

Morrison argues that the traditional notion of the "melting pot" no longer holds; "Its ingredients have separated into a complex racial and ethnic mosaic in which groups of people cling to their separate identities." He points out that in the 1990 census, upward of 250,000 unique entries were reported in addition to the conventional 16 categories of "White," "Black," "Chinese," and the like.

A Growing Disparity Between the Rich and the Poor

The global trend of the rich getting richer and the poor becoming poorer exists in the United States as well. During the 1980s more of America's wealth became controlled by a smaller number of people. This trend was not just in the white community, but was also reflected in African-American families. The percentage of African-American families making more than $90,000 more than doubled from 1967 to 1990, according to new Census Bureau figures. At the same time, the proportion of African-American families at the lowest income level grew by 50 percent. In 1990, more than one African-American family in nine earned less than $5,000 a year. The widening gulf has meant a marked decrease in the proportion of middle-income African-American families.

"The deepening of poverty, which affects whites and Hispanics as well, is particularly true among a substantial segment of the black community, and is cause for real concern," Robert S. Greenstein, of the Center on Budget and Policy Priorities, has said. Mr. Greenstein and other economists and sociologists believe the trends will continue, particularly in a sluggish economy. The real question is whether the government is going to ask the increasingly wealthy to support the increasingly poor.

An Aging Population

Americans are also getting older. Although less than 13 percent of the nation's population is presently 65 or older, that segment will rise to about 20 percent by 2025, and the number of elderly will have doubled. The main effect of the aging of the population will be felt during a short period of intensive change that will commence in the year 2011, when the first members of the baby-boom generation reach age 65.

Population aging will affect the lives of both the elderly and the non-elderly. Social Security taxes will rise, and more of the federal budget will flow to the elderly. The most palpable effects will be felt locally and within families, as chronic health problems and limitations on the routine activities of daily living increase the need for long-term care.

Immigration Worries

The United States also has an immigration problem. As seen in Figure 5-8, during the 1980s the United States received about 9 million immigrants, including 3 million Mexicans.

All indicators point to a migrant intake system near overload. New legal and illegal immigration to the United States has surpassed 1 million annually. Some 2.5 million are on waiting lists abroad for visas. A recent study by the Census Bureau found that there are 20 million immediate relatives of American citizens and resident aliens living abroad, potentially eligible for entry with an immigration preference. A 1989 *Los Angeles Times* poll in Mexico found that 4.7 million Mexicans—about 7 percent of the total population of 67 million—intended to emigrate to the United States.

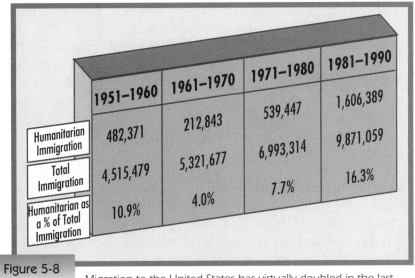

	1951–1960	1961–1970	1971–1980	1981–1990
Humanitarian Immigration	482,371	212,843	539,447	1,606,389
Total Immigration	4,515,479	5,321,677	6,993,314	9,871,059
Humanitarian as a % of Total Immigration	10.9%	4.0%	7.7%	16.3%

Figure 5-8 Migration to the United States has virtually doubled in the last 40 years. Source: Immigration and Naturalization Service

Worldwide demand for settlement in the United States is expected to continue surging in the 1990s. The growth of the working-age population of the Third World will accelerate; the earlier immigrants now in the United States will strive to bring in family and friends by any available means; and political and social unrest will most likely continue to trouble much of Africa, Latin America, the Middle East, Eastern Europe, and the former Soviet Union. Admissions under refugee and other humanitarian provisions, which are not limited by law, could become a much more important source of new settlers during the present decade, adding as many as 2.5 million to 3 million newcomers.

A Changing Attitude

In the recent past, political conservatives have repeatedly been unsuccessful in pushing through any measures restricting the legal flow of immigrants. Nonetheless, since 1991, in political campaign rhetoric, magazine articles, and legislative proposals, the tenor of public conversation about immigration has changed, with emphasis shifting from romantic rhapsodies about the melting pot to anxiety attacks about the dwindling resources of an economically strapped nation.

In California, the Sierra Club, concerned that immigrants are causing a population explosion harmful to the environment, joined forces with three groups that favor immigration restriction to create the Coalition to Stabilize Population. And in Congress, a proposed Constitutional amendment that would deny citizenship to American-born children of illegal immigrants was sponsored by 12 Republicans and 2 Democrats who are civil rights advocates.

It has become particularly trendy in California for politicians to blame the state's economic woes on immigrants, and especially on illegal ones. With Governor Pete Wilson, a Republican, claiming that immigrants are bankrupting the state by using more in services than they pay in taxes, Los Angeles, San Diego, and Orange counties all commissioned studies to determine just how much new and illegal immigrants cost taxpayers.

The New Jersey legislature has eliminated public assistance benefits to illegal immigrants and appears to be moving swiftly to deny them the right to a driver's license. In New York's suburban Nassau County, the welcome of more generous times has given way to such negativity that when a school principal in Elmont, New York reported two of his students, the children of illegal immigrants, to immigration authorities, he was applauded by his local school board.

THE CHANGING AMERICAN FAMILY

One of the most far-reaching aspects of American demographic change is the alteration of the American family. The family is the institution that most fundamentally shapes and nurtures personal values. Children historically have gained their sense of self worth and positioned themselves in the larger society through the implicit and explicit teachings of their parents and extended family. This social unit has always provided the basic equipment—the stability—that allowed our citizens to deal more or less effectively with the major changes in our country's history.

No more. The family, as it has traditionally been understood, is evolving fast in both structure and function. The result is sobering, especially as we enter the era that will include the most acute and threatening change in our history.

A Rise in Single Parenthood

The problem starts with relationships at birth. Demographer Peter Morrison suggests that one reason why children's families are changing is that more of the women having children are not married.

- Nationwide, in 1988, unmarried women bore 1 million children, or 26 percent of all births that year, the highest proportion ever.

- In African-American and Hispanic families, the rates of single-parent families are almost 63 percent and 30 percent, respectively; among white women, 18 percent.

- In the past 30 years, the divorce rate has tripled.

- Of every 100 children born today, only 41 will reach the age of 18 living continuously with both parents.

- Among children who were born in 1980, as many as 2 of every 3 white children and 19 of every 20 African-American children will live in single-parent families at some time in their youth.

The traditional family, a married couple living with their own children, has become a distinct minority. In New York City, for example, such families constitute only one in six households, and declined from 19.2 percent of all households in 1980 to less than 17 percent in the 1990 census. If these trends continue, by the year 2000:

- More than two of every three children under age 6 will have a mother who is employed outside the home.

- Fewer than three of every ten adolescents will have lived in a continuously intact family through all 18 years of their youth.

This instability and lack of both mother and father figures in children's lives is producing problems at best, and dysfunctionality at worst. The 1988 National Health Interview Survey of Child Health found, for example, that "young people from single-parent families or stepfamilies were two to three times more likely to have had emotional or behavioral problems than those who had both of their biological parents present in the home."

Children from broken homes have more trouble in school and with learning, getting along with other people, getting and keeping a job, and maintaining relationships in marriages. In what has been labeled the "new morbidity of childhood," an increase has been noted in developmental delays, learning difficulties, and emotional and behavioral problems. The prevalence of emotional and behavioral

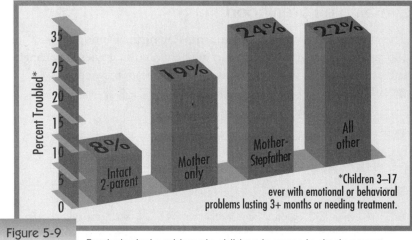

Figure 5-9

Psychological problems in children increase in single-parent families. Source: National Center for Health Statistics—1990

problems, for example, varies from 8 percent among children in intact two-parent families, to between 19 percent and 24 percent among children in nonintact ones, as shown in Figure 5-9.

As David Popenoe of Rutgers University has said, "... in three decades of work as a social scientist, I know of few other bodies of data in which the weight of evidence is so decisively on one side of the issue: On the whole, for children, two-parent families are preferable to single-parent families and stepfamilies."

A Broader Indictment of Society

Other evidence suggests an even broader indictment—of a society that seems unable to control drugs, that cannot even guarantee its children's physical security in school and on the way to it, that fails to reinforce discipline and high standards, that emphasizes instant gratification over working for the future.

The Progressive Policy Institute report, *Putting Children First: A Progressive Family Policy for the 1990s,* gets at the issue with a quote from an article in *Family Affairs.*

Barbara Whitehead illuminated public reactions to family issues through a series of one-on-one and focus group discussions with a cross-section of middle-class parents. Her overall finding is that there are two languages of the family; one is the official language, spoken by experts, politicians, the media, academicians, and other opinion leaders. The second is family language and it is spoken by ordinary citizens. The first language is the language of economics and politics; the second is the language of culture and values. The first is self-consciously relativistic while the second is unabashedly judgmental.

They summarize their findings in this way.

With regard to the family, the views [of the parents] go something like this. A primary purpose of the family is to raise children, and for this purpose families with stably married parents are best. Sharply rising rates of divorce, unwed mothers, and runaway fathers do not represent "alternative life styles." They are rather patterns of adult behavior with profoundly negative consequences for children.

The character of the family, these Americans believe, is the key to raising children successfully. Families have primary responsibility for instilling traits such as discipline, ambition, respect for the law, and respect for others—a responsibility that cannot be discharged as effectively by auxiliary social institutions such as public schools. This responsibility entails a sphere of legitimate parental authority that should be bolstered—not undermined—by society. It requires personal sacrifice and delay of certain forms of gratification on the part of parents. But this responsibility can be fulfilled, even in the face of daunting odds. Generations of Americans have proved that economics and social hardships are compatible with strong families raising competent children—and that such families are the key to overcoming these hardships.

This, then, is the core of average Americans' moral understanding of the family. But these same Americans do not, for the most part, see contemporary society as supportive of this understanding. On the contrary, they see their efforts to transmit moral values to their children counteracted by many of our society's most powerful forces. In sum, they are experiencing not only an economic squeeze, but also a cultural squeeze.

Two principal objects of parental concern are rampant materialism and the dominance of the media, both value-oriented issues. Where do our children receive their values, if not at home? As the parents in the study just cited suggest, popular commercial and entertainment culture play an increasingly central role. Schools and business are also responsible, even though there is a loud chorus that argues for value-neutral education.

Washington Post columnist William Raspberry made the point regarding schools by quoting then-education deputy secretary David Kearns, in an article published on October 7, 1992:

> More and more children are growing up today without the 'nuclear family' that we had ... No matter what sort of family they grow up in, all children need to develop good ethics. The key to these values is education. We are not born with values. They are taught, learned and practiced ... at home, in school, on the playground and in our neighborhoods; by the way we act as adults, by the way we conduct our businesses and by the way we treat each other.
>
> The bottom line is that all of our schools already teach values. They teach them every day in every class and in their halls and gyms." We teach values intentionally, as when, in the wake of the Los Angeles riots, teachers got their students talking about societal neglect and personal responsibility—right and wrong. And we teach them inadvertently—whether by setting solid personal examples or by giving academic credit in spite of skipped classes and indifferent study habits.
>
> There is no such thing as a value-neutral education. Everything is not relative; there are plenty of constants in our American values. Truth is better than dishonesty. Fairness is better than prejudice ... If you exclude values from schools, you will only teach that values aren't important. You send the message that the foundation of America isn't worth teaching, and you provide no alternative to what children see on television.
>
> Yes, children will decide what values are important to them, but they need to know what values are important to *us,* and why.
>
> What is true of schools is also true of companies. As Kearns told his former colleagues, "A company's ethics are reflected in the people it employs, the opportunities it provides them through training and services and the way it conducts internal business ... You either promote good ethics or you allow bad ethics to develop."

There is an increasing chorus questioning the values and ethics of our entertainment industry. Todd Gitlin, a Berkeley sociologist, spoke at a recent conference about the "rage and nihilism" that Hollywood is tossing on screen. He said, "The industry is in the grip of inner forces which amount to a cynicism so deep as to defy parody, 'reveling' in the means to inflict pain, to maim, disfigure, shatter the human image."

James Davidson Hunter characterized it well in the *Washington Post* on September 13, 1992.

> Those who dismiss the conflict over cultural issues as the politics of distraction will miss perhaps the single most important "climatological" change in contemporary American politics: that the culture war is about who we are as a nation and who we will choose to become.
>
> Cumulatively, the disputes amount to a fundamental struggle over the "first principles" of how we will order our life together. Through these seemingly disparate issues we find ourselves, in other words, in a struggle to define ourselves as Americans and what kind of society we want to build and sustain.
>
> Indeed, the cultural cleavages with which we have become familiar have taken shape out of a major realignment in American public culture. It has brought together a wide range of previously antagonistic cultural conservatives (evangelicals and conservative Catholics, for example). It has also united formerly estranged cultural progressives (namely, secularists and progressive religionists) into a new alliance. And each uneasy set of alliances stands against the other as they both try to write into public policy what amounts to opposing visions of what America is and what it should be.

Reprinted with permission of the author.

Writers are beginning to chronicle the tension. *Washington Post* columnist Richard Cohen, recounting his reaction to a well-publicized murder, characterized the numbness that has been brought along by the social change. "It is an awful thing that has happened to us—to me, anyway. When it comes to crime, our hot anger has become cold cynicism. Where once we would have yelled our heads off, now we only murmur our horror to one another at the water cooler and hope something similar doesn't happen to us. The constant taking of life, the very ordinariness of extraordinary violence, has turned us apathetic.

But our loss of anger amounts to more than the loss of innocence: It's the loss of humanity as well."

Our Youth: An Embattled Generation

Who is bearing the brunt of these changes? Clearly, it is our children.

A Country of Poor Children

The 1990 census confirmed that the United States remains a rich nation with poor children. The trends toward marital disruption and single parenthood have contributed most significantly to this issue.

■ In the city of Erie, Pennsylvania 15.4 percent of adults live in poverty; but 35.6 percent of the young children there are poverty stricken.

■ In Los Angeles county, 22 percent of children under 5 years old live in poverty, and in South Central Los Angeles, 44.1 percent of *all* children under 18 live below the poverty line.

Children's poverty has come to be concentrated in families headed by women. By 1989, well over half (57 percent) of all poor children lived in fatherless families. As Peter Morrison says, "Poverty curtails education. Eventually, it erodes future workforce productivity. A rich nation that tolerates poor children in its midst wastes the means to enrich itself further."

Most Stressed-Out Generation in Recent History

This could be the most stressed-out generation in recent history, says Tufts University child psychologist David Elkind.

■ Over 30 percent of 15-year-old girls have experienced sexual intercourse today, as compared with 2 percent in 1979.

■ The sobering consequences of teenage sexual sophistication will be a soon-to-come explosion in teen AIDS cases. *Omni* magazine recently reported that teen pregnancy is greater in the United States than in any other Western society.

■ SAT scores have declined.

■ Suicide and homicide rates are triple what they were 20 years ago.

■ Children are even less healthy than they used to be: The last two decades have seen a 50 percent increase in obesity among children and adolescents.

■■■ Academic achievement has plummeted. "Although there's no overall difference in intelligence, the differences in mathematical achievement of American children and their Asian counterparts are staggering," explained James W. Stigler, coauthor of *The Learning Gap: Why Our Schools Are Failing and What We Can Learn from Japanese and Chinese Education.* American businesses, the authors report, spend some $25 billion each year on remedial education for their employees—virtually all of whom attended public schools.

The stress in our youth generation manifests itself in many ways.

■■■ Eight million junior and senior high-school students drink alcohol every week.

■■■ There is a 1 in 10 chance that a teenage boy will attempt suicide, and a 1 in 5 chance that a girl will try to kill herself.

■■■ Of 1 million teenage mothers, every year 25 percent will have an abortion.

This alienation from the mainstream of American life is reflected in the confidence our children have in our country's institutions. The *Washington Post* recently reported that children are losing trust in government. Less than half of the more than 300,000 children in grades two through six who were surveyed in the spring by *Weekly Reader,* a nationwide classroom newspaper, said they believe their government can be trusted to do what's right.

Character is fundamentally influenced by the individual's view of the future. If young people don't see opportunity on the horizon, they won't do well in school or in most other endeavors.

When young people with this same empty outlook cluster together, a negative synergy develops. Richard Carlson and Bruce Goldman, in *2020 Visions,* have summarized a major aspect of the problem.

Some American communities border on the pathological, imparting ruthlessness, dependency, and despair to their impressionable young instead of skills and values useful to the surrounding society. No single ethnic group has a monopoly on community dysfunction. But inner-city African-American enclaves, victimized not merely by poverty per se but also by rapid economic change, have proceeded farther and faster down the road toward breakdown than any other easily identified communities ...

African-Americans have the shortest life expectancies, the highest rates of teenage pregnancy, and the highest rates of children growing up with only one parent. While African-Americans constitute 12 percent of the population of the United States, they account for more than a quarter of all cases of AIDS reported to date in the U.S.—a fact for which a higher incidence of intravenous illicit-drug use is chiefly responsible.

One in four American black men in their twenties—as contrasted with less than one in fifteen young white men—is either in prison, out on bail, on parole, or on probation. Blacks are likewise much more likely than whites to be victimized by violent crime.

© 1990. Reprinted with permission from The Stanford Alumni Association.

A new study has found that while the number of adults arrested for murder has declined since 1985, there has been a stunning increase in the number of boys under 18 charged with homicide.

"Murder is plunging to a much younger age group," said James Alan Fox, dean of Northeastern University's College of Criminal Justice and a coauthor of the report. "What is so dangerous about this is that a 15-year-old with a gun in his hand is a much more volatile individual than a 40-year-old or even an 18-year-old." According to Fox, the figures suggest that the United States is on the verge of a vast new epidemic of murder, similar to one in the late 1960s and early 1970s, when the rate of violent crime doubled in five years.

THE AMERICA OF THE NEXT TWO DECADES

Rand's Peter Morrison in a 1993 *Rand Note* summarized the American trends in this way:

1. *Families' capacities to meet the needs of dependents will become increasingly narrow.* The family settings in which children grow up will continue to pose enduring problems for social legislation that confronts inadequacies in prenatal care, childcare, and parenting.

2. *By the year 2000, proportionally more Americans will be members of a minority group.* Each minority group will have growing political clout but will also continue to live in much the same areas as it currently does. Most Hispanics and Asians will be geographically clustered in only a

few states; most African-Americans will be isolated residentially within the metropolitan areas in which they live.

3. *Americans will live longer than ever before and elderly people will become far more numerous.* This shift will be gradual in the next 20 years, followed by a period of intensive change that will commence in the year 2011, when the first members of the baby-boom generation reach age 65.

4. *The aging of the population will affect the lives of everyone.* The prevalence of acute and chronic health conditions rises sharply at more advanced ages, and with them the nation's Medicare bill. The limitations on routine activities of daily living, such as eating and bathing, that accompany those conditions can dramatically increase the need for long-term care. The greater number of elderly people and the rise in their life expectancy also mean that more of the "young elderly" (people in their 60s and early 70s) will themselves have very old surviving parents.

5. *At regional and local levels, rapid changes in population size will exacerbate infrastructure and human capital concerns.* Growing areas will experience automobile traffic congestion and the need to replace or add to the infrastructure. Declining areas will experience a wastage of infrastructure and a loss of higher-quality workers.

FORTHCOMING ISSUES

Demographic changes may subtly shape policy issues and occasionally lend urgency to them. They may also increase or decrease the possibility of government action. The following issues illustrate the future policy concerns that the demographic developments discussed here will precipitate.

1. *The decade of the 1990s represents an Indian Summer for the Social Security Trust Fund,* a transitional period during which the large baby boom generation's contributions as workers will boost the fund's size considerably. Starting in 2011, this favorable demographic context will begin to turn sharply unfavorable as the baby boom generation becomes eligible for Social Security. The fund will have to squeeze more dollars out of a slowly growing or possibly shrinking workforce to pay benefits to the swelling number of retirees.

2. *Demographic factors that are causing an increasing number of children to be brought up in poverty raise long-term concerns* because the future competitiveness of the U.S. economy hinges directly on the productivity of

today's youth. Poverty among children curtails educational attainment, thereby reducing the children's future productivity as workers. The issue of economic competitiveness will intensify the congressional focus on childhood poverty and its effect on future workforce quality. This problem also raises the issue of the possibility of increasing social instability, as more and more people become a part of a system in which they don't have much of a vested interest or hope for the future.

3. *As support structures within families narrow, issues of both child care and elder care will evolve and intensify.* The needs of children in vulnerable or disintegrating family structures are already spilling over into the public sector and probably will increase, broadening the demand for various forms of early childhood intervention.

These great forces of exploding numbers of people and the changes in values that they bring with them are fundamentally twisting our country and our world. They are guaranteeing that we will have to radically adjust, in a short period of time, to cities, policies, and cultures with which we are not familiar. It will not be easy.

There are, in this bleakness, points of hope. Supporting these great numbers of people may become easier with some of the breakthroughs that appear on the energy horizon. Let's take a look in that direction.

CHAPTER

6

Energy:

Big Shifts

Fundamental progress has to do with the reinterpretation of basic ideas.
—Alfred North Whitehead

The fuels that allow us to manufacture our technology, pollute our environment, and supply our populations are all just different forms of energy. And because energy plays such a central role in how we live, it is a major driver of global power relationships and the economies of the future. As in the other areas that we have addressed, big changes are afoot in how we will obtain both future electricity and heat. Those shifts are, in large part, reactions to our absolute dependence on energy, and to the paradoxical fact that we are also the victims of the pollution it produces.

Countries like the United States and Japan, which are highly dependent upon other nations for fossil fuels, must always keep an eye on the accessibility of energy sources and the time when these traditional resources are likely to run out. At the same time, the environmental pollution produced by these fuels has become a serious global problem. Developed countries are scrambling to find alternatives and are legislating incentives to spur research into new, cleaner sources.

Lesser-developed countries find themselves squeezed between the need to use increasing amounts of energy to fuel economic development, and the pressures (often primarily from large foreign countries) to find different energy sources than the dirty ones used in the development of the major countries. The developed countries are saying: Don't do it like we did it—but we don't have any alternative ideas yet about how to do it differently.

These pressures have produced a constellation of developments that offer hope for long-term solutions to the world's energy problems, but short-term dependence on conventional energy sources will continue.

CONVENTIONAL SOURCES

If you take an "official" view of our energy future, the Department of Energy believes that United States energy demand should grow slowly over the next two decades as a result of energy conservation measures and advances in energy-efficient technology. According to the *1993 Annual Energy Outlook,* that projection translates into an annual growth rate of 0.9 percent to 1.4 percent, "far below the overall economic growth rate." Nevertheless, if current policies and energy-use trends continue until 2030, national energy consumption will rise 41 percent.

A look at projections for use of common sources of energy will suggest that this "official" scenario is quite possible. But we will also see that absent any revolutionary technology, energy use, particularly in the United States, could decrease substantially with a new set of energy policies.

Oil: A Political Powerhouse

Oil currently supplies 40 percent of the world's energy, and that share may not be reduced for the rest of the decade. As Figure 6-1 shows, in 1991 oil consumption averaged 60 million barrels per day (MMB/D).

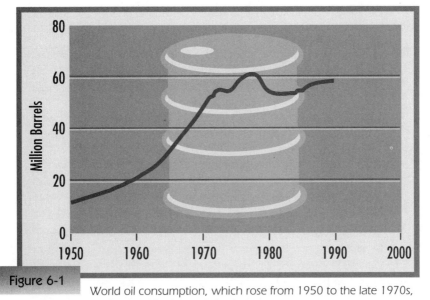

Figure 6-1 World oil consumption, which rose from 1950 to the late 1970s, has flattened out. Source: Worldwatch Institute

Energy analyst A. W. Jessup believes that world oil demand will reach 72 MMB/D by 1996, an increase of nearly 6 MMB/D over 1991.

A quick look shows that East Asia will account for the largest share of the demand increase over this period, a little over 35 percent. The United States will also be a major contributor to the growth in oil demand, consuming about 1 MMB/D more in 1997 than in 1990. According to the United States Energy Information Administration's 1992 Annual Energy Outlook, declining domestic production will cause U.S. imports to increase nearly twice that amount, or by 1.7 to 2 MMB/D.

Gulf Oil Reserves and OPEC

There are plenty of oil reserves to meet the conventionally assumed growth in demand well into the next century—about 1 trillion barrels of proved and probable reserves, 77 percent located in OPEC, 65 percent in the Persian Gulf.

Every barrel of increased oil consumption will be a barrel for OPEC to supply, principally by its Gulf members. United States production will fall, driven by the advent of exclusionary zones that prohibit future domestic prospecting. There are also real questions about the ability of the former Soviet producers to reorganize and overcome problems of low morale, shortages of oil field supplies, and lack of investment.

■ *If demand increases as assumed, OPEC production expansion plans will just cover it;* but since there will be little worldwide spare producing capacity, pressures for an increase in real oil prices could begin as early as 1995.

■ *Within five years, the Gulf producers will have solidified their roles as the Number 1 oil powers.* Other producers will be at maximum sustainable capacity or beginning to decline. Only the Gulf producers will have scope for expansion, and only Saudi Arabia will have almost unlimited capacity to expand to meet the steadily growing world demand. Saudi Arabia will become the swing producer; how fast it expands production will determine how well oil supply and demand will be balanced, and the pressure on prices. According to *Geopolitics of Energy—Supplement,* by Conant and Associates, Ltd., without Saudi expansion beyond its present 10 MMB/D sustainable goal, prices will be under severe upward pressure by 1997.

Presently the global economic slump has driven demand and prices down to uncomfortable (for the producers) lows. The anticipated growth in demand will only come with a decent, and relatively quick, recovery in the global recession—which in 1994 had not yet happened.

Russia has been the largest oil producer at about 9 MMB/D, and the liquid is its largest export, responsible for $13 billion in 1992. But Siberian oil field equipment is in bad shape, morale of workers is very low, and the industry is in trouble. Production dropped to 7.9 MMB/D in 1992 and is moving down. The income generated by oil exports is the principle source for funding of the economic reforms advanced by Boris Yeltsin, yet all indications are that decreasing production will bring the country to the place that it will not be able to supply its own needs, let alone sell to others. "If Russia fails to turn around the energy industry, the reform effort will fail," says David C. Roche, a senior economist at Morgan Stanley.

In some important terms, this is not a pretty picture, leading to:

■ A Russia less stable than it already is

■ A growing dependence on Middle East producers (The Gulf War should have shown us that this dependence is not the best way to supply America's future energy needs.)

■ Continued burning of oil and gasoline, contributing to global warming

Natural Gas, the Clean Energy

A far cleaner fuel, natural gas, exists in abundance. The United States has been producing about 20 trillion cubic feet of natural gas per year for the past 25 years. The Department of Energy believes that the United States has about 8 years worth—167 trillion cubic feet—of proven reserves of natural gas, but it may be much higher. A new report by the National Petroleum Council, supported by the oil industry, estimates that some 1,200 trillion cubic feet of gas in the United States is economically recoverable—60 years worth. Virtually all United States gas reserves have been produced as a counterpart of oil exploration.

Globally, natural gas production has (with one exception) increased quickly since 1950, as shown in Figure 6-2. There are a number of good reasons why the demand for natural gas may well increase in the coming years. Natural gas produces only half of the carbon emissions associated with coal, so growing environmental concerns will encourage more of its use. In an attempt to wean themselves from dependence on Mideast oil, Japan, for example, has shifted its electric production to natural gas and nuclear power. A consortium of Japanese companies plans to build a $20 billion undersea pipeline network that would link eastern Siberia with Japan and most of the rest of the Far East, including South Korea and the Philippines.

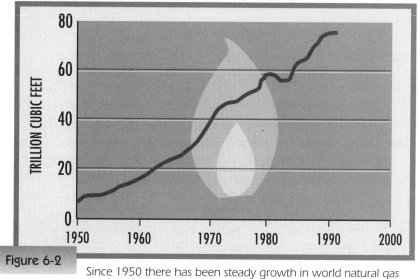

Figure 6-2

Since 1950 there has been steady growth in world natural gas production. Source: Worldwatch Institute

If fuel-cell-powered electric cars become successful, natural gas will be the likely feed stock that is converted to the hydrogen that fuels the cells. This would greatly increase the demand in the first decade of the next century.

Coal: Dirty, Cheap, and Plentiful

The major fuel for United States electric power plants and the major source of greenhouse gases and acid rain is coal. But because of its price, coal is a barrier to the use of other fuels. American coal is plentiful, dirty ... and cheap.

The Christian Science Monitor, in "Saudi Arabia of Coal," from its reprint *Powering the U.S. into the 21st Century,* reported that in 1959, electric utilities accounted for 44 percent of the coal consumed in this country. In 1991, that had increased to 96 percent. They suggested that coal's growing importance in the United States energy mix can be measured in a number of ways:

- Since 1984, coal has been the largest source of domestic energy production, passing 33 percent in 1990. (Because of energy imports, coal accounts for only 23 percent of domestic consumption.)

- Coal production in 1993 reached a record 23 quads, with the excess going to exports that earned $3 billion.

- Fifty-six percent of electrical generation (shown in Figure 6-3) comes from coal—almost 3 times more than nuclear, over 5 times more than natural gas or hydroelectric, and 16 times more than oil.

- The United States has the world's largest coal reserves—25 percent of the total. Ninety percent of the nation's store of fossil fuels is coal. The United States has 6,000 quads of recoverable reserves, 10,500 quads of reserves potentially mineable with existing technology, and identified deposits of 89,000 quads.

Additional demand for coal will come from new power plants and the replacement of old ones. By the year 2000 more than 25 percent of generating capacity will be 50 years old or more and ready to retire. And electricity generation, which accounted for 36 percent of total energy consumption in 1990, could rise to 45 percent by 2010. A midrange projection in the national energy strategy puts U.S. coal consumption up another 65 percent by 2010.

The problem with coal is the sulfur dioxide and nitrogen oxide it gives off when burned. In 1990, burning coal put 2.4 billion tons of

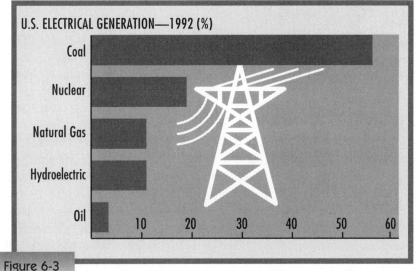

U.S. ELECTRICAL GENERATION—1992 (%)

Coal

Nuclear

Natural Gas

Hydroelectric

Oil

10 20 30 40 50 60

Figure 6-3

Most of our electricity comes from coal-fired power plants.
Source: *Christian Science Monitor*

carbon into the atmosphere worldwide. Government and industry are looking for new methods to decrease these emissions. The Department of Energy launched a $5 billion program in 1986 to develop highly efficient "clean coal" technology for new plants. Thirty projects have been funded so far. One, a "pressurized fluidized bed" combustion system, captures more than 90 percent of coal's sulfur emissions. These advances will be helpful in those places where these new, more expensive plants are being constructed. But for many countries, development is more important than pollution. In the near term, it is likely that more coal will be burned and more atmospheric pollution will result.

China, for example, is the leading user of coal. It presently gets 75 percent of the energy that is powering its explosive economic growth from burning the black nuggets. Many new power plants are being constructed there, and even now the air in some major cities is dangerously laden with pollutants. Until some of the new energy production technologies become mature and competitive, coal will continue to be the major source of fuel in the world.

Nuclear Production Is Flat

It appears that we have reached the peak of world nuclear power plant production. There are more plants being decommissioned than built and, as shown in Figure 6-4, electricity generated from nuclear plants has flattened out. At the same time older plants (whose average age is 17 years, by the way) are being closed at greatly increasing rates. Only 45 nuclear plants are under active construction worldwide, the fewest in a quarter century. Most will be completed by 1996. For reasons having to do with technical problems and nuclear waste storage, dozens of plants may be decommissioned in the near future. National Public Radio recently reported that by 2000, one-third of the United States nuclear plants will run out of space to store their waste in local cooling space. Unless local approval is obtained (which is becoming very hard to do, with the concern that citizens have about the potential effects of nuclear waste dumps), these plants will have to close.

Utilities are finding that the costs of dismantling a nuclear plant are sometimes greater than those of building the plant in the first place—another significant disincentive to the construction of additional plants. Most other countries are having problems with existing plants and are, in the face of increasing public opposition, downscaling any expansion plans. It appears that problems intrinsic to large scale nuclear

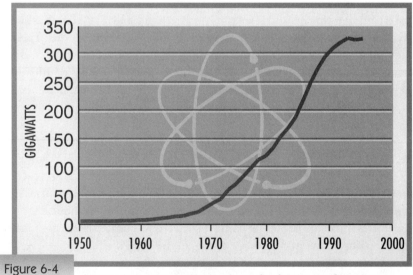

Figure 6-4

Net nuclear construction has been flat for the last few years.

Source: Worldwatch Institute Database

production—cost, waste, operation and technical problems, and catastrophic failure—are finally coming home to roost.

New Designs Probably Too Late

Even though the industry has big problems, designers have produced several new nuclear-based electricity generation concepts that largely eliminate the problems of the earlier designs. They are either on the drawing board or are now being tested.

These models rely for safety not on "active" measures, such as the automatic closing of a valve or an operator turning a wheel in the event of an emergency, but on "passive" features, such as gravity and convection. Even in worst-case scenarios, instead of melting down the reactors simply run down, like a car out of gas. One model not only runs on uranium 238—an isotope 100 times more plentiful than the uranium 235 today's reactors use—but actually eats radioactive waste; specifically, it consumes those long-lived by-products that we're now looking for ways to store underground for 10,000 years or more, and its own wastes decompose within a more workable timeframe of hundreds of years.

The new reactors are small and standardized; thus they can be factory-built and subjected to rigorous quality control, then shipped to their destinations in trucks for on-site assembly. Reduced public concern about safety will speed up the licensing process, which will make the new models competitive with conventional fossil fuel plants.

Although new designs that produce no waste seem appealing, it is unlikely that nuclear power production will ever come back. Public sentiment is seriously against it. The installed base of power plants have immense and increasing waste problems. Existing old plants in Eastern Europe may well fail in the coming years, and new technologies may make them even more obsolete.

New Production Estimates: Many New Plants

The United States government has developed an energy strategy that essentially does more of the same thing that has been done for many years. They assumed a regular escalation of energy requirements to 2030, which would necessitate:

▬ *commercial electricity*—260 new coal and nuclear plants

▬ *industrial and other electricity*—200 new coal and nuclear plants

■■■ *residential electricity—140 new coal and nuclear plants*

America's dependence on foreign sources of energy would, of course, continue to grow, roughly doubling over the next 35 years. It would seem that with the kinds of problems that these methods of generating electricity have produced not only for the United States, but for the world, the American government would be seriously looking for new and better ways to provide for our power needs, rather than doing more of the same thing that got us into this situation.

Change in Carbon Production

Although it will not make any significant difference in the short- or mid-term, the carbon release of burning fossil fuels, as shown in Table 6-1, decreases as humans move toward hydrogen, which now appears on the horizon. Every ton of carbon in fuel combines with oxygen in the atmosphere to release 3.66 tons of CO_2. Absent any new legislation or other action to curb them, the Department of Energy expects carbon emissions to grow by 0.7% to 1.3% annually between 1993 and 2030—an increase of 58 percent.

Fuel	% Hydrogen	% Carbon	Ratio H_2/C
Firewood	9	91	0.1
Coal	50	50	1
Oil	67	33	2
Natural Gas	80	20	4

Table 6-1. Decarbonization of fossil fuel sources

SOLAR: UNLIMITED, CLEAN, BUT EXPENSIVE

Converting the sun's energy directly into usable electricity or heat is the objective of a great many researchers and environmentalists. It has always seemed like the cleanest and best solution to the great problems of pollution and economic development that confront the world. In the past, solar technology has generally been quite expensive and rather unwieldy. Just connecting to the grid has always been easier and cheaper. But in the last few years, great progress has been made in the development of two familiar solar technologies, photovoltaics and wind-generated power.

Photovoltaics Are Dropping in Price

Science reported in 1989 that the cost of photovoltaic power generation has shrunk by a factor of 40 in the last decade, bringing it close to

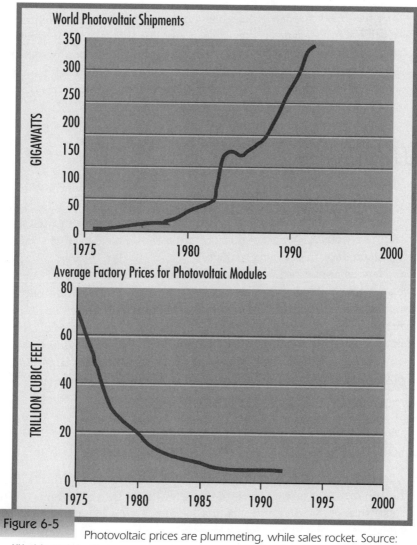

Figure 6-5

Photovoltaic prices are plummeting, while sales rocket. Source: Worldwatch Institute

competing with other sources of electricity. As Figure 6-5 shows, as the price has fallen, the shipments have increased. It seems likely that advances in solar cells will be such that within the next few years, it will become economical to generate a significant amount of residential power through this pollution-free source, particularly if the cost continues to fall. Home owners could easily supplement electricity they purchase from the power company with roof-mounted cellular arrays. Already, some new cars can be purchased with installed solar arrays that power fans to offset the warming effect of solar radiation.

A real breakthrough would happen if the cost became significantly less than central-plant-produced electricity. If nanotechnology develops anything like it appears it might, that could easily happen within the next two decades. Eric Drexler's vision of streets paved with tough, durable solar cells begins to give one an idea of the relative cost of this kind of manufacturing.

Wind Power Competes with Coal

New technology has also made windmills, known as wind turbines, competitive with fossil fuels for producing electricity. Windmills are pollution-free; and now, with advances in aerodynamics and microelectronics, significant portions of the world have been opened up to the production of clean electricity.

New computer technology allows much smoother air flow over the blades and maintains the frequency of the alternating current output, resulting in much higher levels of efficiency. Nevertheless, the problems of size, location, and noise remain. Only certain locations have an average wind velocity high enough to drive a wind turbine efficiently; and tower and wind vane structures are quite large. Wind power will always be uniquely applicable to only a relatively small set of applications, but it is a godsend in those situations.

Renewable Sources Could Make a Difference

Approaches that use the energy of the sun more efficiently than fossil fuels, and that are renewable, are gaining in acceptance and sophistication. Hydropower, biomass (using a crop like corn to make fuels like alcohol), and waste-to-energy technologies, along with geothermal and solar thermal facilities, are becoming increasingly viable. The *Christian Science Monitor* reported that J. Michael Davis, Assistant Secretary of Energy, said that "Collectively [renewables] offer a diverse and virtually inexhaustible resource … It is substantially less harmful to the environment … It can contribute significantly to our economic and energy security." Davis said that the size of the resource is orders of magnitude larger than foreseeable demand.

Presently, renewables supply just 8 percent of the U.S. demand (13 percent of U.S. electrical consumption). But a recent study by five national laboratories concludes that even without any change in policy, this portion will double over the next 40 years because of accelerating technological and economic trends. The government white paper predicts that doubling or tripling federal research and development efforts (spending another $3 billion over the next two decades) would nearly quadruple the contribution of renewable energy sources.

EFFICIENCY

Perhaps the largest single source of new energy lies in the efficient use of electricity and heat. We began the chapter on the environment by noting that we have pollution problems because humans waste so much. We also waste huge amounts of energy; and even rather small successes at stopping that waste add up to giant savings.

As the economy grows and the need for electricity increases, this country and the world can either build more generating capacity, or increase the efficiency of the way we use the energy that we already produce. There are clear advantages to taking the efficiency route.

New Technologies Make It Possible

With new energy-saving technologies, some only a year or two old, it is possible to save as much as 75 percent to 80 percent of the electricity used in a typical office building. These techniques produce the same office environment for much less cost. As a matter of fact, the new technology usually pays for itself in savings over a period of one to six years. Other benefits of this approach are manifold: smaller requirements from power plants that produce pollution, smaller capital expenditures for increased capacity (the money can be used elsewhere in the economy), less fuel required, and so on.

Modern "superwindows," for example, can now insulate as well as 8 to 12 sheets of glass (or a solid, insulated wall) and let in three-fifths of the visible light but only 2 percent of the infrared (heat rays). These energy-efficient windows, coated with low-emissivity glazing that keeps in heat, have saved $3 billion worth of energy since they were introduced in 1981. Amory Lovins says that from the initial "oil shock" in 1973 through the 1980s, more "new" energy was obtained through efficiency than from all other sources of supply combined—seven times as much. "New technologies, most of the best less than a year old, can save twice as much electricity as five years ago, at a third of the cost," he says.

Similar savings can be realized by replacing motors (which use half of all U.S. electricity) with new efficient ones, buying energy-efficient office equipment, and downsizing heating, ventilating, and air conditioning systems to compensate for savings in other areas.

Behavior Change

Enormous differences in the requirement for energy can be made when people change their minds about how they use it. After the oil embargo in 1973, Americans became much more concerned about energy, and the U.S. automobile fleet increased its efficiency by 5 miles per gallon. Lovins's Rocky Mountain Institute has shown that between 1977 and 1985, the United States steadily and routinely saved oil four-fifths faster than it needed to do in order to keep up with both economic growth and declining domestic oil output. This 5 percent per year increase in national oil productivity cut total oil imports in half.

The California Energy Commission estimates that cost-effective investments could reduce total U.S. electricity demand by 40 percent to 75 percent, while improving the quality of life through cleaner air and lower energy costs. Computers are a case in point. More energy-efficient machines could decrease U.S. commercial energy consumption by as much as 10 percent. Amory Lovins asserts that about 6 percent of all the electricity used for commercial purposes in the country goes to power our 30 million to 35 million computers and attached peripherals. A roughly equal amount of power is consumed by the heating and air-conditioning systems in office buildings that deal with the heat that the office automation equipment gives off. Laptop computers eliminate most of both of these requirements; and when flat panel wall displays are available that can be driven by a laptop, there will be no need for the power-hungry machines that we are all accustomed to.

"Nationwide installation of just one fixture—low-flow showerheads that conserve hot water," said Worldwatch vice president Sandra Postel, "would save as much energy as oil drilling in Alaska's Arctic National Wildlife Refuge would be expected to produce, and at a far lower economic and environmental cost."

High-Efficiency Cars on the Horizon

Energy guru Amory Lovins likes to say, "There's a whole Saudi Arabia under Detroit." The amount of petroleum saved by implementing presently available gas-saving technologies in automobiles would be the same as discovering an oil field the size of the Saudi reserves. The Rocky Mountain Institute has shown conclusively that fresh designs using existing technology could easily produce new cars that would get over 100 miles per gallon of gas. More on this is found in Chapter 7.

These cars would use composite fiber construction (rather than steel) and would be stronger, more crash resistant, peppier, and far more economical to run than the current output of Detroit, Japan, and Germany. They would probably cost less than current models. They would have more interior room than present cars and would be powered by a hybrid power plant that used both electrical and internal combustion components. Power from braking, for example, would be shunted back into a battery rather than being converted into heat, as today's cars do. The good news is that Lovins is consulting for some of the major auto manufacturers, and his ideas are being seriously considered.

International Solutions

Efficient use of energy can also make a huge difference in developing countries. Some years ago, the People's Republic of China decided it was time that people had refrigerators, and built more than a hundred refrigerator factories. The fraction of Beijing households owning a refrigerator rose from a few percent to more than 60 percent from 1981 to 1986. Unfortunately, however, through mere inattention, an inefficient refrigerator design had been chosen, thereby committing

China to billions of dollars' worth of electric capacity to serve those refrigerators.

A partial solution to the problem of growing energy requirements in developing countries is energy-efficient design, not only of individual appliances and factories, but of whole electrical systems.

Clearly, we use far more energy than we need to. Not only does it cost us many times more than it should, it also seriously contributes to the destruction of the biosphere. Efficiency wins all around.

POSSIBLE TECHNOLOGY BREAKTHROUGHS

The really exciting potential for attacking the twin issues of dependence and pollution lies with a number of new technologies that appear to be on the near horizon. Within the next two decades, they could have profound, overnight implications for the world's use and production of energy.

Room-Temperature Superconductivity

A great amount of work is being done in the area of superconductivity, the phenomenon that allows materials to transmit electricity without any resistance. If room-temperature superconductivity were discovered, it would make almost all electrical equipment and power distribution systems obsolete. A good part of the energy that we do need (that we don't waste) is required to offset the resistance in wires and other conductors. When electricity interacts with this resistance, it is converted to heat and uselessly vented into the atmosphere. Highly efficient superconducting wire, lighting, and motors would decrease the need for power plants, many of which contribute to the atmospheric pollution problems that the globe is now experiencing. It would be a particular boon to third world countries, helping them to get around the waste and inefficiency that characterized the development of the world's more advanced countries.

Since it was first discovered in 1911, superconductivity was thought to exist only at temperatures very close to absolute zero. In 1986, working with entirely new classes of materials, researchers developed a material with a superconducting transition temperature of 39 Kelvin. Rapid progress increased the temperature to 125 Kelvin within two years. With the amount of time and resources being given to this area, it is quite likely that important breakthroughs will occur in the coming years.

Scientists don't understand why some materials superconduct, so the technique for experimentation in this area is to try as many combinations of materials as possible, hoping to hit on the one that generates encouraging results. Advances in computational chemistry could well be responsible for the quick discovery of a substance that shows no energy loss at room temperature.

If there were no resistance at common temperatures, it would usher in a whole new generation of products that were not possible before (like magnetic levitation trains with no need for cryogenic cooling), and would greatly enhance the efficiency of products like computers (because there would be much less heat loss in microprocessors) and motors. Over time, the need for electricity would plummet, as the internal inefficiencies of electrical equipment approached zero.

Zero-Point Energy ... The Future

What if you were able to "take energy out of the air" and convert it directly into heat or electricity, with absolutely no other by-products (that is, pollutants) produced in the process? The energy source would be essentially unlimited: You could turn on a generator or battery and it would run without any apparent need for fuel. Sound too much like science fiction? It may be that, but it's also true—and close to commercial production.

Quantum mechanics says that most of the energy in the universe is in "space." The great physicist David Bohm once opined that "There is more energy in a cubic centimeter of space than in all of the known matter in the universe." We humans are actually walking around in a sea of this very high-level "zero-point" energy, very much like a fish swimming in the water of the ocean. It is called "zero-point" because it is the ambient energy left in space after all of the heat has been removed—absolute zero.

Taking energy out of the electromagnetic fluctuations in a vacuum seems too good to be true. But, at least two zero-point energy (ZPE) generation experiments have reportedly been operating successfully in this country, and research programs are underway in Japan and Germany as well. One approach, taken by the Institute for Advanced Research in Austin, Texas, is protected by international patents and has been discussed with a wide variety of government and corporate representatives. The present experiment is generating twice the energy that is put into it. The inventors hope to have a working model by 1996 that needs no input and can be used as the basis for full-scale engineering. They believe that within a decade it will be the most widespread type of energy generation.

This technology is revolutionary, and would change the whole equation of global energy. It could solve the economic development problem for the poorer parts of the world by providing low-cost pollution-free energy. Over time, it could eliminate most of the planet's sources of atmospheric pollution. It would also immediately begin to depreciate the value of petroleum as a fuel, and make it available as a primary feedstock for nanotechnology-based manufacturing.

The significance of this discovery should attract extraordinary interest and effort once it becomes established as credible. That kind of reaction should result, very quickly, in practical products. It seems reasonable to assume that by 2012 a major industrial segment will be built around this technology. Perhaps an analogy would be to think of the progress that has been made in computer technology in the past 20 years and project that kind of effort out for about the next two decades for the development of zero-point energy generation.

Cold Fusion

As mentioned in the technology section, cold fusion, or whatever the reaction is, continues to produce enough success to have the interest of segments of the scientific communities in Japan, India, and the United States. One of the inventors of a successful zero-point generator believes that the cold fusion phenomena may well be a manifestation of zero-point energy. In any case, it does appear that something of interest is going on here, although at very early stages of development.

If, in the next few years, cold fusionists come to believe that what they are seeing has to do with zero-point energy, it could be a real push for the whole ZPE endeavor.

ENERGY POLICY

Although it seems reasonable to think that as our economy grows we will need to consume more energy, the idea is fallacious. It is wrong because we waste so much energy and have incentives in place that encourage wasteful behavior. If government (and personal) policies were put in place that changed the attitude of energy users to one that valued energy efficiency, huge differences in consumption would result. Engineers would design equipment with power consumption in mind. Architects would have energy efficiency at the top of their list of building priorities. Automobile and engine designers would approach their jobs from a far different perspective. Consumers would search for the most efficient electrical appliances and lighting equipment. It would be a revolution that would clean up the atmosphere and produce as much as $2.3 trillion in net savings for the United States over the next 40 years—money that could be invested in other, more productive areas.

A change toward an effective energy policy aimed at stabilizing the degradation of the climate would take into account every area of energy use. Recently the Natural Resources Defense Council joined with a group of similar organizations interested in building a strong economy and clean environment to produce a landmark report, *America's Energy Choices, Investing in a Strong Economy and a Clean Environment,* which deals with the policy aspects of energy, sector by sector. Their findings are an excellent example of systems-based planning.

Buildings

Tremendous cost-effective energy savings would result from the use of more than 60 types of conservation technologies and measures currently available. These range from more efficient lighting, windows, and appliances in existing residences, to more efficient heating, ventilating, and air-conditioning systems in new commercial buildings.

Industry

Large contributions to energy supply can be had from cogeneration, solar, and geothermal resources. Cogeneration uses the by-products (like heat) from one generation process (like a fossil fuel power plant) as the fuel for another factory or industrial process.

Transportation

Energy efficiency can be increased by improving vehicle technology by shifting to more efficient transportation modes, by changing land-use patterns, and by implementing measures that reduce wasteful travel (such as single-occupant commuting). At the same time, emissions of CO_2 and other pollutants can be reduced by improving efficiency and switching to less polluting fuels.

Much of the energy for personal transportation could be supplied by electricity and by biofuels such as methanol, ethanol, and hydrogen. Biofuels could be produced from wastes or energy crops, such as short-rotation trees and grasses, that would be grown on a large scale and converted to fuel using thermochemical and biochemical processes now under development.

Electricity Supply

Near-term conventional and advanced fossil technologies and electric-generating facilities that use renewable resources, and the penetration of more advanced coal technology (fuel cells and magnetohydro-dynamic facilities), could be coupled with advanced renewable energy technologies to produce significant savings.

New Energy Policies

The policies that put in place the above changes must be comprehensive, fair, and enlightened, and they must:

■ harness market forces

■ make efficiency the standard

■ invest in the future

These three basic approaches can be expanded into a series of policies, detailed below.

Harnessing market forces:

■ *Promote least-cost planning.* Eliminate regulatory incentives for increased energy sales, require all utilities to develop least-cost plans that allow supply-side and demand-side measurers to compete on an equal footing, and ensure that least-cost investments are the most profitable investments for the utility.

■ *Establish a production tax credit for renewable energy supplies.* To help correct for the different tax treatment of fuel expenses versus capital investment (which biases energy choices away from capital-intensive fossil technologies), and to help the renewable energy industries expand their levels of production so as to achieve significant economies of scale, the federal government should establish and expand production tax credits for renewable energy supply.

■ *Use market incentives to promote efficient technologies.* Charge fees on inefficient technologies or give rebates for efficient ones. When both are combined, the practice is known as "feebates."

■ *Shift some of the tax burden from income to pollution.* To reflect the environmental and national security costs of various energy sources, the government could assess fees on fossil fuel consumption, with part or all of the revenues used to reduce income or other taxes.

Making efficiency the standard:

■ *Increase automobile fuel-economy standards to cut U.S. oil dependence.* Raise the fuel economy of new cars from 28 mpg to 46 mpg during the next ten years, while maintaining vehicle size, performance, and safety.

■ *Set building and equipment efficiency standards to minimize life-cycle costs.* Standards should be set, and gradually raised over time, in such areas as new construction, existing building retrofits, appliances, lamps, and motors. The federal government should update and strengthen the national model energy code, require states and localities to meet or exceed this code, and require that federally financed or subsidized buildings also meet it.

■ *Require effective energy management at federal government facilities.* Conservative estimates show that the federal government can save more than $850 million per year in its own buildings by making cost-effective efficiency improvements. Federal, state, and local governments should invest in such efficiency measures, as well as in cost-effective renewable energy production.

Investing in the future:

■ *Give energy efficiency and renewables their fair share of federal research and development (R&D) dollars.* Federal R&D efforts should shift away from the current heavy emphasis on nuclear energy and fossil fuels, and more priority should be given to energy efficiency and renewable energy R&D.

■ *Develop an integrated transportation network to increase access and cut congestion.* These policies include the market-based measures discussed above to ensure that automobile users pay the full costs of driving, and encompass zoning changes that would discourage sprawl and encourage in-fill development in cities, towns, and surrounding suburbs; high-occupancy-vehicle lanes and ride-sharing programs that would increase passenger occupancy in personal vehicles; and substantial increases in funding for rail- and bus-transit projects.

■ *Expand education, training, and certification programs in energy-efficient and renewable energy design and construction.* Expand support for educational programs that increase the number of qualified designers of national energy programs, conservation program managers at utilities, inspectors of construction sites for compliance with energy-efficient building codes, and other such professions.

BIG CHANGES IN THE NEXT TWO DECADES

An emerging convergence of attitude shifts may radically change the global energy landscape within the next two decades. A large-scale response to the environmental problem will, of necessity, focus on the way we use energy. It will become clear that we cannot continue producing it and using it as we have done in the past. Whatever happens, fossil fuels will decrease in importance. The change will be dramatic if the environmental problem is seen as a threat to the security of humankind. Advances made in the zero-point energy field may exacerbate the shift to new sources, while a real sense of threat would produce extraordinary short-term increases in efficiency.

One only hopes that these changes come fast enough to effectively allay the major problems that our present energy systems and policies have produced.

As with so many other aspects of the larger system, energy issues are married to others like pollution and transportation. Transportation is particularly key, for huge amounts of money and energy are used to move people and products around the earth, sea, and sky. But, as is the case across the board, great changes are emerging in the transportation sector.

CHAPTER

7

Transportation: Moving in New Directions

Being in a ship is being in a jail, with the chance of being drowned.

—Dr. Samuel Johnson

A small number of decisions we make play a major role in shaping many other areas of our lives. For example, when we decide what (and how) we will eat, a huge system of farms, distributors, stores, manufacturers, and restaurants responds directly to those desires. One of the most important decisions we make concerns the way we move ourselves and our commodities. Our system of transportation greatly affects how we use energy, develop technology, affect the economy and environment, and shape our social relationships.

Today, significant advances are taking place in all sectors of transportation. As we will see, these will dramatically change the way we work and travel in the next two decades.

PUBLIC TRANSPORTATION

Compared to other forms of transportation, cars are expensive and very dirty. In the long run, it looks like the area where the greatest contribution to society can be made is public transportation. As Vice President Al Gore has written in *Earth in the Balance,* "We should be emphasizing attractive and efficient forms of mass transportation.... New and improved forms of mass transit, like the magnetically levitated trains in Japan and [rapid trains in] France, should be enthusiastically encouraged."

Some exciting developments in transportation technology may some day help us travel quickly and efficiently while treading lightly on the environment. These include magnetic levitation, high-speed trains, supersonic transport aircraft, and magnetohydrodynamic ship propulsion.

Magnetic Levitation

In 1912, Emile Bachelet, a French-born New Yorker, received a United States patent for a magnetically levitated train. However, it wasn't until the advent of the large superconducting magnets that the repulsion scheme of magnetic levitation, as it is now known, became practical.

The technology employs the opposing force that develops between a moving magnet and the eddy currents it induces in stationary conductors fastened in the guideway, as shown in Figure 7-1. The advantage of magnetic levitation, or maglev, is that it eliminates mechanical contact between a vehicle and the surface over which it rides, thus eliminating wear, contact noise, and problems of precise alignment. The vehicle floats as much as half a foot above the surface, supported and guided entirely by magnetic forces.

The initial development of a practical high-speed maglev system took place in the United States from 1971 to 1976 under Federal Railroad Administration and National Science Foundation sponsorship. The Japanese soon embraced the technology, and proceeded to break the tracked vehicle speed record (still unbeaten) with a 320 mile per

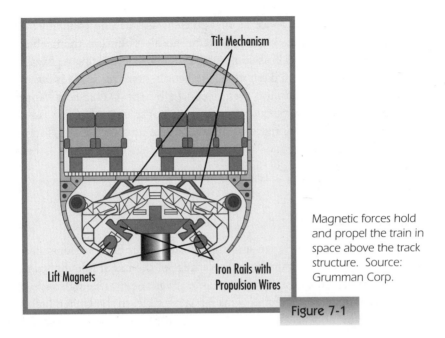

Tilt Mechanism

Lift Magnets

Iron Rails with Propulsion Wires

Magnetic forces hold and propel the train in space above the track structure. Source: Grumman Corp.

Figure 7-1

hour run in 1979, using a full-scale research vehicle at the Miyazaki test track.

The Germans have developed a prototype based on the somewhat different concept that employs the familiar force between an ordinary electromagnet on the vehicle and an iron rail on the guideway. Since this is an unstable force, it requires the gap between magnet and rail (typically less than half an inch) to be maintained by continuous adjustment of the magnet current. The prototype is expected to be operated in Orlando, Florida, in the next few years. The Japanese and Germans have spent approximately $1 billion each on research.

After a hiatus of 15 years, the U.S. government has reentered this competition on a much smaller scale by way of the National Maglev Initiative, a partnership among the U.S. Departments of Transportation (DOT) and Energy (DOE) and the U.S. Army Corps of Engineers.

A network of maglevs could shuttle passengers between American cities at over 300 miles per hour, using far less energy and time than automobile and air travel. One could go from a downtown office to a weekend cottage 100 miles away in just 20 minutes, or take a portal-to-portal trip of about an hour and a half between the air-shuttle cities of Los Angeles and San Francisco, Washington and Boston, and Chicago and Minneapolis.

Maglevs would be twice as fuel-efficient as cars and four times as efficient as airplanes, while producing no air pollution themselves. Commuter maglev systems could be built alongside existing highways, decreasing construction disruption. The requirement for space is far less than for aircraft: The land area occupied by the Dallas-Fort Worth airport is equal to a 60-foot swath from coast to coast. The trains would be considerably more comfortable than aircraft. As fast, roomy trains in Japan and France have shown, maglevs could grow to be a significant segment of the public transportation sector.

High-Speed Trains

Many countries, like Japan and the Western European nations, have very well-developed train systems. Because of the major role that trains play in those economies, considerable investment is being made to push passenger train technology as far as possible. In the United States, except in the northeast corridor, the car and plane are kings. Few new passenger train routes are being planned, but some significant advances are being undertaken to make the present service more efficient.

The National Railroad Passenger Corporation (AMTRAK) has undertaken a major program to increase the speed of passenger trains in the routes between Washington, New York, and Boston. Reducing the travel time is expected to make train travel much more attractive.

Much of the high-speed capability of the Japanese and French "bullet" trains comes from electrification and significantly upgraded or even dedicated right-of-way coupled with lighter-weight vehicles and microprocessor train control systems. For high-speed service, track curvatures are normally shallow and banked, making it possible for conventional train technology to transverse the curve safely with a high ride quality for the passenger. This is typical of the French Train à Grande Vitesse (TGV), the German Intercity Express (ICE), and the Japanese Shinkansen "bullet" train operations.

A tilting train technology has been developed that will run on the existing trackbed. An example is the Swedish X2000 train, shown in Figure 7-2, which has been tested up to 155 mph but travels at 135 mph in its demonstration service along the northeast corridor of the United States. This train has axles that automatically adapt to the curvature of the track, thus allowing significantly increased speed on existing track curvatures. An automatic system tilts the car while it goes around a

Figure 7-2

The Swedish X2000 train tilts as it goes around corners.
Source: ABB Traction, Inc.

curve, to reduce the lateral force experienced by the passenger. This train was evaluated in 1993 in once-a-day round trips between Washington and New York, and later New Haven, in an effort to determine rider acceptance.

The X2000 tilt train was followed in 1993 by a demonstration service with the German ICE, which is a more conventional, nontilting design. The ICE regularly operates at 150 mph in service in Germany, but will also operate at 135 mph in the northeast corridor. Both of these trains are being studied by AMTRAK as it prepares to solicit proposals for new equipment that will be needed to service the Boston-to-Washington corridor in 1997.

The French TGV (Atlantique), traveling at speeds up to 200 mph will be operating in the "Texas Triangle" (Dallas/Ft. Worth-Houston-San Antonio). The first operational phase between Dallas/Ft. Worth and Houston is planned for 1998.

Five existing rail corridors have been selected for development as high-speed corridors under the Intermodal Surface Transportation Efficiency Act of 1991. These corridors are being studied for their potential for upgrade to 90-mph service initially, with gradual increases thereafter. The principal limiting factor will be the existing infrastructure, which includes roadbed, alignment, signaling, highway-rail crossings, and nonelectrified propulsion.

Supersonic Transport Aircraft

Twenty years ago, America decided against supersonic transport because it was too expensive, too dirty, and too noisy. New technological advances, however, are now dealing with all of these objections. Furthermore, the air travel market to and within Asia is expected to boom during the next two decades.

NASA, working with aircraft and engine manufacturers, is at the halfway mark in a seven-year, $400-million initiative to develop environmentally compatible technology. The goals of this project are to:

- develop reliable predictions of the effect of HSCT (high speed civil transport) on stratospheric ozone

- reduce engine emissions of NOx (Nitrogen oxides)

- develop quieter aircraft and engines

- determine how well sonic booms can be softened to permit limited supersonic flight over unpopulated land corridors

Flying at mach 4, the HSCT would make a trip from Los Angeles to Tokyo in only 2 hours, instead of the present 12 hours. If the costs were kept in the same ballpark as current air travel, such a vehicle would, of course, revolutionize air travel.

National and international air transportation systems are growing. Increases of about a trillion revenue passenger-miles are projected for each decade between 1993 and 2020, resulting in 2 trillion revenue passenger-miles in the year 2000, 3 trillion in 2010, and 4 trillion in 2020. Much of this growth is projected to be in international markets. The Europe-Asia market is projected to experience significant growth and the North Atlantic market is expected to double by 2005; but more important, the Pacific market (with its longer ranges) is forecast to quadruple during this time, to about the same size as the North Atlantic market. China's economic growth is causing air travel to expand very fast in that area. Estimates call for Asian travel to grow at least twice as fast in the next decade as air travel in Europe and North America. China has launched a massive effort to build new airports, with more than 20 major facilities now under construction or in the planning stage across the country. While the rest of the global airline business is in a major slump, new airlines and joint ventures are being formed to serve the burgeoning China market.

Based on these market projections, if a reasonable fare premium is assumed, an HSCT is optimistically thought to be able to attract about 300,000 passengers per day away from advanced subsonic transports by the year 2000, and about 600,000 passengers per day by 2015. This translates into a worldwide potential market for 600 to 1,500 HSCTs, depending on economic returns, aircraft specifications, operating constraints, and subsonic flight over land. The aircraft would be introduced about 2005, cruise at speeds of mach 1.6 to mach 2.5, have ranges between 5,000 and 6,500 miles, carry 250 to 300 passengers, and operate in the existing infrastructure (airports, runways, and air traffic management systems) to maximize productivity.

Magnetohydrodynamic Ship Propulsion

A revolutionary technology being tested in Japan for ship propulsion, magnetohydrodynamics (MHD), contains the seeds of a major shift in the way humans travel on the ocean. The principle is based on a fundamental law of electromagnetism: When a magnetic field and an electric current intersect in a liquid, their repulsive interaction propels the liquid perpendicular to both the field and the current. In seawater, the salt conducts electricity. The prototype, *Yamato 1,* works like this: The seawater, through which an electric current is being passed, is channeled through the magnetic field produced by superconducting magnets cooled with liquid helium. The water is then propelled out the rear, moving the boat forward.

This propulsion system has no moving parts to break down, and is quiet and vibration free. At present, however, the system cannot move the prototype boat faster than 8 knots, with a maximum efficiency of 4 percent. The efficiency of commercial ships ranges between 22 percent for hydrofoils and 60 percent for cargo ships.

Initial research on this application of MHD was done in the United States, but was abandoned when researchers found that then-current metal magnets were too heavy to be efficient. Kensaku Imaichi, the designer of *Yamato 1,* is a specialist in superconductivity, which makes the current prototype possible. He anticipates that if new ceramic or other supermagnetic material can be found, ships can be propelled at speeds of 40 to 50 knots, or even higher if hulls can be made more stable.

Such a combination of breakthroughs would revolutionize ships in general, and ocean shipping in particular. Japanese technologists believe this will happen. They predict that full-sized ocean freighters traveling at over 100 miles per hour will ply the seas by the year 2007, shortening the trip from Japan to California to two days.

PRIVATE TRANSPORT

As we have seen, one of the major sources of atmospheric pollution is the automobile, with its internal combustion engine. The oil shock of the 1970s sent car designers looking for alternatives, and for a while the electric car seemed just around the corner. Then gas in the United States got cheap again. But now new advances in technology and changes in government regulations are again pushing hard toward an electric or hybrid car and appear to be precipitating a revolution in automobiles.

The Electric "Zero-Emission" Automobile Is Coming

The primary push comes from a new California law that mandates that 2 percent of the cars sold by any manufacturer in the year 1998 must produce zero emissions, and that by 2003, 10 percent of sales must produce no pollutants. Since California is the major market in the world for automobiles, manufacturers are now scrambling to produce electric cars—apparently, the only kind that produces zero emissions. The federal government is supporting new research, and almost every major automaker plans to introduce a model by 1998.

In contrast to 15 years ago, there are lighter and stronger materials available, and electric motors and batteries have improved in efficiency. Electric motors are 90 percent efficient and battery packs are about 80 percent efficient. If we assume that the batteries are charged by plugging them into an electrical socket, then the electricity is ultimately being generated by fossil fuels, and the average efficiency of electric plants is only about 32 percent. This makes the current energy efficiency of an electric car about 23 percent—less than that of a high-mileage gasoline car on the highway.

These cars are planned primarily as commuter cars. A study done by the Electric Power Research Institute (EPRI) in 1989 compared nearly identical gasoline-powered and electric-powered minivans. They found

Figure 7-3 This ultralightweight Swiss Esro e301 car gets 120 to 150 miles per gallon of gasoline. Source: Rocky Mountain Institute/Horlacher

that in urban use, electric vans required only 60 percent to 75 percent of the energy consumed by the gasoline vans. A converted Geo Metro is about 63 percent more efficient. And the Impact, by GM, which was designed from the ground up as a high-performance sports car, is even more efficient because of its lightweight, aerodynamically designed body and low rolling-resistance tires.

The Swiss have been working in this area as well. Figure 7-3 shows a prototype ultralightweight, two-place car with a body made almost completely out of composite fiber materials. The curb weight is only about 400 kilograms (880 pounds).

Drawbacks to Batteries Remain

Some of the drawbacks that stood in the way of economical electric cars 15 years ago still remain: battery expense, life, and weight; recharge time overnight as opposed to a few minutes filling up with gas; the availability of recharging stations; and short range without recharge. And if the electric car is really to reduce pollution significantly, then it is necessary for the plants that generate the electricity for recharging batteries to be clean as well. The whole system must be clean.

This simple battery approach has only moved the pollution source from the car back to the power plant. The lack of efficiency of the whole system translates into increased pollution—but not on the highway.

There is an alternative, though, that is quite different: hydrogen fuel cells. Working somewhat like batteries, fuel cells produce electricity directly and cleanly (the only by-product being water) from the H_2. Hydrogen, which is the most plentiful energy source on the planet, can be produced from water and also from natural gas. Present technology fuel cells potent enough to power a car are smaller than many current automobile engines. A diagram of the drive train of a typical hybrid fuel-cell/capacitor/electric car is shown in Figure 7-4.

Studies have shown that by the turn of the century, present technology will make it as safe and cheap to convert and distribute hydrogen for use in fuel-cell-powered automobiles as it is for gasoline now. Small units could be installed in residential garages that convert natural gas—already present in most homes—directly to hydrogen. Alternatively, H_2 could be trucked (as gasoline is now) to service stations, for distribution there.

According to Worldwatch Institute's Christopher Flaven, "Fuel cells are the most obvious alternative, since they allow the efficient production of electricity ... with an efficiency about twice that of today's engines.... Solar hydrogen could eventually become the

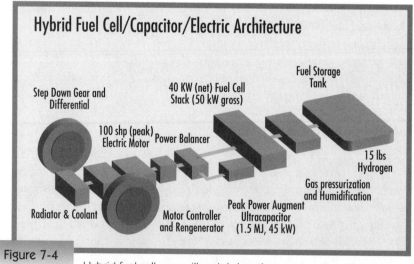

Hybrid Fuel Cell/Capacitor/Electric Architecture

Fuel Storage Tank

Step Down Gear and Differential

40 KW (net) Fuel Cell Stack (50 kW gross)

100 shp (peak) Electric Motor Power Balancer

15 lbs Hydrogen

Gas pressurization and Humidification

Radiator & Coolant

Motor Controller and Rengenerator

Peak Power Augment Ultracapacitor (1.5 MJ, 45 kW)

Figure 7-4

Hybrid fuel-cell cars will weigh less than conventional internal combustion cars. Source: Directed Technologies, Inc.

foundation of a new global energy economy." If fuel cells become the choice of automobile buyers, we could see the end of the age of internal combustion engines and the entry of the hydrogen era.

Further out, there is the possibility of zero-point energy generators producing the electricity, thus eliminating all of the upstream production associated with any other fuel.

Alternative Fuel Vehicles

Other fuels are being assessed for automobile use. Vehicles powered by compressed natural gas produce minimal amounts of key pollutants. Natural gas can be burned in high-compression engines, which allows efficiency to improve 15 percent to 20 percent and CO_2 emissions to be cut 30 percent. The exhaust from a hydrogen-powered car contains only water vapor and small amounts of nitrogen oxide (NOx). NOx is a greenhouse gas; but since natural gas burns cleaner than gasoline, engineers believe that a simple catalytic converter can eliminate virtually all emissions.

Policy Implication of Efficient Cars

The above examples of technical efficiency suggest that efficiencies of about ten times those of present vehicles would be possible. These kinds of numbers would have profound implications on the internal and external cost structures that describe our transportation system. For example, Figure 7-5 shows inventor Paul MacCready's expression of the historically declining real-fuel cost of driving a new U.S. car. If the trends continue, the real cost is likely to approach zero as cars use 5 to 20 times less fuel and the world oil price falls in real terms.

Of course, global oil-related politics and economics would shift radically if this scenario plays out. One way or another, the existing trends clearly telegraph a major shift in the private transportation systems of the world. Both technology and environmental pressure are conspiring to produce a dramatically different world.

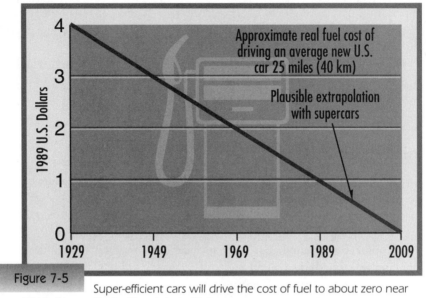

Figure 7-5 Super-efficient cars will drive the cost of fuel to about zero near 2010. Source: Rocky Mountain Institute

INTELLIGENT VEHICLE HIGHWAY SYSTEMS

The relative inefficiency of the automobile technology itself is not the only problem. Traffic congestion is estimated by the Department of Transportation to cost the United States almost $100 billion a year in lost productivity. A recent survey found that vehicles travel an average of 7 miles per hour during peak hours in the nation's biggest cities. The U.S. highway system is so mature (and so expensive to expand) that new infrastructure-based efficiencies for automobile and truck travel are going to come not from building new, larger roads, but from using our present road and highway structure more intelligently.

Increasing the level of interaction between the road infrastructure and an individual vehicle is what the Department of Transportation's Intelligent Vehicle-Highway Systems (IVHS) is about. This project, originally centered in various Massachusetts Institute of Technology labs, is based on forming partnerships with industry to develop a road and highway system that "knows" its state of use and can communicate transparently with individual vehicles so they can use the system in the most efficient way. A number of defense contractors are seriously involved in this project, seeing it as an alternative to declining defense budgets. DOT believes that this new technology will be commonplace on America's highways by 2005, followed in 10 to 20 years by automatic highways, where drivers would give control of the car over to the intelligent system built into the highway.

Essentially, the IVHS system (responding to the initiatives of human highway controllers) would, through signal lights, control the flow of traffic, and through direct communications with vehicles, alert them to problems on the road. Drivers, on the other hand, would have far more information available to help them make decisions about routes to a destination, location, and road information.

There are many interesting problems associated with such a system. The interface with the driver, for instance, could be accomplished in a number of ways. The "back seat driver" version would use a voice simulator to tell the driver, "Turn right next corner, then make a sharp left on the street with the red house on the corner." Then there is the need for computer-generated maps (Japan has already digitized maps of all of the roads in the country in preparation for more intelligent cars), or interactive maps that can report on the condition of the road ahead. One can now buy cars in Japan and the United States that use the satellite Global Positioning System (GPS) as an input to a small television-like moving map display on the dashboard that always shows where the car is located. GPS will certainly play a central role in a number of these new schemes. All of the proposals require a very high degree of accurate positioning information to be available, not only to drivers, but also to highway controllers who manipulate the flow of traffic.

This is a new regime, with new ground being broken. But many human-factor questions will need to be answered before a working system can be put in place. On the traffic control side, there is the need for models of how people are likely to use such a service so that the system doesn't, for example, simply shift all of the congestion caused by an accident from a highway to a secondary road.

Within two decades, it is likely that there will be places where you can get in a car, tell it where you want to go, and sit back and let it take you there—generating almost no pollution in the process.

COMMERCIAL TRANSPORT

Big changes are also happening in the way we move materials and products; people are beginning to understand the value of integration and cooperation. The watchword is *intermodality*. The idea is that transport is arranged door-to-door, and rail, truck, air, and ship lines pool their resources to give the most efficient service. This cooperation is a direct derivative of the innovative use of information technology. Intermodality results in savings of cost, fuel, and time, all of which mean savings for the consumer and profits for the transport companies.

There are two major components to this trend. One is the physical and procedure-oriented issues associated with moving an item easily and seamlessly from one location to another. This includes the technology, regulations, multilateral agreements, tracking systems, and so on. The other significant segment is the change in the marketplace that these capabilities will make possible.

Cooperation Between and Among Carriers, Customers, and Government

At its base, an intermodal system involves the close cooperation of many different types of carriers. As Ralston Purina's vice president Marty Tendler says, "Partnerships between railroads and trucking firms bring a new level of efficiency and economy. That efficiency adds value. It makes the United States a competitive entity in the world."

An example of the power of this new intermodal information tracking is the partnership between the Stride Rite Corporation, American President Lines (APL), and the U.S. Customs Department. In combination, these players have put together a system that will cut the time required to move products from manufacturers in the Far East to customers in the United States.

New product styles are shown to customs officials twice yearly and duty rates are set. APL scans the bar code labels on cases as they are loaded into containers for shipment. All the information is consolidated and sent electronically to Stride Rite in the United States. The unit price and factory of origin are added and forwarded to the customs broker. This data is used to make an automated broker interface (ABI) entry, which clears the goods through customs while they are still on the ship.

Stride Rite benefits by knowing exactly what the costs will be and exactly what is in each container. They can look at existing inventory and know which container to process first. There is no wait for customs clearance.

The key to this system is information technology and coordination between the various companies that handle Stride Rite's goods. According to Dan Wolf, director of transportation for Stride Rite, "All parties work together well, contributing in their areas of expertise. We're using what each party does best. My job is to coordinate."

This rather simple example illustrates a national and international trend toward a new intermodal system that will be made possible by the new information technology that is coming into the marketplace.

A New Marketplace

In time, the infrastructure should be in place to allow us to send most anything to most any place without talking to a person. Although one can now arrange with a freight forwarder to take care of all the details of a particular shipment, the intermodal arrangements that are made are ad hoc, designed for only one transaction or a specific group of transactions. New information technology will soon allow the evolution of a permanent international intermodal marketplace.

As the information needed for each step of a shipping process becomes increasingly standardized and available in digital form, it will begin to be communicated and manipulated exclusively in electronic form. This will open the door to automated transactions.

The stock market is a good analogy. Originally, financial equity transactions were between individuals. In time, with the standardization of instruments, there came into being a marketplace—a clearinghouse—where the financial "products" could be bought and sold. Initially, all aspects of the business (offer to buy/sell, record keeping, buy/sell transaction, billing, analysis, and knowledge of the market) were manually produced. But with the advent of sophisticated information technology, every piece of the marketplace became automated except for the simple buy/sell transaction (which was maintained for a unique set of reasons). Today a broad digital stream encompasses every single aspect of the business that leads to and from the trading pit.

The client interface with the marketplace is also completely electronic. In the largest, most sophisticated cases, the client's trading decisions are made by computers, and the complete transaction is initiated, confirmed, and reported without any human intervention. It is a seamless, almost organic system that allows the automatic purchase or sale of any of the thousands of varieties of products that are bought and sold in that marketplace.

The intermodal shipping marketplace is moving in the same direction. Think of it as an organic system, composed of space- and land-based communications and positioning capabilities that move and provide the information needed for any transaction that is allowed in the marketplace. It seems that ultimately one will be able to access the marketplace (via computer) and offer to buy shipping services for just about any given commodity. Automatically, all of the shippers in the marketplace will bid (electronically, of course) on the business. Perhaps the client's computer will analyze the offers and automatically select and initiate one option. At the least, the offers will be presented to the client, who will decide which option to take. The rest of the process would be completely automatic—production of shipping documents, intershipper coordination, customs clearance, billing, exchange of funds and fees, tracking of the shipment, and so on. Humans would deal with the exceptions—the problems.

This is not just speculation. There are many highly complex activities in other areas that are moving inexorably in this direction.

TRANSPORTATION AND INFORMATION TECHNOLOGY

It may well be that advanced information technology will do away with many travel needs. This is likely to be particularly true with the advent of virtual reality and projection holography. When people are able to make and maintain long-distance personal working relationships, they need to travel less. On a scale never before seen, technology is *moving information instead of people.*

In his book *Earth in the Balance,* Al Gore identified the first simple manifestations of the trend: "We can also replace conventional commuting wherever possible with what is now known as telecommuting. This technology is already in widespread use, as increasing numbers of people work at home but keep a direct connection to co-workers through a communications link between their computer stations. As the capacity of computer networks increases, this trend is likely to accelerate."

Technology and Transportation Regulation

It is an understatement to suggest that technology will have a profound impact on transportation in the next 20 years. But to make the case clearer, and show how some particularly powerful information technology will cut across all aspects of transportation, let us briefly consider the implications of virtual reality (VR) on the different pieces of the U.S. Department of Transportation transportation puzzle. Keep in mind that any of a number of other technologies mentioned in earlier chapters (like chaos theory, nanotechnology, and zero-point energy) will similarly sweep through all aspects of our lives, changing them forever.

One important aspect of VR is that it allows very sophisticated simulation. Almost any situation that can be modeled in a computer can theoretically be simulated, from the smallest atomic environment to large, even global or cosmic, contexts. Because they are more flexible and do not involve the expense of full-scale models, VR applications allow researchers to try out designs and evaluate human factors before prototyping or building. This saves expense and time, and often is much safer. Of course, some contexts (like the aforementioned atomic environment) that could never be actually experienced can be virtually experienced. VR can be a real advantage in both research and training. Consider how it is working its way into a variety of DOT areas.

Federal Aviation Authority (FAA)

The FAA has a dynamic modeling system of air traffic, airspace, airport area, surfaces, and buildings, which helps with airport design, air traffic flows, and design changes. It also uses simulator modeling as a tool for analysis and contingency planning for dealing with bottleneck delays, geographic sector saturation, and airport gate holds. In the future, the FAA plans to link its systems together to achieve less expensive distributed simulation.

Already some virtual reality applications, like helmet displays and cockpit and flight-deck simulations, have been found to be a less expensive alternative to large physical simulators. The FAA may use virtual reality in the analysis and prevention of accidents by re-creating activities where the human-machine interface is poorly understood.

National Highway Traffic Safety Administration (NHTSA)

Here the use of simulation, models, and virtual reality has the capability to enhance research on the relationships between vehicles and between vehicles and pedestrians. This may help in the understanding and prevention of accidents. Safety situations can be "experienced" without exposing anyone to physical harm.

Federal Highway Administration (FHWA)

The highway administration has a long history of using computer simulation, especially in the area of traffic optimization, on both micro and macro scales. They expect virtual reality to be an especially useful tool for evaluating a complete range of high-risk safety situations involving driver/vehicle/highway interactions because there is no risk to lives or property.

The design and modeling of the Intelligent Vehicle Highway System will provide applications for VR. A researcher could drive a "test car" on a prototypical highway system in different stages of development without leaving the office or lab.

Merchant Marine Academy (MARAD) and Coast Guard (USCG)

The Merchant Marine Academy uses computer-aided operations research as a training aid to mimic ship maneuvers and evaluate harbor designs. Their system can accommodate a large range of weather, traffic, channel, and environmental conditions.

Vessel traffic control simulator systems are used in the same way as air traffic control simulators and help in the evaluation of human factor issues. Vessel simulators are also similar to those used for aircraft pilot training. Three-dimensional virtual reality simulators may be used to assess the design of ship systems, especially of limited spaces like engine rooms. There are already simulators in use as training aids at the Coast Guard Academy in New London, Connecticut, and at the Reserve Training Center in Yorktown, Virginia. They have been quite successful and should produce long-range savings in training costs.

Federal Railway Administration (FRA)

The FRA uses a full-scale locomotive control simulator to evaluate human factors and work standards related to fatigue and alertness. VR could be helpful in simulating many different safety situations, particularly in advanced systems collision avoidance and accident survivability studies to evaluate proposed new maglev and high-speed rail systems under various operating scenarios and accident threats, thereby reducing developmental design risks.

Office of the Secretary of Transportation (OST)

Although it will not be practically available for a number of years, VR may someday produce the ultimate telecommuting environment. You can transport yourself into any other virtual office, at headquarters or at some other location, without leaving home. There is no travel time and none of the overhead costs and expenses associated with maintaining a work space in an office environment. Time can be used much more efficiently.

DOT has found that there has been a 20 percent improvement in worker productivity since the introduction of a telecommuting program. It is sponsoring research to identify areas where expanded telecommuting might be successful as early as mid-1995.

TRANSPORTATION PLANNING AS A SYSTEM

In all that we have considered, one hard truth colors almost all transportation planning: *We don't see our transportation as a system.*

We don't see it as a system because we haven't designed it as one. Instead of establishing a rational land use and transportation policy, transportation decisions have often been made on the basis of a reaction to overcrowded roads and political lobbying.

The San Jose, California, light rail case is illustrative. Five hundred million dollars was invested in light rail to ease congestion. But now that it is built, the rail line doesn't run near anything. It goes near the airport—three-quarters of a mile—but not near enough for people with baggage to take advantage of it. It doesn't connect with the railroad, nor does it connect with the subway. This is because the system wasn't designed to serve concentrations of populations; it was designed to hit as many political districts as possible. As a result, it serves fewer than 11,000 people, although it was designed to serve 40,000.

Successful transit must follow the pattern of Toronto, Paris, and Stockholm, where the location of stations was linked to residential and commercial development. Transit projects need to be designed to make it easy for people to use them. For example, bus and train routes can be connected with bike paths within the city, and provision made for carrying or storing bicycles. This would give people the convenience of efficient inner city transport without parking problems, and a traffic-free commute.

These principles work. In Curbita, Brazil, a city of 1.5 million people, an efficient mass transit system was designed based on integrating land use and making provisions for bicycle and pedestrian traffic and a network of express and local buses. As a result, gasoline use is 30 percent lower per vehicle and people spend only 10 percent of their income on transport, among the lowest in Brazil.

Building Relationships

Looking at transportation as a system in the context of the larger society also means facilitating communication between the different participants in the system. Relationships must be built between policymakers within the transportation community—for example, departments of highways and rail must work together—and between agencies; such as housing, land use, and transportation. Cities like Toronto, Portland, and Amsterdam have already linked their transportation and land use planning, and the efficiency is noticeable.

Considering Life-Cycle Costs

At issue here is not just the operating costs and by-products of a given transportation system, but also the costs and benefits that attend the construction and dismemberment of the system. Today, when governments everywhere are pressed to stimulate economies and help produce jobs, one of the questions relative to investing in transportation is, where does a dollar (or franc) spent produce the most economic return? As it turns out, the most efficient and environmentally benign forms of transportation also produce the greatest number of jobs during their construction. German figures show that highway construction generates the fewest jobs of any public infrastructure investment. Spending 1 billion deutsche marks ($580 million) on highways yields only 14,000 to 19,000 jobs, compared with about 22,000 in railway tracks, or 23,000 in light rail track construction.

One of the most important employment questions is the extent to which the skills now used in the automotive industries are adaptable to the operation of rail systems. Markus Hesse and Rainer Lucs of the Institute for Ecological Economics Research in Wuppertal, Germany, conclude that given some overlaps and similarities in skill patterns, the shifts should not be too difficult. Both motor vehicle manufacturing and railroads require a broad distribution of occupations. The skills needed to construct highways, railway tracks, and bike paths—such as engineering, concrete pouring, and trucking—are relatively similar, although workers will need to adapt from one to the other.

Private gasoline-powered vehicles have gotten us into much of the trouble we presently face. Efficient transportation alternatives must be found in order to allow for sustainable economic development and a cleaner environment—both in the United States and in the world. Some of those alternatives will involve moving information instead of people. In that sphere, satellites will play a very important role. Space will be key in enabling and facilitating much of the change we see on the horizon. Let's take a closer look.

CHAPTER

8

Space:

Linking Everyone

If the stars should appear one night in a thousand years, how would men believe and adore.
                                        —*Ralph Waldo Emerson*

The technology revolution that we will experience in the next two decades will be about information collection, manipulation, and storage. It will be about moving large quantities of data rapidly from one place to another. In the global system that will accumulate and transport that information, space-based satellites will play a critical part. They will allow information links from just about any place to any other place.

Although space has primarily been used by the military for communications and remote sensing, repeater satellites to beam television signals down to large regions of the globe are now having an extraordinary impact. Telephone systems for conventional long-distance service and more specialized maritime ship-to-shore communications are in place, with far more ubiquitous capabilities on the near horizon.

In the last few years, the commercial use of space has begun to build, starting with more regional television broadcasting units, the private use of the Global Positioning System (GPS), and now, in the planning stages, a number of private global communications systems. Space capabilities are stitching together many components of the rapidly evolving global nervous system.

Technologists and planners see future uses in space for communicating, perhaps generating electrical power, processing materials in ways that can't be done on earth, remotely sensing activities on the surface of the Earth, manned flight, navigation, and providing on-orbit services for visiting space vehicles.

COMMUNICATIONS

A great deal of the utility of satellites is determined by their height above the earth's surface. In *geosynchronous orbits,* where the satellite's orbit matches the rotation of the earth, it remains positioned above one point on the equator. *Low earth orbits* have the satellite constantly flying around the earth in any of a number of possible paths. In some cases, like the Hubble telescope, packages are in orbits determined by the maximum effective altitude of the space shuttle, which is used to deliver and service them.

Geosynchronous Orbits

Because television broadcasting and some telephone communications satellites need to provide constant coverage to one geographic area, they are positioned in geosynchronous orbits (GEOs). As is shown in Figure 8-1, these are high orbits—22,500 miles above the earth—that require greater launch capability for payloads that are usually quite large. A single GEO satellite usually works independently (as in the case of television broadcasting). In some cases, telephone and image

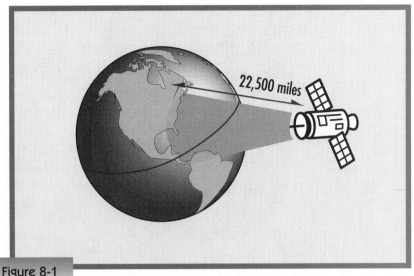

Figure 8-1

A satellite in geosynchronous orbit above the equator can cover a large area of Earth from a fixed position in the sky

information is uplinked from, say, the Pacific, and sent to another geosynchronous system positioned over the Atlantic, before returning to Earth, thus allowing data to be moved from one side of the globe to the other.

Star Television, Rupert Murdoch's extraordinarily powerful Asian transmitter, is in a GEO orbit. Star is the only large satellite network to reach all of Asia, including China and India. Programming is beamed up from Hong Kong to the spacecraft flying motionless, high above the equator. Five satellite channels are broadcast down to an area that includes 38 nations in Asia and the Middle East—from Tokyo to Tel Aviv, from Mongolia to Malaysia. Forty-five million people in that region have the necessary equipment to receive their programming.

Low Earth Orbits

Most of the new growth in commercial space appears to be in low earth orbit (LEO) systems. The United States and other countries have used LEOs for surveillance, because their orbits are much closer to the earth than geosynchronous ones. But that means that the satellite constantly travels around the earth, crossing a given surface location only once each orbit, as can be seen in Figure 8-2.

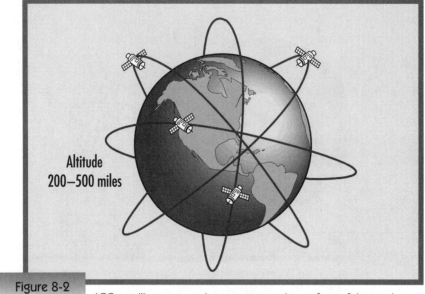

Altitude 200–500 miles

Figure 8-2

LEO satellites constantly move across the surface of the earth

Commercial firms are now planning and beginning to launch constellations of LEO satellites, configured so that a number of spacecraft are above the horizon of any point on earth at any time. These constellations are referred to as Big LEOs and Little LEOs, depending on the number of satellites in the constellation.

Big LEOs use 66 to 77 satellites, all linked together electronically to form a telephone service web that completely covers the earth. A telephone call started with one overhead satellite is handed off to the next one that arrives overhead. In theory, it is very much like the operation of a cellular telephone system, where the signal is passed from one antenna to another as the caller moves from one region to another. The World Administrative Radio Conference has endorsed the use of radio spectrum by two types of small satellite constellations in low earth orbits—one for wireless telephone calls and one for messaging services. Big LEO operators are now negotiating for FCC frequency allocation. They may have approvals by 1996 or 1997 and should begin launching very soon after that.

The best known Big LEO is the 66-satellite Iridium system, which will provide hand-held portable telephone service from any location of the earth to any other one. If the corporation is able to obtain the necessary financing, it should be in operation by 1998 or 1999. The pace of technology is moving so fast in this area that the company assumes that its satellites will become obsolete within two to three years, and therefore plans to have at least one launch per month after the complete constellation is in place just to replace old satellites.

The recently announced Teledesic Corporation, a partnership of Microsoft's Bill Gates and Craig McCaw of McCaw Cellular Communications, is another Big LEO. This planned $9 billion system would include 840 small satellites at an altitude of 435 miles. It would be able to transmit video and sophisticated computer-generated data to 95 percent of the earth starting in 2001.

Little LEOs, which use 8 to 24 satellites, are designed for messaging and positioning services. Some have pioneer licenses and should begin launching in the early part of 1995. There are five applicants to provide telephone service and three who want to supply messaging services. These systems will allow messages to be sent and received from any place in the world to laptop computers with very small antennas built into the covers, and to paging units that can be made small enough to be a part of a wristwatch. These services will be further enhanced by the development of VSAT (very small aperture antennas) for business and home high-definition television.

POWER GENERATION

In an example of the ultimate high-tech solution to a problem (that may well be overcome by other, far more efficient technologies), large satellites may be used to convert solar energy to electrical energy and beam it, in the form of microwave transmissions, to large collection stations on Earth. These surface facilities would then convert the radio energy back to common electricity that could be used to supply the projected increase in the nation's requirement for electricity.

One variation of this scheme is to build the equipment on the moon and move the completed satellites to geosychronous earth orbits from there.

MATERIAL PROCESSING

On Earth, gravity presents serious problems to the manufacturing of certain materials and conducting certain experiments. Space presents an option to earth-based processes through the use of microgravity factories designed for specific applications. Pharmaceuticals are an area of particular opportunity; protein crystals and medicines could be produced and genetic experiments done much more effectively in a microgravity context. Space-based furnaces for mixing alloys and electroplating would also be much more efficient than those available now. At the present time, there is no commercially viable microgravity manufacturing process available; payload processing facilities and launch costs will ultimately determine if microgravity manufacturing becomes a reality.

Again, as in the case of orbital power generation, there are other technologies on the horizon, notably molecular nanotechnology, that could offset and eliminate all of the usual gravity problems associated with manufacturing. In fact, far more effort is being made to develop nanotechnology than microgravity manufacturing. If it is successful, the economics would be so much better that the things that are used in space may well be manufactured there, with nanotechnology the manufacturing process used.

REMOTE SENSING

Satellites have a perspective of the earth that is unequaled by any common vehicle. Many space packages are designed to capture these high-altitude views of specific pieces of geography in a variety of electromagnetic wavelengths. A host of remote-sensing capabilities are used for many different satellite-based applications. Sensors for visible wavelengths, infrared, laser, radar, and millimeter wavelengths are available and can be configured for a variety of missions. Atmospheric sampling equipment can be used to map the chemistry and dynamics of the upper atmosphere with extraordinary sensitivity. Current satellites can also measure winds for the first time, and the altitude and range over which they occur.

One satellite that went up in 1993 measures the circulation of the earth's oceans. The laser geodynamic satellite measures geopotential, the gravitational potential of the earth. Weather satellites are constantly being launched, and instruments to track hydrology and sea ice are included on some defense satellites. The Shuttle Radar Laboratory, which went up in April 1994, makes synthetic aperture radar (SAR) measurements of the topology of the land. The United States and

Canada are jointly putting up a radio detection and ranging satellite, which will measure the topology of ice. A series of two-year missions will monitor the ozone, and the coupling between the oceans and the atmosphere. A joint Japan/U.S. mission will measure the rainfall in the tropics, and other joint projects with Europeans and Japan will observe the polar areas.

Predicting Weather Disasters and Spotting Oil Slicks

These capabilities can be used to predict weather disasters, spot oil slicks, find downed sailors, monitor natural resources, help manage renewable and nonrenewable resources, and monitor global warming and ozone layer depletion.

A practical example will be helpful here. A number of recent events suggest that Arctic shipping routes may be increasingly used for moving passengers and cargo between Europe and the Far East and northern Siberia. The Northeast Passage, paralleling the Siberian coast, has recently been opened for international shipping traffic by the Russian government, along with access to a number of Siberian ports. During a four- to five-month period in the summer, some ships can make the icy transit largely unaccompanied. Depending on their destinations and routes, ships may need the help of Russian icebreakers. This route is a much shorter way to get from the Atlantic to the Pacific than the usual trip through the Panama Canal. As much as two weeks can be shaved from the trip by taking the northern route.

On the other side of the North Pole, a similar Northwest Passage through the islands of northern Canada is being probed by ships using current satellite ice map imagery to determine which routes are least ice-jammed. The ERS-1 satellite, which supplies the pictures, uses a synthetic aperture radar (SAR) device that allows it to penetrate cloud cover and operate at night. The ice charts are faxed to the ship via the Inmarsat satellite-based phone system to give it a two- to three-hour-old picture of the ice dispersion.

Peter Wadhams, director of the Scott Polar Research Institute at the University of Cambridge in England, recently said, "The use of SAR for ships could make it possible to establish international trade routes across the north of Canada and the north of Russia, at least in the summer, if the data can be made available quickly to users ... then it will make it possible to establish trade routes through the Arctic in a way that more likely will be successful."

The Future Is Tied to Government Policies

The current commercial market for remote-sensing satellites is closely tied to government policies, as most of these payloads are operated by governments. The U.S. government recently made a major policy change, approving high-resolution satellite photography for U.S. commercial satellites. This should generate a much larger market for images from privately owned American space platforms. Industry sources estimate that the current remote-sensing market will likely grow from the current $400 million a year to $2 billion by the turn of the century. Spy-satellite quality data is already available from Russia and France.

The U.S. Commerce Department and National Oceanic and Atmospheric Administration are looking for better incentives for private corporations to use existing remote-sensing satellites like LandSat and GeoSat. Japan is interested in the possibility of acquiring fishing industry information. Petroleum prospecting interests believe that these capabilities might be helpful to them. Farming organizations are also using the images for analysis of land use. In Europe and the United States, there is an increasing emphasis on using both commercial and military capabilities to track environmental changes.

The influence of government policy could further decline when lower-cost sensors and launch systems are developed (they are clearly coming), making remote-sensing satellites more affordable for private operators.

The number of future remote-sensing payloads is also strongly linked to the cost of processing the data collected through such systems. Presently, these costs constrain the market for such systems. In many cases, so much data is generated by a sensor that years (decades, in some cases) are required to effectively analyze the huge flow.

These same platforms can, of course, be used for national and military surveillance, and there is an interesting political issue arising around the ability of small countries to launch satellites that are used for surveillance. Some argue that space surveillance and reconnaissance will be affordable to most nations throughout the world, which will result in a new reality in which all countries can have surveillance for the asking. The days when surveillance and reconnaissance from space were the exclusive domain of the superpowers will be gone forever.

MANNED FLIGHT

The fact that an increasingly large investment in hardware is being put into orbit—and largely abandoned—suggests that humans will soon go into space on a commercial basis to repair and refuel these assets, thus extending their useful lives. Industry sources believe that there will be a big new market for maintaining satellites in space and bringing them back for repair. Similarly, as needs change, it will be valuable to move a space craft rather than abandoning it.

One project in the planning stages, COMET, will put devices into space and recover them for repairs and refueling before the end of the century. It is almost certainly a harbinger of similar, more sophisticated services to come. Certain communications satellites will need to be refueled on station. The orbital transfer of other fluids, raw materials, finished products, and cryogens, could also be accomplished from microgravity factories.

Beyond the year 2000, the Japanese are looking at the possibility of hotels in space. There is also interest in mining on the moon, Mars, and asteroids, but the costs of doing so compared to other options that are becoming available are likely to put such expeditions off for more than two decades.

NAVIGATION—GLOBAL POSITIONING SYSTEM

The most significant new advance in navigation in centuries is the Navistar Global Positioning System (GPS), a constellation of satellites that surrounds the globe. For the first time in history, users can now obtain very accurate geographic position information anywhere in the world. A small battery-powered, hand-held GPS receiver can deduce its position to less than 5 meters in three dimensions by comparing signals received simultaneously from up to six different satellites (see Figure 8-3)—and the accuracy will soon be measured in centimeters.

Until now, we have not generally had an accurate method of establishing the location of something if that item was not within sight of someone who knew specifically where he or she was located. We have become used to this, building systems and processes to keep track of where something was last reported and weaving rough estimates deeply into the fabric of everyday life.

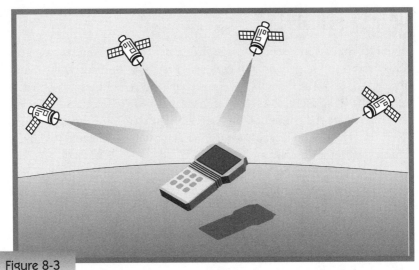

Figure 8-3 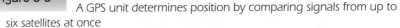 A GPS unit determines position by comparing signals from up to six satellites at once

Everyday positioning problems—such as not remembering where one parked a car in a large lot—are rather easily (if frustratingly) resolved. Things become much more acute when people don't have a good idea of even where *they* are. Such situations, in unfamiliar cities, at sea, or in the air, sometimes carry serious premiums if not resolved in a timely manner. Then there is the matter of things in route between two known locations, or stolen, or lost.

Now, with a small, increasingly less expensive device, position can be known almost exactly. This technology is revolutionizing major aspects of commercial and social activity.

Business, Recreation, and Transportation

GPS was conceived and launched first by the U.S. military in 1978 and became operational with 24 satellites in 1993. The Persian Gulf War was won in part because of GPS, which allowed tank drivers to surely navigate the featureless Iraqi desert at high speed in bad weather. But its greatest benefit in the short term is in business, recreation, and transportation. Aircraft owners are switching over and are, for the first time, able to tell their location, altitude, and attitude with no linkage or initialization from the ground. Fishing captains can return exactly to a spot that brought an earlier catch.

Already some GPS units are equipped with automatic cellular phone responding devices that cue them to report their position, direction of travel, present speed, average direction, and so on. Fleet owners will know exactly where each of their trucks is located, 24 hours a day, as will shippers of containers on trains and ocean ships. Devices on stolen cars will be activated by a telephone call by the police and will immediately give away their position.

Consumer Market Uses

But the greatest ultimate influence may be in the consumer market. *Space News* reported that Japanese electronics manufacturers are actively targeting consumers with their GPS products. Some cars in Japan and the United States are already equipped with GPS positioning devices that feed into a moving-map display in the car, constantly showing drivers exactly where they are.

As unit size decreases with advances in microelectronics, personal units—perhaps built into watches—could become commonplace. Motorola's and Mayo Clinic's laboratories are already working to develop a wristwatch-size GPS receiver using multichip modules. Coupled with personal global cellular telephone systems, these items could assure that, appropriately equipped, a person would never get lost again.

The former Soviet Union, the Commonwealth of Independent States, operates Glonass, a system similar to GPS. Like GPS, it will ultimately have 24 space vehicles; 15 satellites are active now. Some manufacturers are considering designing combination GPS/Glonass receivers to be used primarily for vehicle navigation and tracking, and for aeronautical applications.

GPS Is Transforming Aviation

Satellite-based services are revolutionizing the aviation business. In the past, aircraft transiting an ocean made an hourly voice position report to the appropriate air traffic control agency by high frequency radio. Now some 160 airliners and private jets are equipped to automatically send written reports via the Inmarsat satellite communications system at five-minute intervals. Helicopters are also being equipped with the satellite equipment. GPS-determined position reports are also being coupled to the Inmarsat system to provide automatic position reports, with no crew involvement. Ultimately, pilots want a two-way system that allows bidirectional written communication so that requests and answers can be traded between pilots and controllers.

GPS has greater, much more profound implications for aviation than just position reporting. Recent studies have shown that by using three antennas, located on the tail and tips of the wings, GPS can provide highly accurate attitude information. This input could be coupled to an autopilot that can—also using GPS-derived position information—fly the aircraft over the flight route and through an instrument approach almost to landing. Throughout the process, the pilot can monitor the aircraft's progress on a moving map display that during the approach phase can show both geographic location and altitude information—all without any linkage to the ground. This equipment is likely to be inexpensive enough that it will be easily available to the general aviation fleet.

ON-ORBIT: FIRST STOP TO DEEP SPACE

The physics of space operations make the cost of overcoming the earth's gravity the most fuel-demanding portion of a long-range flight to geosynchronous orbit. It would therefore be advantageous to have a "gas station" in Low Earth Orbit where, having broken free of the braking pull of the earth, a vehicle could top off before continuing the mission. Fuel and other services may therefore be in LEO in less than two decades.

GENERAL TRENDS

Launch Services

Much of the expense of space launch services is associated with infrastructure and vehicle development costs. Therefore there is. a real advantage to finding alternative approaches for launching that offset or bypass some of the usual expenses. China recently entered the commercial launch market with lower costs that directly targeted the dominant French position in the field. Now the Russians are doing the same thing and driving costs still lower.

Zero-Point May Eliminate the Need for Fuel

The need for fuel presumes that the motive force of 2010 will be similar to what we use now. But if zero-point energy production becomes feasible, completely new space vehicle power plants will be possible, with no need to carry along fuel.

In 1992, the State Department approved a request by Lockheed Corporation to work on a joint venture with Krunichev Enterprise of Moscow, builder of the Proton rocket, to provide commercial satellite launch services. Proton launchers, which previously have been used for delivering weapons, are much cheaper than any others on the market, and this move brings a whole new set of economics to satellite operators. Some suggest that launch costs using the Proton could be as small as 20 percent of what past costs have been.

Until now, France's Arianespace, which builds the Ariane rocket series, has controlled more than two-thirds of the commercial launch market and has seen China as its major competitor. This development could spur new space options and open up market segments that would not otherwise have been economically feasible.

Sea-Launching Is an Alternative

An alternative to the expensive launch infrastructure costs on land is to move offshore. Serious planning is underway to provide very inexpensive (about 10 percent of current cost) small satellite launch services from ships or offshore platforms. Ship-based launching has additional advantages in that a launch can be made from any latitude (thus taking better advantage of the earth's rotational momentum), rather than being constrained by the physical restrictions of fixed land-based sites.

A problem with sea launching is getting the rockets and payloads out to the ship so that the ship doesn't need to come into port between each launch. There is also a set of safety problems associated with sea launches that do not attend land-based launches.

Recycling Reusable Vehicles

The great cost of developing and launching satellites will motivate increasing attempts to reuse space launchers and payloads. McDonnell Douglas Space Systems Company has planned a Single Stage to Orbit vehicle (SSTO), which will operate like an airplane; launch into space, drop off a payload, and then land on earth again. It is designed to turn around in days or hours. The prototype was tested in the fall of 1993 with full-scale development scheduled in 1994 to 1996. If successful, this approach will decrease launch costs from $2,500 per pound to hundreds of dollars per pound.

Competition Over Satellite Parking Spots

Because geostationary communications satellites operating at the same frequencies jam each other if they are parked in space too close to each other, only a limited number of orbital positions are available for certain applications servicing certain geographic regions. In the past, satellite operators have petitioned to the International Telecommunications Union (ITU), which is part of the United Nations, for positions, with the assurance that all operators would conform to the ITU decisions.

Now, with more than 15 launches for satellites serving the Pacific in 1993 and 1994, every satellite space in the region is in demand and several disputes over rights to the spacecraft slots erupted. Operators from the United States, Hong Kong and the Philippines have all claimed common positions over Southeast Asia.

John Hampton, deputy director of Intelsat, said that mutual self-interest has sustained voluntary cooperation with ITU guidelines. However, he and other senior officials in the industry are concerned that once one company abandons compromise, the system will slide into an electronic chaos of jammed frequencies.

Space News reports that with widespread confusion and disagreement over which operators have priority to run their satellites under ITU rules, few observers expect an orderly resolution of all the conflicts.

FUTURE PROSPECTS

Analyses carried out for the Office of Commercial Space Transportation (OCST) indicate the following anticipated developments during the period through 2010:

   ▪ *Launch rates will increase* gradually, with most growth occurring in the area of small launch vehicles.

▓ *Spacecraft will get smaller.* At a recent Institute of Navigation meeting, a proposal was made to develop a system of small, low-cost "econosats," that could augment the GPS system.

▓ *The greatest payload growth will be in the area of Low Earth Orbit (LEO)* communications networks, which will require both initial launches of constellations and replacement launches as satellites wear out.

▓ *Remote sensing and microgravity markets could grow,* but only as markets mature.

▓ *An average of 44 commercial payloads will probably be launched annually* during the period from 1993 through 1999; this will rise to an average of 55 per year during the period from 2000 through 2005.

▓ *The number of commercial microgravity payloads will rise steadily* but not dramatically during the two periods.

▓ *Most growth in commercial launch demand appears to be likely in the area of LEO communications satellites.*

▓ *The number of GEO communications and remote-sensing satellites launched annually is likely to remain at current levels* through the end of the decade, and marginally higher during the first five years of the next century.

▓ *Lower launch costs could also greatly affect payload design and operations.* Lower launch costs might lead operators to deploy greater numbers of less-expensive satellites with shorter lifetimes and more limited capabilities; this could, in turn, increase the number of launches.

▓ *The growth in LEO communications systems will favor U.S. launch companies and payload operators,* as most of the interest in LEO communications is U.S.-based. This is in contrast to recent trends, which have favored foreign companies in the areas of launch services, while U.S. companies have maintained market share in the sale of payloads.

COMMERCIAL SPACE AND NATIONAL SECURITY

Strategic foreign policy implications associated with space launch services are technology-transfer-driven because launch services are the gateways that basically provide developing foreign nations and transnational corporations with space-based weapons delivery, communications, and surveillance systems. In the Cold War era, access to these systems was largely controlled by the major developed countries—either the United States and its major allies or the Soviet Union and its major allies.

As a remnant of our containment strategy as well as our associated technology transfer policy, the United States exerted strong influence to deny Soviet space launch services to Western markets. In an extraordinary set of circumstances, in the waning days of the Bush administration, Russian and Kazakhstan space launch officials, in some U.S. officials' opinions, extorted the U.S. State Department into allowing access to formerly Western commercial space markets, with the understanding that advanced missile and surveillance satellite technology would not otherwise be provided to Middle Eastern clients and possibly to terrorist organizations, with potentially adverse impact to U.S. security interests.

Despite the fact that controls to prevent sales of former Soviet space technology to Middle Eastern clients could not be guaranteed anyway, this threat to access to Western space launch markets was sufficient to sway President Bush to approve the policy change over the strong objections of the Department of Defense, the Joint Chiefs of Staff, the Department of Commerce, and the Department of Transportation.

Commercial proliferation of space-based systems became the reality of the 1990s as Soviet space-launch systems became available to an international marketplace, with the primary objective being to raise hard currency to preserve the space technology sector of their devastated economy. China entered into this competition, offering space launch services to Middle Eastern clients and transnational commercial interests of the developing world. France and the European Space Agency have been very active, providing access to space for devices serving the developing world.

Space Is Becoming a Free-for-All

Commercial space access is swiftly becoming a free-for-all, lacking international cooperation, regulation, and enforcement. Space junk orbiting the earth has taken on serious implications for the safety of very expensive orbital devices. Nations staking claims to geosynchronous orbital sites and orbital paths are taking on the unregulated implications of an "Oklahoma land rush," and new international policy implications concerning the inability of enforcing property rights of sovereign nations in space are a serious concern.

Space control, as a concept, is the twenty-first-century equivalent to the concepts of Sea Control and Sea Denial used by major naval strategists of Britain, France, and the United States during the eighteenth through through the twentieth centuries. In Desert Storm operations, U.S. and allied forces enjoyed unprecedented strategic advantage through use and control of space-based systems, including cooperation by Russian and French officials to deny or delay Saddam Hussein's access to space surveillance information.

Access to space surveillance images showing changes in the U.S. force disposition, such as General Normal Schwarzkopf's war-breaking flanking maneuver, might have resulted in substantially increased U.S. casualties against a more sophisticated adversary. It will be a major challenge for our forces to sustain the ability to control or deny access to space-device gathered intelligence, especially with transnational commercial proliferation of such space-borne devices. Such capability will require a coordinated combination of political, diplomatic, and military strategic policies.

In the next chapter we'll come back down to earth and discuss a subject that affects all of us: health.

CHAPTER

9

Health:

Serious Threats…

and Gains

To understand God's thoughts we must study statistics, for these are the measure of his purpose.
—*Florence Nightingale*

So far, we have discussed some "hard" components of the larger system in which we live: technology, energy, and so on. But there is another side to the equation—the side that deals with humans and how they relate to each other in individual and social settings. These "soft" subjects, like economics, politics, and social values, are as important as the more tangible ones—and in some cases they are even more important. So we will give them their due, beginning with a look at trends in health and health care.

Biotechnology

Biotechnology holds forth the hope of dramatic gains in identifying and treating illnesses. The keystone of that area of effort is the Human Genome Project. Over the next decade, this project will identify the whole human genetic code, providing a map for medical researchers that points directly at diseases likely to be acquired very early in life. And in the genetic engineering field, drugs are being designed that hold extraordinary promise and, in some cases, at much less cost. These biotech forces will have a profound impact on health and health care in the next two decades.

In addition to the breakthroughs that we have discussed in biotech and genetic engineering, health and health care trends contain both good news and bad news. The good news involves some amazing new capabilities in medicinal technology, possibilities of lengthening human life, and the hope associated with alternative approaches to medicine. The downside includes the global scourge of AIDS, the resurgence of old diseases thought conquered, and the failure of the American health care system, with its accompanying threat to the greater health of the country.

TECHNOLOGY AND MEDICINE

A revolution is going on in the area of artificial human organs. Technologists and medical researchers are making such progress that industry observers believe that by about 2015, artificial organs will be available to replace every organ in the body except the brain and central nervous system.

In 1990, the Institute for Future Technology in Tokyo studied anticipated developments in technology for the next two decades. Their predictions?

- By 1998, anti-viral agents will be available for widespread treatment of viral diseases.

- By 2001, synthetic organs will be widely used because of the elimination of undesirable reactions by recipients.

- Bionic legs, equipped with computer-controlled actuators and small power sources, will become available in 2002, followed in 2003 by implantable artificial ears.

- That year should also bring a cure for cancer and the advent of bionic muscles—compact robots with actuators in a fibrous form resembling human muscle.

- By 2006, we should have artificial organs from human tissue. Body cells and tissues will be incorporated into artificial pancreases, kidneys, and livers.

- Two years later, implantable health sensors will make their debut. Long-life biosensor implants will monitor disease and manage health.

- Artificial photoreceptors connected to the optic nerve will restore sight in 2011, and diabetes and senility will be eliminated.

- By 2012 we will see the process of human memory elucidated, and by 2014, artificial eyes will end many, if not most, forms of blindness.

Even if these particular assessments are optimistic, it is clear that a major revolution in the way that humans deal with their health problems is in the wind. These trends will be encouraged and enabled by devices like the "nerve chip" (a solid-state device that connects on one end to a nerve and the other to a computer); and new capabilities, such as transforming muscle into hard, well-formed bone. (A surgeon and cell biologist recently molded rat muscle into tiny leg and jaw bones.)

Some of the most interesting new genetically engineered drugs, available by the year 2000, will prevent paralysis due to spinal cord injury. Existing drugs, if administered immediately, can already reduce the damage, but the next generation will be able to repair spinal cords. Some observers believe that there will be almost no new cases of paraplegia and quadraplegia by 2020.

LIFE EXTENSION

One of the most intriguing areas of research is that of the extension of human life. There is reason to believe that we are quickly approaching a number of thresholds that will soon allow people to live to be 100 or more.

Life magazine, in their October 1992 cover article on the subject, reported on advances in genetics and chemistry that have identified genes that control aging in fruit flies, nematodes, and jellyfish. The lives of fruit flies have been doubled by selective breeding. Futurist Jerome Glenn, in his book *Future Mind Artificial Intelligence,* says that a new group of substances—called geroprotectors—has been identified for slowing the aging process in warm-blooded animals by 20 to 100 percent. He also reported that the Soviet publication *Sputnik* claimed that "The drop in temperature of man's body by a mere 2.5 degrees could add 50 percent to his lifespan."

Scientists working in the area seem unanimous in their feeling that we are close—within a decade—to a breakthrough.

Dr. Edward Masoro, a physiologist at the University of Texas Health Science Center in San Antonio, said, "If dietary restriction has the same effects in humans as it has in rodents, then human life span can be extended by at least 30 percent—which would give us an extra 30 to 35 years. But once we understand the mechanisms that control aging, we may find it possible to extend lifespan considerably more, perhaps by 100 percent—which would give us an extra 100 to 120 years."

The foremost authority on aging in yeast, Dr. Michael Jazwinski, at the Louisiana State University Medical Center, said, "Possibly in 30 years we will have in hand the major genes that determine longevity, and will be in a position to double, triple, even quadruple our maximum lifespan of 120 years. It's possible that some people alive now may still be alive 400 years from now." Dr. William Regelson, professor of medicine at the Medical College of Virginia, felt, "With the knowledge that is accumulating now about the nutritional and neuroendocrine aspects of aging, and if we develop ways to repair aging tissues with the help of embryonic cells, we could add 30 healthy years to human life in the next decade. And beyond that, as we learn to control the genes involved in aging, the possibilities of lengthening life appear practically unlimited."

What these researchers say they need is a clear vision of the whole, a grand unified theory of how human beings age. Dr. Judith Campisi, a cell biologist at the Lawrence Berkeley Laboratory in Berkeley, California, believes that such a theory will soon take shape. "Right now," she says, "aging research is where physics was 50 years ago, just before Enrico Fermi split the atom. In the next five years, progress will be exponential."

Profound Implications

If these scientists are right—if human life is suddenly increased by 30 percent, to around 100 years, the implications for society will be profound. All of our systems of work, education, economics, and recreation—our very sense of self—are based on an average length of life of about 70 years. In some cases the change would be catastrophic: The insurance industry, for example, would be seriously jolted. And what about jobs? How would our social systems provide meaningful work not only for more citizens (as the population rises), but also for a growing group that has a productive life that is 30 or more years longer?

Some people find revolting the idea of living significantly longer (they think that it would be horrible to extend one's elderly years), while others would love to have more time to accomplish the things they find interesting and important. Breakthroughs in life extension would almost certainly result in a series of new, very strongly debated, social issues.

THE AIDS DISASTER

Some of the implications of the global scourge of acquired immune deficiency syndrome (AIDS) are obvious and well cataloged. They are taking a tremendous toll in personal torment, economic devastation, and perhaps even political upheaval. Other potential twists in this epidemic are less obvious—but much more sinister.

Global Exponential Growth

The current trends are, by themselves, compelling. Although they differ on their projections, both the World Health Organization (WHO) and the Global AIDS Policy Coalition show a rapidly rising incidence of AIDS (see Figure 9-1).

With no cure in sight, the WHO estimates that at least a million adults were newly infected with the HIV virus that causes AIDS during the first half of 1992, and that 13 million have been infected worldwide since the epidemic began. Most of the new infections—well over 70 percent—involve heterosexuals in developing countries of Africa, Asia, and Latin America. Women are the fastest-growing group of newly infected in the industrialized world. Each week, 15,000 women contract the HIV virus, according to WHO's Global Program on AIDS. WHO predicts that 30 to 40 million people will be infected with HIV by the year 2000, more than 90 percent of them in developing countries

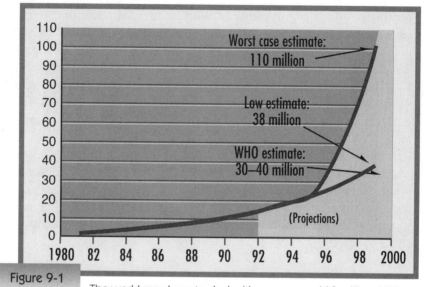

Figure 9-1

The world may have to deal with as many as 110 million AIDS cases by the year 2000. Source: *Boston Globe*, Global Aids Policy Coalition, World Health Organization

that lack the resources to mount prevention campaigns or to treat the ill. The Global AIDS Policy Coalition has developed a computer model that predicts that as many as 110 million people will be infected by the year 2000. In fact, WHO states that its own estimates are conservative.

To put this in a historical perspective:

- The Black Death killed about 25 million in the fourteenth century. But by the year 2000, 30 million to 110 million people will be infected with HIV, the virus that causes AIDS—up from some 12 million today.

- By the year 2000, the epidemic could drain between $356 billion and $514 billion from the global economy.

- In the worst-case scenario, the dollar loss equals 1.4 percent of the gross domestic product of the entire world. That's the equivalent of wiping out the economy of either Australia or India.

- In the United States, *U.S. News & World Report* estimates that the plague will siphon off between $81 billion and $107 billion by the year 2000.

The New York Times confirmed that the disease is now spreading much more rapidly through heterosexual transmission than by any other route, particularly in Africa and Southeast Asia. It is following roads and navigable rivers into rural areas; and as it claims more women each year, many more children are born with the disease or are orphaned by it. The price of caring for AIDS is skyrocketing: The lifetime cost of treating an AIDS patient in the United States in 1993 was $102,000, up from $57,000 in 1988. Disparity between rich and poor is evident in AIDS treatment, as in other things. The United States spends $38,300 per person; $22,300 is spent in Western Europe; $2,000 in Latin America—and $393 in Africa. Clearly, many people are not being treated.

The economic implications of the epidemic are ominous. Michael H. Merson, director of the World Health Organization's AIDS program, said that the alternative to spending more up front on AIDS prevention is political and economic collapse, which will send shock waves rippling through industrialized countries. "Thailand estimates the minimum cost of the epidemic to that country alone by the end of the century will be $9 billion. Imagine that happening throughout Asia, where the economies are thriving," he said. WHO estimates that about $120 million is being spent each year to *prevent* AIDS. Researchers estimate that the effort needs $2.5 billion.

Unidentified Cause of AIDS

In July of 1991, a few new cases of AIDS began cropping up in people who didn't have any trace of HIV, the virus commonly thought to cause the disease. The new patients displayed HIV risk factors (needle-sharing, unprotected sex, or a history of blood transfusions), but they didn't have the virus. This anomaly, now seen in several dozen cases around the world, highlights the fact that scientists don't really know whether the AIDS-like illness is caused by one virus, several viruses, or any infectious agent at all. In fact, some scientists suggest that AIDS is a result of things other than HIV, but their ideas have been deprecated in the past because they were not in the mainstream of scientific thought.

Asia Is the AIDS Epicenter

Asia is now the epicenter of the AIDS epidemic. Africa held that position for a number of years, but as Figure 9-2 shows, the tide has shifted. Two of the worst-hit countries are Thailand and India.

In Thailand, by the year 2000, 3 million to 6 million people may be infected, fully 5 percent to 10 percent of the population. The problem is particularly bad there (as it is in Africa) because the disease will attack those most responsible for the country's economic success—people aged 14 to 44. An entire generation will be at risk. Local sexual patterns exacerbate the spread: 75 percent of Thai men have had sex with prostitutes, almost half before they were 18. There are 800,000 prostitutes in Thailand; 20 percent to 30 percent are already HIV infected. In northern Thailand, the rate is 44 percent. Sixty percent of the Thai budget for public health will be consumed by AIDS-related expenditures during the next five years.

HIV infection in India is hard to pin down. Estimates have 300,000 to 400,000 infected, but the number is perhaps closer to 1 million. Bombay, for example, has 100,000 to 150,000 prostitutes out of a population of 12 million. The HIV infection rate for these women increased from 1 percent in 1987 to 30 percent in 1990. Figuring an average of six contacts per night, or about 600,000 heterosexual prostitute contacts per night, there are perhaps 200,000 exposures to HIV. With HIV transmission rates ranging from 0.1 percent to 1.0 percent, Bombay alone probably gets a minimum of 6,000 new HIV infections each month.

"AIDS is expected to retard much of the progress made in the late 1980s by countries like India," says DRI/McGraw-Hill's Nariman Behravesh. The number of youngsters orphaned by AIDS could more than double in the mid-1990s, to 3.7 million worldwide.

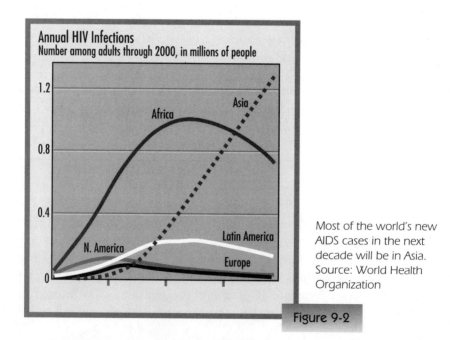

Annual HIV Infections
Number among adults through 2000, in millions of people

Asia

Africa

Latin America

N. America

Europe

Most of the world's new AIDS cases in the next decade will be in Asia. Source: World Health Organization

Figure 9-2

Even Japan is having to deal with the problem. The Japanese government has begun to admit that their country is as vulnerable as any other to the disease and has started new programs to educate its largely uninformed citizens. Behind the new worries is the troubling rise in recent figures and the fact that the pattern of its spread is similar to that in other countries with a tragically high incidence of the disease, such as Thailand.

Only China appears to have controlled the incidence of AIDS. Very strict border checks are made of those coming into the country, and some travelers must undergo mandatory blood tests. Some visitors report that China has been able to cure some of its few AIDS cases using traditional Chinese medicine, which focuses on bioenergy systems—the natural energy of the body.

Africa Devastated

Africa has been devastated by AIDS. In last five years, the number of Africans infected with HIV has tripled to about 7.5 million, and projections indicate 11.5 million victims by 1995. It is reported that the merchant infrastructure is being eliminated in some countries as large numbers of these people die.

The U.S. Problem

In the United States, more people will die from AIDS than have died from all of our wars combined—25 times as many as died in the war in Vietnam. A million and a half will probably die by 1995. About 50,000 Americans now get the AIDS virus each year, and by 1995 about 50,000 will be dying annually. And these figures are conservative. In 1991, federal statisticians estimated that about 18 percent of AIDS cases go unreported. Presently, perhaps a third of the deaths are drug abusers, a third gay men, and the rest heterosexuals, mostly African-American and Hispanic women. Figure 9-3 shows the climb in AIDS cases in the United States since 1981. *Newsweek* reported that AIDS is spreading unchecked among the nation's adolescents, "regardless of where they live or their economic status." In 1992, it was the sixth leading cause of death among 15- to 24-year-olds.

Americans have not yet come to grips with the likely and possible implications of this disease. In *The Catastrophe Ahead,* a book based on a two-year research study by the Hudson Institute, William B. Johnston

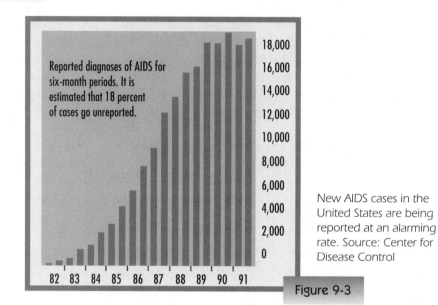

Reported diagnoses of AIDS for six-month periods. It is estimated that 18 percent of cases go unreported.

New AIDS cases in the United States are being reported at an alarming rate. Source: Center for Disease Control

Figure 9-3

and Kevin R. Hopkins say, "The HIV epidemic is currently at an early stage. As the epidemic grows during the 1990s, it will dramatically alter the American economic, political, and social landscape."

AIDS threatens our already reeling health care system. It could well change our social mores and the permissive attitude that has been associated with sexual conduct. Already a tide of lawsuits is making its way through the courts as the result of 500 new statutes, inspired, sometimes in fits of panic, by the epidemic.

By 1994, the annual cost for care of those dying of AIDS could be over $10 billion. The economic cost of this disease will peak at a time of extraordinary pressure on our economy from other sources, and could well be one of the events that galvanizes the conservative response by the baby boomer generation.

AIDS may well change the way we trade and interact with some countries, and who we allow into the United States The fact that we don't know exactly what causes it opens the door to a number of potential scenarios. One, advanced by Michael Ledeen of the American Enterprise Institute: "The day we learn that AIDS has been spread by a fly or mosquito is the day we see the first quarantine of an entire continent."

ALTERNATIVE MEDICINE

Perhaps as a reaction, to modern medicine's high-tech, reductionist orientation, Western nations are seeing significant growth in alternative medical practices, some many centuries old. In a 1992 cover story, *The New York Times Magazine* said, "In recent years, unconventional therapies such as meditation, acupuncture and homeopathy have begun to gain a foothold in American medicine."

This alternative approach to wellness is based on a variety of techniques that encourage healing without invading the body and that take advantage of natural body repair functions. It is holistic and systems-based in that the practitioner takes into consideration many aspects of a person's life, not just bodily symptoms. Much of it is based on concepts that assume that the mind has significantly more influence on health than mainline medicine believes.

These alternative approaches represent a very large change from the direction that medicine has been going for most of a century. If they are embraced by mainstream medicine, they will revolutionize both the practice of medicine and the role the patient plays in his or her own recovery. Most physicians would have to fundamentally rethink the underpinnings of the theory that supports their practice.

Relationship Between Mind and Body

Numerous studies support the validity of many of the underlying concepts of alternative medicine, particularly the relationship between the mind and body. In a landmark 1989 cardiac study, Dr. Dean Ornish found that patients could reverse their heart disease through diet and exercise—and the love of their friends. People with many friends or family ties tend to live longer than loners. Good relationships seem to protect the human immune system from the negative effects of stress. Mononucleosis in teens has been linked to stress in school. Herpes has been linked to loneliness. Positive mood, hope, and social support have been linked to cancer survival; tough-mindedness and a will to live have been linked to survival in AIDS.

Heart attack victims who have emotional support survive longer than those who do not. Among medical students under the stress of examinations, those who reported close relationships with family and friends had a stronger immune response to vaccination.

Theodore Melnechuk, who helped organize psychoneuro-immunology conferences in the 1970s, has cited dozens of studies showing that psychological factors are linked to the four broad types of immune dysfunction—cancer, infections, allergies, and auto-immune disorders.

The National Institutes of Health recently established an Office for the Study of Unconventional Medical Practices to investigate a wide range of treatments, including herbal medicine and massage therapy. Harvard Medical School plans to offer a course on unorthodox medicine. Similar courses and lectures are already available to medical students at Georgetown University, the University of Louisville, the University of Arizona, and the University of Massachusetts at Worcester.

Many physicians now speak of a transition from the narrow biomedical model of Western medicine to a "biopsychosocial" one. More than 2,000 physicians use acupuncture in conjunction with conventional medicine, according to the American Academy of Medical Acupuncture, and 5,000 use hypnotherapy, according to the American Society of Clinical Hypnosis. About 1,000 doctors practice homeopathy, the treatment of disease by using minute, highly diluted doses of the very substances that, in large doses, can cause the condition.

BIOELECTROMAGNETICS AND HEALTH

Some new theories about the interaction of humans with electromagnetic fields (EMFs) are changing certain aspects of health care. Appliances, computer monitors, and portable cellular phones are all designed with increasing consideration for the amount of electromagnetic radiation they produce.

Some scientific studies suggest that the risk of leukemia and other malignancies rises with exposure to electromagnetic fields, which are generated in varying degrees by all electrical devices, from hair dryers to high-voltage power lines. Two studies in Sweden suggested that children who live near high-tension lines have a higher risk of leukemia, and on-the-job exposure to electromagnetic fields increases the risk of cancer in working men in proportion to the strength of the electromagnetic field. Men who use electric razors appear to have a higher cancer rate than those who don't.

Only a few studies have been done to date, and none are conclusive. Clearly, we need more research on this subject if we are to continue living safely in a world connected by powerlines.

VIRULENT DISEASES REVIVED

A number of diseases, thought long destroyed, are making a comeback—with a vengeance. Many traditionally effective agents no longer work against these newly acclimated bugs.

The most publicized "superbugs" are the strains of drug-resistant tuberculosis bacteria that have caused outbreaks of the disease in U.S. hospitals and prisons in the past few years. And in a sobering series of 1992 articles in *Science* magazine, researchers point out that the problem of drug resistance is not limited to a few germs, but spans an entire spectrum of disease-causing microbes, including those responsible for gonorrhea, meningitis, streptococcal pneumonia, and staphylococcus infections. These microbes are spread by the enormous increase in tourism and business travel in recent decades. Overuse of antibiotics has accelerated the evolution of superbugs; hospitals and day-care centers in particular are major breeding grounds.

In a 1992 survey at Cook County Hospital in Chicago, 46 percent of a sample group of doctors in training to become internists had become infected with the TB germ. The recommended remedy: Wear scuba-like masks of thick rubber connected to a motorized air pump on the belt, and redo ventilation systems with expensive filters. To the prisons and inner-city clinics that serve the majority of tuberculosis patients, the adjustments mean huge new expenses at a time when their coffers are already bare. And because there is no precise science dictating how to adapt an old building to prevent the spread of TB, there have been many false starts.

The Associated Press recently reported a surge of malaria. Thought conquered 15 years ago, it is on rise again, killing millions of people worldwide. Presently there are about 2 million deaths annually in 102 countries, including the United States. The parasite has become resistant to most drugs and the carrier mosquito has become less sensitive to insecticides. At the 1994 annual meeting of the American Association for the Advancement of Science, microbiologist Alexander Tomasz of Rockefeller University warned that many common bacteria are evolving resistance to antibiotics. As a result, we are facing "nothing short of a medical disaster," he said.

Our increasingly complex and interdependent world provides many new avenues for the spread of viruses. Every decision made anywhere, in any sphere of life—environmental, political, demographic, economic, military—carries with it implications about disease that resound around the world. When the Aswan High Dam was built in Egypt, the new body of still water allowed mosquitoes to thrive, and the viruses they carried became a new threat. When used tires were shipped from Japan to Texas, mosquitoes hitched a ride in the wet rims—mosquitoes that carried viruses never before seen in Texas. And when the city borders of Seoul were pushed farther into the countryside, urban Koreans were exposed to a virus that rats had been carrying for centuries. Many contracted a raging hemorrhagic fever that kills at least 10 percent of its victims.

THE U.S. HEALTH CARE PROBLEM

In the United States, national health care expenditures have risen to some $800 billion per year, an amount approaching 13 percent of the gross national product (GNP), as shown in Figure 9-4. If past growth rates continue, health care will bankrupt the entire government before the end of the decade. The American health care system is an inefficient patchwork of 1,500 health insurance programs, in which 22 cents of every dollar goes to administrative costs.

In 1940, health care absorbed $4 billion, a mere 4 percent of our GNP. In 1990, such expenditures equalled $666 billion, or 12.2 percent of the GNP. In 1992, the country spent more than $800 billion on medical care, or 13.4 percent of the GNP. In 1990, business spent 61 percent of pretax profits and 108 percent of after-tax profits on health care benefits for employees (as opposed to 20 and 36 percent, respectively, in 1970). The United States also spends more of its gross domestic product—the value of items produced solely within U.S. borders—on health care than any of the 23 other members of the Organization for Economic Cooperation and Development (OECD).

The history of federal health care legislation has been a dismal cycle of failed "reforms." Every effort to control federal expenditures has succeeded only in shifting costs by opening new loopholes. Special interests and bureaucratic inertia have prevented any significant overhaul of the system. State legislatures are more creative, but it is too soon to determine if these measures will prove to be solutions or will repeat federal experience by shifting the costs to new areas.

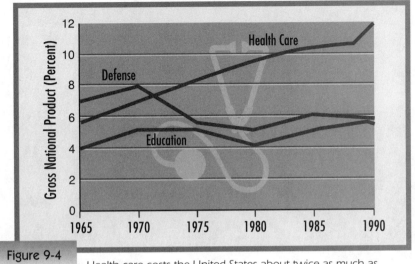

Figure 9-4 Health care costs the United States about twice as much as defense. Source: *Consumer Reports*, U.S. National Center for Education Statistics, U.S. Health Care Financing Administration

It is clear that without rapid reform, the entire U.S. health care system, as well as the U.S. economy, faces the possibility of financial collapse. It remains to be seen whether or not the version of the Clinton health care plan that gets through Congress will result in any significant change.

As the world wrestles with the by-products of the population explosion, new ideas and big changes in science and technology, and major adjustments in public policy, the health and health care of some groups will increase—but for many others, it will decrease. In both cases, these issues will be major considerations that will flow over into many other areas. One of those areas is social values.

CHAPTER

10

Changing

Social Values

The minority is sometimes right; the majority always wrong.

—*George Bernard Shaw*

As has been mentioned, the four most fundamental drivers of the future are information availability, technology, the physical environment and social values. The availability of information is most influential, for it is the valve that determines what a person has access to, or knows, out of all of the knowledge in the world. A member of a primitive tribe in New Guinea who has never seen a television or heard a radio would not know much, if anything, about Europe, or the United States, or automobiles, or computers, or conditions in the larger world in general. This is why information technology is so important—it is explosively expanding the amount of knowledge that is available to those of us in the developed world.

Technology gives us the tools—the mechanical advantage—to do things we wouldn't otherwise be able to do. These technical devices not only make our lives fuller and easier (and in so doing dramatically shape the systems we design to support and enable modern life); they also change the way we think. They reconfigure the grid through which we see and understand our world. We have only to think of the effect that cars, airplanes, and television have had on our families and the way we work and govern ourselves to know that that is true in spades.

But not all technology is broadly embraced. We humans make decisions about what we like, need, and think is important. And those decisions are fundamentally influenced by the basic set of values that we have assembled throughout our individual lives. These values are extraordinarily powerful, leading, in the extreme, to the sacrifice of one's life for an idea or belief.

As social values change, so also does behavior. When human beings do things differently, the future becomes something different from the present and the past. It is impossible to try to model value shifts across the whole planet, particularly when there are so many groups who see the world in such different ways. But we can work with some fairly good-sized pieces that will give us a feeling for some major forces for change.

TWO APPROACHES

There are two broad, and particularly interesting models for tracking social change: the generation model and the paradigm shift model. One looks to history for its key to the future, and the other looks to the horizon.

The Generational Model

William Strauss and Neil Howe, in their book *Generations*, "posit the history of America as a succession of generational biographies, beginning in 1584 and encompassing everyone through the children of today." They theorize that each generation belongs to one of four types, and that these types repeat sequentially in a fixed pattern. The vision of *Generations,* they say, "allows [one] to plot a recurring cycle in American history—a cycle of spiritual awakenings and secular crises— from the founding colonials through the present day and on into the next millennium."

Each generation, a social unit that dominates the society for about 22 years, has a special role in history. At any given time, four different generations are living together: youth (0 through 22 years old), rising adults (23 through 44), midlife adults (45 through 66), and elderhood (67 through 88). Each group has a unique set of characteristics and a unique name, and influences the other groups in a generally predetermined way. As Figure 10-1 shows, we are now in the midlife era of the Boomers. Strauss and Howe believe that Boomers act a lot like the Missionaries (who preceded them by four generations); and that the Thirteeners—the children of the Boomers—will respond like the Lost group that was born before the turn of the century. Future national moods can be projected based on the common personalities of today's generations as they age into new phases of life.

Strauss and Howe's basic assumption, that peers share the same "age-location" in history, is beginning to be shared by other researchers. For example, Douglas Coupland, author of *Generation X,* says, "Hippies were searching for something valuable. Benetton youth are looking for that same timeless essence but with a radically different

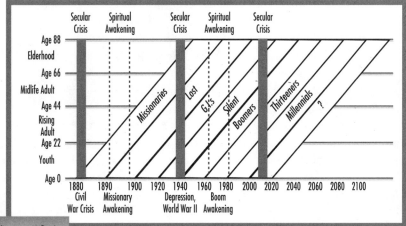

Figure 10-1

Each generation rises to influence the society during its midlife years.
Source: *Generations* by William Strauss and Neil Howe © 1991 by William Strauss and Neil Howe. Reprinted by permission, William Morrow and Company, Inc.

sensibility. Generations really do exist. And it's a weird, almost solipsistic, conceit on the part of their parents to say, 'Hey, we understand you kids completely.'"

There Have Been Regular Social Cycles

Generations says that the United States has had a series of regular social cycles that moved between eras of *spiritual awakening* and *secular crisis.* After an awakening, the country would enter a time that was largely *inner-directed.* This inward orientation would lead to a period of crisis, which would be followed by an *outer-driven* era, and then the cycle would repeat itself. Each of the eras has a unique set of characteristics.

- *Crisis Era.* During this time, a grim preoccupation with outer-world peril grows to maximum intensity, as spiritual curiosity declines, wars are very likely, sex-role distinctions widen, public and family order strengthen, and personal violence and substance abuse decline.

- *Outer-Driven Era.* The sense of community reaches its peak, the ideals that predominated in the crisis era are secularized and institutionalized, the emphasis is on planning, doing, and building, and wars tend to be an unwanted carryover from the recent crisis. Emphasis on the spiritual decreases.

- *Awakening Era.* The focus on inner life grows during this time, as secular interest in outer life declines. Wars are unlikely, artistic culture is high, and crime and substance abuse rise.

- *Inner-Directed Era.* Confidence in established institutions sinks, while satisfaction with personal and spiritual life is high. Individualism flourishes, wars become more likely, and open hostility emerges between risk-taking adventurers on one side and moralizers on the other.

Associated with each era is a paradigmatic, or typical, mood. The characters of the four generation types (Idealist, Reactive, Civic, Adaptive) work together to generate the mood of the era. Table 10-1 shows the composition of each era.

The Idealist Lifecycle (at midlife during Inner-Directed Era): A youth spent amid secular confidence and coming of age during an awakening, in a postcrisis era of mellowed Reactive elders, vigorous Civic midlifers, and conformist Adaptive rising adults, these generations travel a *prophetic lifecycle,* with their coming-of-age passion and their principled elder stewardship in times of crisis.

The Reactive Lifecycle (at midlife during Crisis Era): A youth spent during an awakening and coming of age amid spiritual confidence but secular uneasiness, children to an era of still-powerful Civic elders, torn

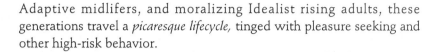

Adaptive midlifers, and moralizing Idealist rising adults, these generations travel a *picaresque lifecycle,* tinged with pleasure seeking and other high-risk behavior.

	Awakening Era	Inner-Directed Era	Crisis Era	Outer-Driven Era
Elder	Civics	Adaptives	Idealists	Reactives
Midlife	Adaptives	Idealists	Reactives	Civics
Rising	Idealists	Reactives	Civics	Adaptives
Youth	Reactives	Civics	Adaptives	Idealists
Cycle Calendar	Year 1–22	Year 23–44	Year 45–66	Year 67–88

Table 10-1. Composition of eras

From *Generations* by William Strauss and Neil Howe © 1991 by William Strauss and Neil Howe. Reprinted by permission, William Morrow and Company, Inc.

The Civic Lifecycle (at midlife during Outer-Driven Era): A youth spent amid spiritual confidence and coming of age during a secular crisis, in a post-awakening era of sensitive Adaptive elders, values-oriented Idealist midlifers, and pleasure-seeking Reactive rising adults, these generations travel a *heroic lifecycle,* with a clear collective mission and high ambitions for cleaning up and rebuilding the outer world.

The Adaptive Lifecycle (at midlife during Awakening Era): A youth spent during a crisis and coming of age amid secular confidence but spiritual unease, this cohort enters childhood surrounded by stern Idealist elders, pragmatic Reactive midlifers, and aggressive Civic rising adults. These generations travel a *genteel lifecycle,* with a cult of professional expertise and critical gestures of conscience and humanism.

Throughout the country's 18 generations, the strands of four recurring personalities have been woven together, following each other in a fixed order. Each predominates for about 22 years, and plays a direct role in defining the characteristics of the other three lifestyles.

Different Approaches to Life's Challenges

The unique mood of an era results in different general approaches to the major issues of life. Table 10-2 shows the broad spread of reactions.

	Awakening	Inner-Directed	Crisis	Outer-Driven
Nurture of Children	Underprotective	Tightening	Overprotective	Loosening
Sex-Role Divisions	Narrowing	Narrowest point	Widening	Widest Point
Tolerance for Personal Risk	Rising	High	Falling	Low
Individualism vs. Community	Rising individualism	Maximum individualism	Rising community	Maximum community
World View	Rising complexity	Maximum complexity	Rising simplicity	Maximum simplicity
Behavior Toward Ideals	Discover	Cultivate	Champion	Realize
Behavior Toward Institutions	Attack	Redefine	Establish	Build
Sense of Greatest Need	Fix inner world	Do what feels right	Fix outer world	Do what works
Vision of Future	Euphoric	Darkening	Urgent	Brightening

Table 10-2. Character of eras

From *Generations* by William Strauss and Neil Howe © 1991 by William Strauss and Neil Howe. Reprinted by permission, William Morrow and Company, Inc.

Recent Generations

Strauss and Howe name a generation for the time in which the cohort is middle-aged and most influential. *Everyone who lives a normal lifespan experiences every era once,* whether at the beginning, middle, or end of life. Almost everyone alive today in the United States is a member of one of the following generations:

■ *G.I. elders,* born between 1901 and 1924; (glorious, Civics): firm believers in public harmony and cooperative social discipline, accustomed to being looked upon (and rewarded) as good, constructive, and deserving. A rationalist generation.

■ *Silent midlifers,* born between 1925 and 1942; (progressive, Adaptives): Other-directed, more appreciative of the mind-sets, virtues, and flaws of those born before or behind them. No elected president among this generation. They bring nonjudgmental fairness and open-mindedness to American society.

▪ *Boomer rising adults,* born between 1943 and 1960; (awakeners, Idealists): An authentic generation with a unique vision, a transcendent principle, a moral acuity more wondrous and extensive than anything. Typically exert their most decisive influence on history late in life; have a capacity for great wisdom, terrible tragedy, and insufferable pomposity.

▪ *Thirteener youths,* born between 1961 and 1981; (lost generation, Reactives): Named for the thirteenth American generation. Low expectation is a game this generation can play to its advantage; they know the odds. An ill-timed lifecycle. A popular Thirteener put-down is, "That's history," which means, that's irrelevant.

▪ *Millennial children,* born between 1982 and 2004; will be civic achievers.

The 1990s: An Inner-Directed Era

The 1990s are an Inner-Directed era in which Idealist endowments of principle, religion, and education are likely to rise. The Reactive endowments of liberty, pragmatism, and survival may wane, while the Civic characteristics of community, technology, and affluence will become dormant. Adaptive endowments (pluralism, expertise, and social justice) should peak and then fall later in the decade.

History suggests that a Crisis is due by 2020, about half-way through the cycle dominated by the Millennial Generation (about 2010 to 2040).

To understand the principal influence of the coming decade, we must understand the dominant generation—Boomers, rising adults, born between 1943 and 1960, are entering midlife in an Inner-Directed era (1991 to 2003) and elderhood in a Crisis era (2004 to 2025). Boomers will always listen to 1960s music, debate the "lessons" of Vietnam, and show a weakness for granola and mineral water. All will be steered by their coming-of-age experiences.

Boomers will assert their midlife values. They will subject their coming-of-age Awakening—what it did and did not accomplish—to growing scrutiny, and they will generate stormy peer-on-peer invective (following the script of every prior Idealist generation entering midlife).

▪ *Boomer perfectionism* will begin to express itself less in the realm of personal fulfillment than in the realm of social virtue.

▮ _Boomer politics will become more intensely value laden._ Members of the generation will grow increasingly pompous, intolerant, uncompromising, snoopy, and exacting of others, as well as more dutiful, principled, and demanding of themselves.

▮ _The Boomer's era of political remission ended when the last G.I. president departed._ Bill Clinton's presidency is the signal for a new activism.

▮ Notwithstanding their current reputation for personal selfishness, Boomers will not mobilize around appeals to collective self-interest (tax, labor, trade, retirement issues), but will look for lofty commitment on matters of principle. This will produce an attitude that will help to _revitalize a sense of national community._

▮ The Boomer _share of Congress and governorships_ (now 21 percent) _will expand rapidly_ in the middle 1990s and become a plurality following the 1994 or 1996 election. They will reach their lifetime peak share of national leadership around the year 2005, just as the Inner-Directed era is ending, 62 years after the birth of their first cohort.

▮ Some of the promising _Boomer politicians and presidential candidates will spring from outside the ranks of law, government, and party politics._ Ross Perot, though not of the Boomer generation, may well be the harbinger of this movement. Their elite will maintain individual identities apart from institutions.

▮ In Congress, _resignations over matters of principle will become more common._ Throughout the top echelons of government and business, interest in philosophy, literature, and the arts will rise—and interest in "how-to" manuals will fall.

▮ _Seeing new virtue in community,_ Boomers may see advantages in taxes on consumption, regulation on speculative investment and pleasure-seeking leisure, and public intrusions into what others will consider matters of personal and business privacy. Similarly, an antidrug and proenvironmental alliance may emerge as the nation's most potent lobby. In all aspects of civil life, they will insist on enforcing a new sense of local community.

▮ Boomers will _remain a hard sell for political and commercial marketers,_ taking less interest in flesh-and-blood candidates than in abstract issues. To reach them, aspiring politicians will have to demonstrate candor, simplicity, moral rectitude, serenity of soul, even a hint of detachment. They will seek high purpose in what they buy: quality over quantity, uniqueness over comfort, inner satisfaction over outer popularity.

■ Boomer manager-owners will try to *turn firms into agents of public and private virtue.* Focus on the "bottom line" will not just mean profits, but principles about what companies should mean to owners, employees, customers, and neighbors. Boomer executives will be prepared to accept a narrowed pay gap between themselves and their workers.

■ *A culture war will develop between the Boomer and Thirteenth generation* because the Boomers will push an austere and stripped-down version of their New Age morality into mainstream social life. Around the year 2000, Boomers will settle in as the more cerebral "older" generation, seeking the classic and the enduring over the faddishly popular. They will challenge sex, profanity, and violence in the media, and will mount attacks on all forms of substance abuse.

■ *The midlife African-American elite will assert moral leadership in troubled neighborhoods,* forcing younger people to "build character" and accept more responsibility for their own condition. African-American Boomers may ultimately make their most enduring contributions in letters and cultural leadership.

■ *Boomer women will have an explosion in public life;* aging Boomer women will rewiden sex role distinctions, and push women back toward the pedestal of family life.

■ *Boomer judgmentalism will land heavily* on the criminal justice system as well as in civil law. Society's leaders will find it easier to condemn individuals and harder to condemn "society."

■ Boomers have the capacity *to age elegantly,* in their own eyes and in the eyes of others, but if they cling to a youth-fixated narcissism into their forties and fifties, the United States will be heading for trouble. The split between the New Age (modernist) and evangelical (traditionalist) camps should be watched carefully.

2004–2025: Crisis Era

Whether Boomer leadership will end in triumph or tragedy will hinge on their capacity to restrain (or let others restrain) their latent ruthlessness. Faced with crisis, this generation of one-time draft resisters will not hesitate, as elder warrior-priests, to conscript young soldiers to fight and die for righteous purposes. Let us hope that old Boomers will look within themselves and find something richer than apocalypse.

The Paradigm Shift Model

Another model for looking at changes in social values, one that takes in much more than just the United States, has been developed by Kirk and Christine MacNulty, principals in the Arlington, Virginia-based strategic planning firm of Applied Futures, Inc. The MacNultys believe the Western world is in the middle of a profound social change in the very framework that is used to describe reality—a paradigm shift—the likes of which has not been seen for over 400 years. The last time this happened was when the world shifted from the medieval era to the Industrial Age. In this case, they believe that we are moving from the Scientific/Industrial period to a Social/Consciousness age.

Three Driving Forces for the New Paradigm

New scientific discoveries (by Newton, Copernicus, Galileo, and others) in the fourteenth to seventeenth centuries (and spread by the printing press) fueled a basic shift in the most fundamental terms of how humans understood reality—themselves, the world around them, and their organizations. Similarly, modern physics, analytical and developmental psychology, and research into consciousness are precipitating an overhaul of the basic outlook of a growing segment of developed societies.

The New Physics

The new ideas are anchored in quantum mechanics and are now beginning to work their way into everyday life. They revolve around the powerful notion that consciousness is required to explain the existence of matter. No longer do leading physicists like David Bohm believe that reality exists outside of human involvement. *Consciousness is causal*—a chair exists because it is observed—someone is required in order for physical reality to exist. In *Taking the Quantum Leap* (winner of the National Book Award), physicist Fred Alan Wolf says, "Fundamentally, the observer creates reality by observing it, asserted Neils Bohrs and Albert Einstein in their 'Copenhagen interpretation,' which has been a mainstay of physics ever since." Wolf goes on to say, "It is precisely how we observe that creates the reality we perceive. Change the how of it and you change the what of it."

Furthermore, mathematics prove that matter can go both forward and backward in time; that all reality is connected to everything else through instantaneous connections; that matter can appear and disappear (many times very rapidly); and that a given piece of matter can split into two pieces that are the same size and weight as the original one. Time does not flow in at a fixed rate, and it is an integral part of space—one does not exist without the other. These ideas threaten the very essence of the Newtonian explanation of reality, which is the basis of Western beliefs.

Some of the first inklings of the practical implications of quantum mechanics can be found in the field of medicine. Some cancer patients in mainline hospitals are now often told to meditate and to visualize tiny soldiers in their bodies searching out and killing cancer cells.

Analytical and Developmental Psychology

Psychology, which came into being only during this century, also supports these ideas. Both Maslow and Jung suggested that people are more than their egos. Maslow included levels above those of self-actualization in his hierarchy of needs. Jung posited that people develop from instinct to ego to self, self being the best personal and transpersonal aspects of the psyche.

It is this detached, transpersonal orientation that allows one to see the reality from outside of a narrow personal perspective. It is the realization of the existence of something greater than mere physical life, for instance, that allows a person to offer his or her life in the place of another. In more mundane terms, this perspective allows a "systems" view that accepts personal loss or pain in order to accomplish a larger good.

Consciousness Research

As a response to these ideas, more and more major universities and research institutions are exploring the mind/body relationship and finding that the mind has ultimate control over the body. The discipline of psychoneuroimmunology has shown a causal relationship between physical health and mental attitude. Alternative medicine based on nonphysical forces is now being taught at Harvard Medical School and other similarly prestigious institutions.

The common concept that is arising from all of these areas is that consciousness is evidently the complete equation of reality—consciousness is causal. Futurists Marvin Cetron and Owen Davies say that we are redefining what it means to be a human being. "We are beginning to distinguish between being human and being a person, between the body and the functioning individual who may—or may not—inhabit it. And the rights we once granted to all humans are now being limited only to persons."

The Inner-Directeds Are Leading

Although some of these ideas have been around for centuries in the East, they are just beginning to take hold in the Western industrialized world. In particular, they are being embraced by an increasing number of *inner-directed* people, who look largely within themselves for direction. They are not significantly influenced by the attitudes and actions of others. They march to their own drum, and as a group they produce and nurture most of society's new ideas and value shifts. They are innovators who maximize individual potential and whose needs are primarily "growth needs." Research in Europe and the United States shows that the inner directed segment is growing significantly in all major Western countries. This is the group that is embracing the beginnings of a "consciousness is causal" perspective and starting to see the world in holistic terms. The net effect is that a radical new understanding of reality is working its way into Western societies.

The information technology explosion is spreading these ideas and their derivatives throughout the developed world.

As the inner directed values increasingly establish a more influential position in society, a new paradigm will evolve: Because people can directly influence their reality, there will be decreasing tolerance for those who do not take the responsibility of doing so. Those individuals, for instance, who are a burden on society because of poor health or a form of dependency (drugs, alcohol, and so on) may find themselves without the traditional sympathy or support that they previously were accorded. No one can any longer blame "them"—one's problems are not the fault of society or of external circumstances.

The paradigm shift perspective suggests that in the next two decades there will a number of fundamental new trends:

 Dependency will be overtaken by independence and interdependence.

 Autonomy will subvert collectivism.

 Socialism, already discredited, will increasingly give way to capitalism.

■ Materialism as a metaphysics will increasingly be overcome by the idea that consciousness is causal.

A New Renaissance

This model argues for the blooming of a "super Renaissance" that will be many times more significant than the last one, producing major changes in every significant aspect of life. The very underpinnings of reality—philosophy, theology, ethics, sociology, and so on—will all be assaulted by this new set of ideas.

In his book, *The American Future,* Wm. Van Dusen Wishard writes:

We are well into a Quantum Age of Uncertainty and Unpredictability; that in the realm of quantum mechanics, "objective experiment" is a contradiction in terms; that the physical world may not consist of structures built out of independently existing (and unanalyzable) entities, but rather a web of relationships between elements whose meanings arise entirely from their link to the whole; that a "complete understanding" of reality lies outside the capabilities of rational thought, and must include subjective, intuitive insights; that consciousness/mind did not appear late in the evolutionary process, but were always here; that far from mind being housed in the brain, mind exists independently of the brain (and possibly independently of the body); and that subatomic particles may contain some form of consciousness enabling them to transmit knowledge faster than the speed of light, over distances measured by light-years.

The above assumptions form the greatest shift of scientific worldview since Galileo's work in the 17th century. Despite their startling implications, they evolved [in the Western world] during the past century. They still have to work their way through the philosophy, knowledge structure, culture, education and general worldview of the rest of our society. But these new assumptions, asserting their authority, are *causing* the upheaval we are seeing in our society today.

GENERATION OR PARADIGM?

In looking at the United States and, to a lesser extent, other parts of the developed world, we have considered two different perspectives for the same period of time. They are not mutually exclusive; they describe the coming era from two different—and equally valid—perspectives. In fact, perhaps the best model for exploring changes in U.S. social values is a synthetic one that includes both generational and paradigmatic components.

The generational approach is essentially a "short-wave" analysis: Every 22 years, a new generation comes on the scene with a set of predictable characteristics. The paradigm model is a "long-wave" perspective: The last shift of this kind was some 400 years ago. *It therefore seems to make sense to superimpose the two trends, and take as the major social value driving force a paradigm shift modulated by generational change,* as shown in Figure 10-2.

This also offsets intrinsic shortcomings of the generational model, in that it represents an analysis of trends during a period between paradigm shifts (that is, a period with no major value shifts), which does not reflect the insertion of a technology that even approaches the profundity of the current wave of information technology or the introduction of fundamentally new concepts in science.

The United States in the next two decades will see a number of new social trends, driven by a constellation of value changes.

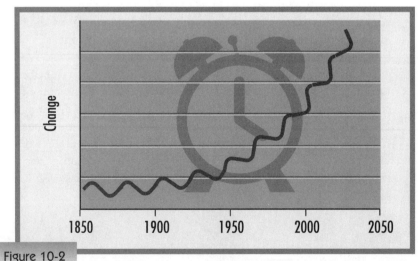

Figure 10-2

Social values in the United States may represent a paradigm shift modulated by the cycles of the generational model

- Two major groups, sustenance-driven traditionalists and inner-directed progressives, will be in open conflict for the mind of the society.

- Holism and interdependency will increase significantly as a principle of operation and decision making.

- Religious denominations and other conservative institutions will dig in deeply and defend their principles vigorously.

- Conservative groups, in the face of rapid increases in threatening information, will try to revert to simpler, more familiar times.

- Individuals will become increasingly autonomous, unlinking themselves from institutions (which are naturally conservative).

- There will be a growing intolerance for those who do not show personal responsibility, both in this country and abroad.

- There will be major changes in the structure and function of government, business, and education.

- Large numbers of people will be confused about the rapidly emerging new ideas. Many will find this destabilizing, producing an increase in compensating behavior.

THE REST OF THE WORLD

To the extent that one buys into the paradigm shift model, it probably has relevance to most of the developed world—certainly that part of humanity that will be hooked up to the information network and flooded with new ideas. But a good part of the world—most of it, perhaps—will not participate in this revolution any time soon. Both economically and in terms of information technology, most of the world's people will find themselves cast as have-nots, looking over the fence, as it were, by television—and not liking what they see. Whether they respond negatively to the disparity in the standard of living or, for religious or other reasons find the Western lifestyle threatening, the ubiquitous TV will assure that they will know that their situation is different from that of the rest of the world. History tells us that people respond in one of two general ways to large amounts of new information. For some, many new ideas coming at a rapid pace is exhilarating. They see hope and opportunity in the change and embrace it with a gusto. Many people in the developed world will see change in this way.

On the other hand, many people find change threatening. New images that they don't understand, or that they believe fly in the face of traditional values, generate quite different responses. If they haven't been part of the evolutionary process that convinced others that a radically different lifestyle was a better way to live, the poor and isolated will find the electronic images startling and shocking, very much at odds with the traditions that their lives are built around. And they will respond accordingly, by reverting more strongly to the conservative principles and social structures that have always given them comfort and meaning.

That is exactly what is happening in many parts of the world; and as the rate of change accelerates, so too will this response.

But more than that, if people deeply believe that they are being "screwed" by the system, or that these new ideas are a threat to religious principles that they presume to be God-given and universal, they will attempt to change the situation. In the past, even if poor people knew they were deprived, there wasn't much they could do about it. But now, not only do they know they're on the bottom of the ladder, but the ability to do something about it is working its way down to them—and they have no reason not to attack the system. Lack of hope means that one has nothing left to lose.

A Proliferation of Weaponry

For decades now, people have been pumping huge numbers of weapons into the world system. At one level, both industrial and developing countries have been building conventional guns and bombs at a staggering pace and selling the common systems to just about anyone who would pay for them. The most developed countries, like the United States, produce very sophisticated, high-cost devices and discriminate somewhat in who they will sell to; while companies in places like Eastern Europe, Brazil, South Africa, and China manufacture millions of smaller weapons that are distributed broadly. In the spring of 1994, there were 24 violent ongoing conflicts (mostly subnational civil wars and the like) that provided an ongoing market for this deadly materiel.

This proliferation of conventional arms means that many of the poorest and least stable places in the world (like Angola, Somalia, Sudan, and Afghanistan) are awash in weapons. And the weapons are in the hands of the young men—the manifestation of the global teenager boom—who find fighting for local warlords or insurgency groups to be a significantly better life than they would otherwise have.

Although all manufacturers are in this business for the money, for some countries—like Russia and Eastern Europe—building and selling conventional weapons is the only (or major) way they have of obtaining hard currency, which they need to buy other foreign-made necessities. They would have far worse problems than they already have if they quit selling arms.

Exotic weapons of mass destruction—nuclear, chemical, radiological, and biological—also appear to be becoming dislodged from the hands of the countries that built them. There are scattered reports that small numbers of former Soviet tactical nuclear warheads are being quietly sold to Middle Eastern groups. Parcels of enriched uranium are being circuitously moved out of places like Russia and sold for large amounts of money.

The interesting, and scary, part about this is that these weapons were originally built by countries that didn't want to use them. They were a deterrent to their own use. Now, if reports are true, these extraordinarily destructive devices are finding their way into the hands of people who *want to use them.* They have no reason not to threaten the very fabric of the developed world—and now, they have the means to do so.

We are witnessing an attitude shift on the part of a significant number of people—a hardening of their opinions about those who are living better than and differently from themselves. In part, it is a reaction to the flood of new information and images that is sweeping the world and their inability to reconcile their own lives with what they are seeing and hearing. It seems that the situation will get worse before it gets better.

SOCIAL FRAGMENTATION

The same alienation that we see in some of the poorer parts of the world is also growing in countries like the United States. Again, we are seeing a backlash against the change that is being embraced by the leading edges of society. Religious and ethnic groups are swinging toward conservatism—harkening back to times and tools that have worked in the past rather than looking forward to the future.

As change increases, a major ideological conflict ensues between the progressive and regressive groups until the progressive ideas (promoted by the inner-directed leading edge) gain mainstream dominance (are embraced by the outer-directed group that finds meaning from external indicators). The new ideas then become conventional wisdom that is subject to attack by a new group of progressives.

Such a conflict is now in full bloom in the United States. It played a major role in the 1992 presidential campaign, for example, with George Bush trying to appeal to conservative "family values," and Bill Clinton offering a new alternative to the status quo.

Growing Tribalism

Tribalism, one of the most significant manifestations of this retrenchment in the face of change, is showing itself both domestically and globally. In this country, the most obvious example is the fragmentation of the society into cultural subgroups. In the past, the idea of America was one of a melting pot—as historian Arthur M. Schlesinger, Jr. has written, "the creation of a brand-new national identity, carried forward by individuals who, in forsaking old loyalties and joining to make new lives, melted away ethnic differences." But now, as the result of a variety of pressures, there is a major push by segments of our society to highlight minorities at the expense of the whole.

Dr. Schlesinger summarized the trend well.

> The hostility of one tribe for another is among the most instinctive human reactions. Yet, the history of our planet has been in great part the history of the mixing of peoples. Mass migrations have produced mass antagonisms from the beginning of time. Today, as the twentieth century draws to an end, a number of factors—not just the evaporation of the cold war but, more profoundly, the development of swifter modes of communication and transport, the acceleration of population growth, the breakdown of traditional social structures, the flight from tyranny and from want, the dream of a better life somewhere else—converge to drive people as never before across national frontiers and thereby to make the mixing of peoples a major problem for the century that lies darkly ahead.

A Loss of Communal Ties

The manifestation of this trend in the United States is not simply nationality or race. As Charles Sykes (presenting a classic Boomer critique) has suggested,

> The increasing tendency of Americans to fragment themselves along the lines of race, sexual preference, gender, ethnicity and psychological infirmities may reflect their sense of the loss of more traditional communal ties—family, church, community. But rather than defining themselves in terms of a shared culture, these new communities of grievance are animated by their shared conviction that they are victimized by "heightism," "lookism," "sizeism," or "toxic" parents.
>
> Our victim culture is fueled in large measure by the desire to redefine inappropriate conduct as disease or "addiction."

Minority groups want to study together, live in universities apart from the rest of the students, and even rewrite the conventional view of history and change curricula to emphasize their particular view of the world. In Atlanta, for instance, the *Washington Post* reports that nearly all of the city's 109 schools and more than 80 percent of its teachers are using Afrocentric curricula in the coming school year. Third-grade children are taught math problems in the East African language of Ki-Swahili. In Maryland's Montgomery County, outside Washington, D.C., a committee of Korean, Chinese, and East Indian residents advised the school system on "what perceptions we want our kids to have about Asia" when a three-year world history sequence was overhauled.

Other minority groups are also asserting themselves. In a major political fight in New York, angry school chancellor Joseph A. Fernandez laid down an ultimatum to a Queens school board that had refused to adopt a plan to teach elementary school children to respect and appreciate gay people. In the end, Fernandez was fired as the result of an uproar by parents (Boomers) against his policies.

Global Fragmentation

Parallel issues dominate the international sections of our newspapers. The ethnic violence in the Balkans, the continuing disharmony in the Middle East, the threatening religious war in Northern India, and the

Northern Ireland struggle are all examples of areas of groups that are fixated on the past rather than the future.

Three antimodern religions, Islamic fundamentalism, Maoism, and fanatic environmentalism also offer a harbor for those who find the pace and composition of change menacing. Islam was once the world's cultural and technical leader, but the new version is overwhelmingly antimodern and anti-Western. It has great appeal to the underdeveloped world, and it may reconquer the entire Middle East, from Morocco to Pakistan. Maoism has far fewer adherents, but Maoists are proactive killers and may succeed in taking over a faltering Latin American nation or two. Fanatic environmentalism has the greatest appeal to Western intellectuals. In *Power Shift,* Alvin Toffler describes these eco-theologues as "wish[ing] to plunge society into pre-technological medievalism and asceticism... . [they] insist that there can be no technological relief, and that we are therefore destined to slide back into preindustrial poverty, a prospect they regard as a blessing rather than a curse."

Where does this tribalism lead? Schlesinger points out that at some time in the past most ethnic groups, like the Irish, have attempted to influence curricula and literature in partisan ways, but ultimately those efforts have died as the group became more completely integrated. Also, if the generational approach is to be believed, as the Boomers begin to dominate, they will increasingly deprecate these kinds of programs.

What are the implications of information technology and its effect on tribalism, as information is more broadly and quickly communicated? Some have suggested, for instance, that television may play a major role in the integration of Europe, in that it more quickly exposes the different societies to each other. On the other hand, the information overload and threats of the unfamiliar may well generate additional stress and strengthen the resolve of subgroups to find stability within themselves.

CURRENT ATTITUDES

All of these forces and trends are reflected in some of the current attitudes of the American people. In their book, *The Day Americans Told the Truth,* Kimm and Paterson identified some of them.

- Americans generally have lost faith in authority of government, the corporate sector, churches, and education.

- On the whole, we believe less in others, trust less, and dislike our fellow citizens.

- We believe less in ourselves and the actions that we take with others and ourselves.

- There is much less belief in the traditional patriarchal family.

- We believe less in work as a calling. Work is something that is necessary and holds few other rewards.

- The majority of those sampled believe that the United States in the future will be colder, meaner, greedier, and more selfish than in the past.

We have the highest illiteracy of any industrialized country, as well as the highest divorce rate, highest number of single parents, highest debt per household, highest crime rate, highest homicide rate, and highest per capita expenditures on crime. We have one of the highest adult mortality rates, the highest infant mortality rate, and yet the highest expenditure per capita for medical bills. We also now have the greatest economic disparity between the rich and the poor.

Newsweek magazine, in a March 1992 article about the changes we are confronting, noted that,

> Our new era lacks a name, but its central challenge is clear: to restore the American Dream, we must reconcile our ideals with today's economic realities. We need to rethink private and governmental responsibilities. Counting on prosperity as a panacea bred irresponsibility in government, Corporate America and even our personal lives. To some extent, things correct themselves. Tougher competition has forced many companies to improve. There's a renewed awareness of the irreplaceable importance of families in rearing children into self-reliant and responsible citizens. But the one place where change can't occur automatically is government.

NEW STRUCTURES FOR DEALING WITH CHANGE

We have suggested that the great changes we will experience in the next two decades will threaten the current paradigm at its most fundamental level. The early signs of that change are becoming obvious as progressive thinkers actively explore new models of organization, government, and education.

Heterarchies—Virtual Corporations

Business is reorganizing away from hierarchies to structures like heterarchies, where employees acquire a much broader variety of skills and use those abilities in differing roles, depending upon the job or project. One week a worker might be a team leader, at another time a technician. Working groups are brought together on an ad hoc basis, by picking and choosing among the available pool of people—always trying to put together the strongest team for that particular task.

This highly dynamic approach is made possible by advanced information technology. Databases can keep detailed information on the skills and experiences of individual workers, and that data can be used to form the working groups required for a particular task or project.

Communitarians

At a more basic level—perhaps responding to the pull described in the generational model—new groups are attempting to redefine the individual's relationship to society. A new collection of thinkers, both liberal and conservative, calling themselves Communitarians, are pointing to the need to curb the minting of "rights" and to balance existing rights with greater willingness to shoulder responsibilities and commitments to the common good. They emphasize the importance of community, the moral claims staked by shared needs and futures, as distinct from the claims of various subgroups and individuals.

Holistic Theories

Some Communitarians would resonate with holistic approaches (supported by quantum theory) that suggest that humans have direct links with all around them, not only other people but plants and animals as well—that we all exist in a very large and complex interdependent system. New generations of school children, who have grown up with ecological principles, implicitly take this view.

All of these shifts in attitudes and values saturate the other social sectors that describe modern life. An economy, as we will see in the next chapter, is nothing, in broad terms, but the manifestation of a group's basic values in its dealings with money. When values change, economies shudder. And in this period of great change, economies are shaking.

CHAPTER

11

Economies:

Fundamental Shifts

If all of the economists in the world were laid end-to-end … it would be good.

—*John L. Petersen*

The major economic problem of the future stems from the fact that we don't know how economies really work. Economic activity is nothing more than the manifest behavior of groups of humans; the behavior of economies is therefore at least as complicated as human behavior. It is not, for example, described by a set of simple mechanistic supply-and-demand equations. The economic jungle is teeming with uncertainty, unpredictability, and chaos. It is not linear.

This is not the common perspective. Economists, like weather forecasters, are constantly trying to use their equations to predict how global and national economies will behave. Like their meteorologist brethren, they're best at reporting what has already happened, marginal at predicting anything further into the future than a couple of days, and in the dark if the objective is months or years away. The true principles of economic behavior are almost certainly closer to sociology or biology than they are to physics.

Nevertheless, decisions affecting economies are almost always made with the assumption that changes in one parameter, such as interest rates, will almost certainly result in parallel changes in other parameters, such as inflation rates. But since the behavior is not linear and mechanistic, the intended results often never quite arrive. And if they do, they are accompanied by any of a number of unanticipated companions that wreak further havoc on the stability of the system. For example, there is no provision for valuing waste, and therefore so much of the present problem with the environment can be attributed to the incentives that are an integral part of the underlying economics. Because the system only values money, it has no way of quantifying the experience of workers, or their attitudes, or the power of an organizational vision or objective. We look only at a narrow set of "numbers," and find ourselves constantly surprised and at the mercy of this extraordinarily complex organism that is more creative than we are.

This is a problem—particularly so in a world that is becoming more complex, more unpredictable, and, because of information technology, faster reacting. And so, increasingly, we find ourselves along for the ride, with less and less direct influence on the direction that the system is taking and on its ultimate destination—all because the framework within which we look at the problem is fundamentally flawed. The next two decades will bring major change to our economic theory as we begin to see the behavior of the system in more holistic terms. As discussed at the end of this section, the conversion has already begun; a number of new theories are addressing the shortcomings of our historic deterministic approach.

A NEW PARADIGM

Not only are we looking at economic problems through the wrong grid, but we have entered a time in which the driving forces are quite different than they have been in the past, exacerbating our inability to understand what is going on. As with the printing press at the time of the Enlightenment, new information technologies are changing the very underpinnings of all aspects of life. This will only become more acute in the coming years, highlighting the major flaws in the present approach.

The early 1994 United States economic recovery is illustratative. *Fortune* called it a "duck of a different feather." Even though productivity is increasing, employment is flat. Companies are working hard to keep their costs down, and the composition of existing jobs is changing. Conventional wisdom is being "blown out of the water."

The next 20 years will see the following trends:

■ *Major Shifts in Required Skills.* As information technology makes deeper and deeper inroads into the system, more and more knowledge workers will be required. People without a high school diploma will find it very difficult to get a job as the composition of the workforce changes from industrial to information. By the year 2000, factory workers will probably be less than 16 percent of the American workforce, having been caught in the same kind of shift that happened to farm workers. (A century ago, nearly half of the workforce was farm workers; now it is only 3 percent). Almost all of the growth will be in the service sector.

■ *Big Changes in Structures and Processes.* Information technology is forcing fundamental changes in the structures of organizations that we use for commerce. The hierarchical structure is being replaced by an array of new trends that emphasize flatness, speed, and responsiveness. People are increasingly working away from the office, connected to everyone else by computers and phones. Workers are changing jobs more often. The old ideas of stability do not lend themselves to agility. Workers are being brought together into work teams for a specific project, and when it is completed, they go on to another project, with another team. Layers of vice presidents and managers are being eliminated to shorten the communication path from the bottom of an organization to the top.

■ *External Threats to the System.* Major changes in the world's weather, increases in natural disasters, the erosion of social and educational systems, and serious concerns about the effects of pollution are combining to reshape the objectives (and the incentives) of the economic system.

■ *Very High Rates of Change.* The organization that is effective and responsive in a context where the total amount of information is doubling every year, and products become obsolete in months, will of necessity be very fast and very smart. Lifelong learning will be required for workers to keep themselves current and engaged. Organizations will have to make decisions faster and faster as the metabolism of the larger system increases.

■ *Big Problems.* There are big systemic problems with how our societies reconfigure themselves to deal with the effects of the paradigm shift. It appears that our ideas about schooling may not be compatible with the needs of a marketplace that increasingly values knowledge workers. Our system does not yet place a value on the waste that it produces. Changing that perspective will radically affect a parallel revolution in our manufacturing and marketing processes. The very purpose of business will change. Instead of being about making money, or about making and selling things, a new definition is required. As businessman Paul Hawken says, in *The Ecology of Commerce,* "The promise of business is to increase the general well-being of humankind through service, a creative invention and ethical philosophy." The solution to some of our big problems will certainly require a rethinking of this magnitude.

■ *Weakened Social and Economic Infrastructure.* The country's lack of economic vitality manifests itself, of course, in grassroots social ways. In 1970, only 20 percent of full-time working Americans 18 to 24 years old could not earn a wage higher than the poverty level. By 1992, according to economist Lester Thurow, this had deteriorated so that 40 percent of workers in this category could not earn above a poverty-level wage. Stated another way, in 1955 the minimum wage was equal to 105 percent of the poverty level. In 1992 it was 55 percent of it. *There appear to be no long-term dynamics to reverse this trend. The sociological pain, increased crime, and urban violence that are its by-products are inevitable in America entering the twenty-first century.* One indication of this trend can be seen in the number of people filing for bankruptcy protection. As shown in Figure 11-1, this number has reached record levels. For the year ended June 30, 1992, there were 972,490 filings, a 10.5 percent increase over the previous 12 months. In the first nine months of 1993 there were already 897,231 personal financial failures.

■ *Changes in Relationships.* As shown in a later section, conventional tools that have always influenced the economy may not work in the future.

The relationship of changing interest rates to the national debt and the rate of inflation is reaching the point at which far less control will be available to the Federal Reserve in the future if present trends continue.

MAJOR AMERICAN PROBLEMS

A series of trends exists that individually might not be so serious, but that in combination raise ominous questions about the U.S. economy in the next two decades. We are entering into an era that operates differently than the past. The rules will be different. Getting from here to there will not be easy, as old relationships and experiences are cast off and much effort and time (and mistakes) are invested in learning how the new era "works."

Some of these trends are direct derivatives of the underlying social change being driven by information technology, shifts in social values, and so on. Others are the result of past mistakes or the nature of our systems (like the political color of all government decisions). In any case, the aggregate of wholesale contextual change, added to the mistakes and the shortcomings of our social systems, may well produce an unhappy situation that cannot be effectively managed.

To get the flavor of these trends, let's look at them in general, keeping in mind that they may interact in a large number of ways that

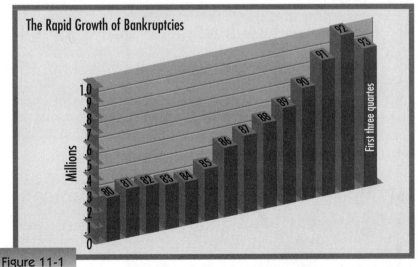

Figure 11-1 The number of people filing for bankruptcy protection has tripled in the past decade. Source: American Bankruptcy Institute.

are not obvious now. The rate of change will increase exponentially in the coming years, further stressing the system. Additionally there may be other issues (like a series of natural disasters) that could quickly emerge and magnify latent weaknesses that would otherwise not be problems.

The Trade Balance: Buying More Than We Sell

All other things being equal, the pool of funds that is available to business, government, education, and individuals for investment in our economy rises and falls with our balance of trade and the interest rates charged by the Federal Reserve Bank. Money that comes into the country in return for American sales abroad is available to be invested in this country. When we buy foreign goods, we send money out of the country and decrease the amount that is available in the pool for investment here.

If we send out more than we take in (the case with Japan, China, Canada, and OPEC, as shown in Figure 11-2), the difference must be made up in some way in order to maintain an adequate pool for reinvestment by local businesses and organizations. A government can print more money, thereby decreasing the total value of the money (producing inflation), or it can raise interest rates, thereby increasing the incentive for foreign traders and investors to move their money into the

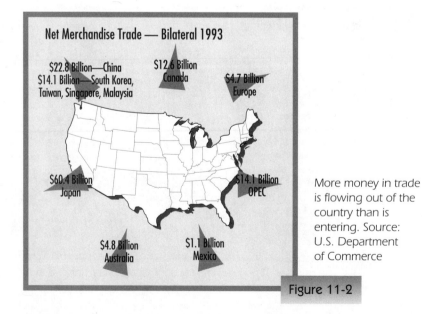

Net Merchandise Trade — Bilateral 1993

$22.8 Billion—China
$14.1 Billion—South Korea, Taiwan, Singapore, Malaysia

$12.6 Billion Canada

$4.7 Billion Europe

$60.4 Billion Japan

$14.1 Billion OPEC

$4.8 Billion Australia

$1.1 Billion Mexico

More money in trade is flowing out of the country than is entering. Source: U.S. Department of Commerce

Figure 11-2

United States for the higher return. We have mostly used the latter approach to deal with our imbalances when other forces, like currency exchange rates, have not been playing a major role in the mix.

The opportunity for the greatest change in U.S. trade exists with Europe, Japan, and China. Many economists predict that Europe will be in a slump for a number of years, driven by the reunification costs that Germany must work off. If Europe's slump gets much worse, it will become harder for the United States to make inroads into European markets, not so much because of European protectionism, but because of plunging demand.

At the same time, the People's Republic of China (PRC) presents a rather dicey, but opposite, trade problem for the United States. China may be the world's most significant future economic force. World Bank officials predict that China will be the third largest economy by the turn of the century (if it isn't already), and the largest by about 2020. These projections are partly a function of China's vast population, but they also reflect an economic growth rate that has averaged 8 percent since 1985. China's economy grew 12 percent in 1992, and 13 percent in 1993. The Chinese government plans for growth rates to average 10 percent through the end of the decade, doubling every nine years.

The weak links in these projections may be the environment (pollution is very bad in many places and will only get worse with new industry and power generation plants), domestic social stability (the number one concern of the government), and China's ability to provide infrastructure fast enough to support the high rate of growth.

Explosive growth in the PRC is largely enabled by exports to the United States. If China meets its goal of 10 percent a year for the rest of the decade, it will be six times larger in the year 2000 than it was in 1978. That would equal the performance turned in by Japan and Taiwan in the 23 years following 1950. But China's growth is occurring in a country not of 20 million or even 120 million people, but in one that is home to more than a fifth of humankind.

If this growth rate happens, it would substantially increase our trade deficit. In the period from 1990 to 1991, Chinese exports to the United States tripled. At the present rate of increase, China will bypass Japan in 1995 as the country with which we have the largest trade deficit (while Japan generally maintains its levels of exports to the United States).

There are powerful political reasons why we should let this happen, allowing capitalism within their own country to be the force that erodes away the authoritarian nature of China's government. The alternative, of course, is some kind of protectionism, with its attendant set of problems. Then there is the problem of human rights abuses, and the fact that the United States has tied most favored nation status to progress on that front.

In a 1992 *Time* essay, former President Richard Nixon argued strongly against protectionist measures: "More than ever, trade is the key to prosperity. The recession of 1931 became the Great Depression of 1932 after the Smoot-Hawley tariffs contributed to the collapse of world markets. Since trade accounts for 25 percent of U.S. GNP today, a trade war would trigger a depression that would make the present downturn look like a minor blip."

Inflation in the Wings?

In 1990, economist Paul Krugman, in *The Age of Diminished Expectations,* wrote:

> The Federal Reserve is currently in a strong position, based upon its perceived success. Yet there is in that position a basic vulnerability of which the Fed is all too well aware.
>
> The problem is that the United States has two major economic worries—the trade deficit *and* inflation—while the Federal Reserve has just one policy instrument: control over money and credit. The textbooks tell us that monetary policy needs to be supplemented with fiscal policy to achieve macroeconomic goals. Translated, that means that you can't count on having both acceptable inflation and acceptable trade performance unless you are willing to do something about your budget deficit as well as your money supply. With the Federal deficit trapped in political amber, however, the Federal Reserve bears the entire burden of stabilizing the economy.
>
> So far, the Fed has been both lucky and skillful in reconciling these goals. It has kept inflation under control, and the trade deficit has remained tolerable. But there is lurking danger that growing pressures to do something about the trade deficit will undermine the commitment to keeping inflation down. There is continuing political pressure on the Federal Reserve to adopt "soft money" policies that would keep interest rates and the dollar low, even at the risk of inflation. Should the Fed give in to these

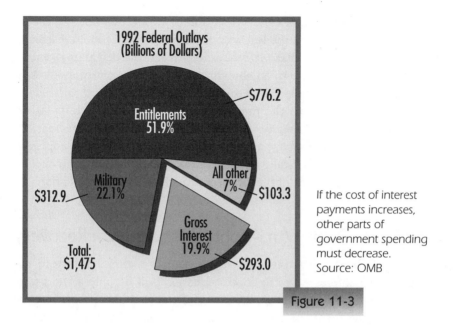

1992 Federal Outlays
(Billions of Dollars)

$776.2

Entitlements
51.9%

All other
7% — $103.3

Military
22.1%

$312.9

Gross
Interest
19.9%

Total:
$1,475

$293.0

If the cost of interest
payments increases,
other parts of
government spending
must decrease.
Source: OMB

Figure 11-3

pressures, the end result could easily be an inflationary resurgence—squandering the gains won at such enormous cost.

This is not academic speculation. The recent experience of Britain shows that a seemingly stable monetary situation can unravel with sickening speed.

Manipulating Interest Rates Will Become Increasingly Ineffective

So, on one hand, inflation must be controlled, but on the other, there is the national debt that must be serviced. As Figure 11-3 shows, the size of the federal debt is such that interest payments alone in 1992 accounted for 20 percent of the total federal budget. Fifty-two percent goes to entitlement programs, and the balance of almost 30 percent is spent on funding the whole of government operations (defense, commerce, state, and so on). The 20 percent is based on a current interest rate of 5 percent—the rate that is being charged for the three- to three-and-a-half-year notes with which the debt is being financed. (The average maturity of the federal debt is 3 to 5 years.)

If, in an attempt to control inflation or to increase foreign capital flow into the country, the Fed were to increase average interest rates so that the three-year notes yield, say, 10 percent, the deficit debt service could similarly double to an amount equal to 36 percent of the present budget, leaving only 12 percent available for all of the rest of government—half of the previous amount, an untenable position. Therefore, for the first time, there is an effective (and decreasing) interest rate ceiling above which the Fed cannot practically go; for in doing so, it systematically eliminates the funding of government—or forces the monetizing of the difference, thereby increasing inflation.

The National Debt—An Anchor to Long-Term Recovery

If the federal debt continues to rise as it has, this inability to use increasing interest rates to control inflation will be only a short-term concern. In the longer term, the size of the debt could become so great that paying for its interest dominates the federal budget. The trends appear to be in that direction.

The nation's total debt from consumers, business, and government more than doubled, to $11.3 trillion, between 1982 and 1992. But, in a development that defies postwar credit history, the economy has been unable in this recovery cycle to "reliquefy," or pay down debt and position itself for fresh spending.

Corporate debt remains equal to nearly 38 percent of gross domestic product, the highest level in at least 25 years. And interest payments, though they have fallen from their 1990 peak, still consume almost 25 percent of corporate cash flow, compared with about 20 percent 10 years ago.

Corporate debt service costs might have fallen even further if business weren't paying a huge price for the federal government's staggering budget deficit, almost $400 billion in 1992 (when everything was counted). These troubling numbers have kept long-term interest rates hovering between 7 percent and 8 percent, or an unusual 4 percentage points above the inflation rate. The deficit is expected to remain at uncomfortable levels in the near future, and this means that real long-term interest rates could very well stay at historic highs despite the fragile, recovering economy.

So we are not in the position to pay down the debt. At best we can decrease the rate of its increase. "Debt is the major impediment to a robust recovery," says economist and money manager Henry Kaufman. "There is simply no precedent for this in our postwar experience."

James Dale Davidson, co-author of *The Great Reckoning* says, "The U.S. government has become so heavily indebted that it can't keep the banks afloat much longer. Today, 62 cents out of every dollar that's paid in *personal* income tax to Washington goes just to pay interest on the national debt. If you keep compounding that, you reach a point of no return, where the government is unable to continue absorbing more and more liabilities."

The Point of No Return

In the 1980s, President Reagan felt the need to increase interest rates to a "global" competitive level so that payments on the accelerating debt could be met by similar increases in foreign capital. That can't be done for long. Once this nation passes the point where debt service equals federal annual revenues and increases of debt service are met only by increased foreign borrowing, we have reached a point of no return. Hyperinflation will soon follow, destroying almost all savings— particularly those of insurance annuities and elderly people on fixed incomes. That is the situation that some people see on the horizon.

In his 1992 book *Bankruptcy 1995,* Grace Commission co-chairman Harry Figgie, argued that if trends at that time continued, the federal government's accumulated debt would reach approximately $6.56 trillion by 1995, as shown in Figure 11-4. That's roughly nine times the amount the government will collect in personal and corporate income taxes in that year. Figgie thought the growth rate of the federal budget deficit would probably accelerate. From nearly $400 billion in 1992, the Grace Commission estimated that the deficit would climb to $640 billion in 1993, to $730 billion in 1994, and reach $850 billion in 1995. Had this scenario played out, interest payments would have exceeded the amount of money the government collects in personal income taxes by 1995. In that year, interest on the debt alone would have reached 103 percent of all personal incomes taxes collected.

Happily, Figgie's scenario did not evolve as he had envisioned. Even taking into consideration the growing segment of our government's business that is "off-budget," the debt in 1993 was much less than anticipated—affected, no doubt, by the tax increase that was instituted in that year. But the basic problems that Figgie described are systemic. Our system has not changed. Perhaps the time schedule just slid a little.

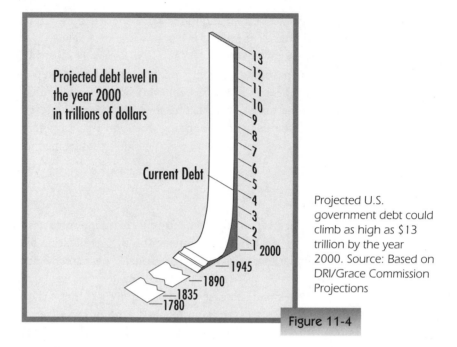

Projected debt level in the year 2000 in trillions of dollars

Current Debt

13
12
11
10
9
8
7
6
5
4
3
2
1 2000
—1945
—1890
—1835
—1780

Projected U.S. government debt could climb as high as $13 trillion by the year 2000. Source: Based on DRI/Grace Commission Projections

Figure 11-4

Look at the trends. In 1964, the national debt was $316 billion. Interest on the debt was $10.7 billion, or 14.8 percent of all personal and corporate income taxes collected that year. By 1988, the national debt had climbed to $2.6 trillion and interest to $214.2 billion. Interest payments took 43 percent of all government income tax revenues that year. In 1992, interest charges on the national debt came to $293 billion. Paying that amount alone took nearly 52 percent of personal and corporate income taxes. The Grace Commission thought the national debt would reach $6.56 trillion by 1995. It won't reach that level for a number of years, but when it does, the interest charge alone (assuming constant interest rates)—some $619 billion—will amount to about 85 percent of all income taxes, *more* than the government collects in taxes from individuals. Interest rates are rising, though, so the debt service will be somewhat greater than projected. As mentioned earlier, the relationship between inflation, interest rates, and servicing the federal debt is a serious new problem for the United States.

In 1991, interest on the national debt was the largest single item in the federal budget. In that year, the U.S. government spent more on interest than on the combined expenses of the departments of Agriculture, Education, Energy, Housing and Urban Development, Interior, Justice, Labor, State, Transportation, and Veterans' Affairs.

In 1982, America's debt stood at 36 percent of the gross domestic product. By the end of 1992, the debt had reached 70 percent of the GDP. The debt is growing three times faster than the size of the U.S. economy. At this rate, by 1996 the U.S. federal debt will total more than the entire industrial output of the United States.

Insurance Companies Weakened

Floods, earthquakes, riots, and hurricanes have together contributed to the largest losses in recent history for the insurance industry. *Best's Review,* characterizing a 1992 industry meeting, said that the shadow of Hurricane Andrew and the rest of 1992's record series of catastrophes loomed over the proceedings in Boston, and representatives of the reinsurance business were in demand. There was a pervasive sense that the worst news is yet to come on Andrew's impact, but tentative hope that the hurricane losses might prompt the long-awaited turn in the property/casualty underwriting cycle. The one certainty, repeated often by reinsurance executives, was that capacity in their industry would tighten and that catastrophe covers would become more expensive, if available at all.

A month later, A. M. Best Co. said that the insurance industry's losses on Hurricane Andrew would be $13.4 billion, or 25 percent more than the American Insurance Services Group, which serves as the industry's official scorekeeper, had earlier estimated. Now the Los Angeles earthquake of January 1994 has added another $20 billion in damages, not to mention the $12 billion Mississippi River flood of 1993—a large amount of which will be paid by insurance companies.

Pension Fund Overhang

There is a potential pension crisis brewing in the United States. On one hand, fewer and fewer workers are provided a pension plan by their employers. Workers actually covered by pension plans peaked at 48.3 percent in 1979 and fell to 43.2 percent in 1988. Most of those not covered work for small businesses. The compliance costs for administering a traditional defined-benefit plan nearly tripled from 1981 to 1991 because of ten major changes that Congress made to the Employee Retirement Income Security Act in that period.

More Defined-Contribution Plans

Of those employers who do provide a plan, many are moving from a *defined-benefit* plan that guarantees retirees a certain payment, generally based on years of service and level of compensation, to a *defined-contribution* plan that does not guarantee a specific pension. Defined-contribution plans have a great appeal for small companies because they are less complex and roughly half as expensive to fund and administer as defined-benefit plans. The U.S. Department of Labor reported that workers covered under defined-contribution plans more than doubled from 1980 to 1987, to 13.4 million. In 1991, some 11,900 defined-contribution plans were initiated, and only 370 defined-benefit plans.

Not Funding All Liabilities

Furthermore, corporations are increasingly not funding all of their pension liabilities, leaving the federal government with the growing obligation. The Pension Benefit Guarantee Corporation, a government agency, protects the retirement income of nearly 40 million participants in about 100,000 private pension plans. It does so by insuring private pension beneficiaries against the loss of promised benefits if a pension plan that has insufficient resources to make good on its promises is terminated. Pension benefit payments currently insured by the PBGC are more than $800 billion. The PBGC insures benefits promised by defined-benefit plans, but does not insure defined-contribution plans.

For a number of reasons, a corporation may end up not funding all of its obligations under its plan. A sudden drop in the stock market can cause a plan that was fully funded last year to be significantly underfunded this year. If a company gets in financial trouble, the IRS can give it a waiver that relieves it of the obligation to either completely or partially fund its plan. In these situations, the PBGC insures the unfunded difference so that the employee knows that his or her pension will be paid at retirement. Congressional leaders charge that cash-strapped companies frequently make pension promises that far exceed the money they set aside to cover them, knowing that if the company doesn't survive, federal insurance will cushion the fall.

At the present time, the U.S. government has a $94 billion unfunded liability, $10 to $13 billion of which is attributable to plans of financially troubled companies. Although it has sufficient cash to continue paying benefits, the pension insurance fund has billions of dollars less than it will need to meet escalating long-term obligations to retirees, according to the General Accounting Office (GAO). Rep. J. J. Pickle (D-Tex.) feels that unless Congress acts now, these problems will worsen and "become the next savings and loan bailout."

If the government's exposure in the commercial area is this great, one wonders what the unfunded pension liabilities are for federal workers, retirees, and the military. Four million retirees receive pension benefits through annuities that have been purchased by their employers from insurance companies. But, according to the GAO, 170 life insurance companies failed between 1975 and 1990. Forty percent of the failures occurred during 1989 and 1990. Since then, California-based Executive Life Insurance Co. has been placed in conservatorship. This is the largest U.S. insurance company failure in history.

If the stock market were to drop significantly, the continued sluggish economy produce more business failures, more insurance companies fail, or the Pension Benefit Guarantee Corporation be inadequately funded to assume the unfunded corporate pension overhang, then the U.S. pension system could be in for a big blow.

The U.S. Educational Problem

As the Information Age matures, it will be increasingly clear that knowledge workers are the most important capital asset of any country. In order to compete effectively in world trade, we must learn how to invest in human capital.

The United States has the best public education system in the world for the top 15 percent of our students; the bottom 25 percent is a disaster. Our schools, particularly in urban areas, are sending out graduates who are ill equipped for our information-based economy— let alone, in many cases, life. In the increasingly competitive global marketplace of the future, the uneducated and undereducated are a severe drain on our future. If we do not provide as much information as possible to our young people, we will find ourselves responding to those societies that have. Information is the key commodity.

The United States needs a revolution in education, and it is almost certainly in the making. The question is whether big change will come fast enough. Americans are increasingly frustrated with the shortcomings of our system. Business and the military spend many billions of dollars teaching entry-level workers the basics that they didn't learn in school. Manual labor jobs are decreasing, and the growth opportunities are in industries that require more intellectual content. Our inner cities are a wasteland, moving young people further and further away from the economic mainstream of the country. Organizational and structural change that is making its way through the business community will, in time, certainly invade education. One hopes it will happen in time.

Finding Educated Workers Elsewhere

The transnational nature of business and the hyperfluidity of information assures that the business community will find the knowledge workers it requires—wherever it can find them. Highly educated people from other countries (at lower costs) are a real incentive to employers. For example, third-party offshore computer programming services to U.S. firms totaled $250 million in 1991, and the business is growing at an estimated 50 percent a year, according to International Data Corporation.

By one estimate, India's computer science departments churn out 20,000 English-speaking graduates a year. What's more, India's programmers are increasingly schooled in the hot languages of the 1990s, C and C++, because their universities can't always afford the mainframes needed to run older languages such as COBOL.

U.S. high-tech companies are hiring Russian programmers in Moscow to develop routines for commercial applications, and similar services are being sourced in Ireland and some Southeast Asian countries.

A WEAK GLOBAL SYSTEM IN RECESSION

The world economic system is in a recession. Germany's growth rate hovers around 1 percent. Great Britain, France, and other countries have been drawn into the vortex initiated by Germany. Japan is having its worst bout with recession since the 1950s, with an extraordinary fall in equity prices. The United States may be recovering, but some observers suggest that the worst is still to come.

Lord William Rees-Mogg, former editor of *The Times of London,* sees these trends in broader, deeper, and more fundamental terms.

A world economic crisis is a type of world revolution. It destroys old structures, economic and political. The Soviet Union, with its rigid inability to adapt, was the first to fall before the full force of the storm now blowing through the international financial system. ... Such a crisis destroys well meaning politicians and promotes men of power ... It destroys respect for government, as people discover that their leaders cannot control such events.

Rees-Mogg noted to *Washington Post* columnist Jim Hoagland that nothing less than the credibility of governance is at stake in this spreading economic crunch.

"Are we entering a full-blown world economic crisis?" asked Jim Hoagland. "Will the politicians in power in the world's industrial democracies pay the price not only in diminished credibility but also in being thrown from office?"

THE NEXT TWO DECADES: A DEPRESSION?

In a December 1991, article in *Across the Board,* economist Shlomo Maital, reviewing books by James Dale Davidson and Lord William Rees-Mogg, Jacques Attali, and Lester Thurow, mentions that the last decade of this century and the approach of the new millennium mark the confluence of two types of cycles. One is the 500-year cycle noted by Davidson and Rees-Mogg: "The end of each century divisible by five has witnessed a major transition in Western civilization." The second type of cycle is the 60-year Kondratieff Cycle, named after the Russian economist who first noticed it. Three depressions have occurred in the past two centuries—in 1814 to 1849, 1873 to 1896, and 1930 to 1939—roughly 60 years apart. The fourth depression is now due, say the cycle's proponents. They believe that the prime signal, instability in financial markets, has been broadcasting loud and clear, with the collapses of U.S. stock prices in 1987 and again in 1990, and the 49 percent drop in the Nikkei Dow Index that same year, a drop far sharper than the one experienced by Wall Street in 1929.

The big winners in the next millennium could be Europe and Asia, Maital reports. In ten years, Attali predicts, half of all world trade will occur in the Pacific Rim, whose member countries will achieve an aggregate gross national product equal to that of Europe or the United States. Access to the U.S. market is absolutely critical to the near-term accelerated growth of the Pacific Rim countries.

In 15 years, Attali says, new high-speed ships will make every Asian port only a day apart. Europe, too, may be a winner, but only if it is able to bring to fruition its dream of a huge, efficient single market—and only if the struggling economies of the former Soviet Union and Eastern Europe do not collapse, sending millions migrating toward the West.

The big losers, according to all four authors, will be Latin America, Africa, India, and China. (As noted earlier, there is a strong counter-argument for China flourishing.) These regions, the authors agree, will be locked out of the major trading blocs, left without capital, skill, or technology. Africa's future is particularly bleak: Attali writes that "it will be the only region on the whole planet that is entirely excluded from abundance."

China, and particularly India, must cope with tremendous transition strains in their social, economic, ethnic, and religious areas. By 2035, assuming current population dynamics, India will surpass China as the most populated nation on earth. China's per capita GDP will increase during the next 20 to 30 years, while India's will decrease, reflecting China's zero population growth policies.

Options: Dependent upon International Political Initiative

The Economist, in a special secion on the year 1993, discussed the possibility of a global depression, and noted, "The best way to reduce the risk of such a calamity is to forestall those preconditions. That is the job of financial regulation—a state of affairs which is not exactly encouraging."

The article continues:

A renewed drive toward more tightly regulated domestic markets may be attempted. (Some recent changes in American banking rules, for instance, seem to echo earlier direct controls of interest rates, and all that.) But this approach is likely to fail for exactly the same reason that domestic deregulation came about: financial markets have knitted themselves together, and it will take more than the wit of regulators to separate them. If one country tries to regulate more tightly by itself, it might find that it has delivered its financial industry into the hands of foreign competition.

What then are the hopes for international regulation? This is undoubtedly the right way forward, but the difficulties are immense.

It has been almost 50 years since the Bretton Woods agreement sought to stabilize the free world's currency rates through a formal market mechanism. The world has changed vastly since those days, and the framework needs to be overhauled, leading some to call for a Bretton Woods II.

NEW MODELS

Obviously, the present system isn't working the way we think it does. And we are increasingly less able to influence it in the way we desire. As the interdependent world searches for better ways to decrease the economic swings that bedevil it, at least three new ideas have surfaced as new ways to understand economics. Jonathon Rauch, writing about government reform in the *National Journal,* touched on it. "The dramatic initiatives and experiments of the New Deal and the Great Society have created their own bureaucracies and constituencies, which now strangle efforts to attune the government to the realities of the present day. Entitlements alone account for three-quarters of all federal domestic spending, but they are engraved in government stone. "Governments ought to work like a capitalist economy," Rauch says, "or a *biological* system—evolution through trial and error."

It's not just government that needs to be reconsidered; it's the underpinning theory that we use to describe the behavior of economic systems. Federal Reserve Chairman Alan Greenspan recently called the U.S. economy a "different animal," because it was not acting like it always had in the past. As we enter this new era that is changing in so many ways, we should be looking for new models that better describe this extraordinarily complex system upon which we are all dependent.

Bionomics: Economy as Ecosystem

Rauch's comment about a biologically operating economic system may well have been drawn from some of the work that is going on in the new science of complexity, or from the work of Michael Rothschild, author of *Bionomics*. Reacting against the mechanistic imagery and structure of classical economics, he has developed a new model for explaining the operation of the economic system that parallels that of the biological world. Instead of the "economy as machine" model, bionomics argues that a market economy works remarkably like an evolving ecosystem—a naturally occurring, spontaneous, evolutionary phenomenon. Just as biology studies the evolution of genes, organisms, and the ecosystem, bionomics studies the evolution of technologies, organizations, and the economy.

From the bionomic perspective, the global market economy of the information age looks like a "capitalist rain forest," populated by vast numbers of highly specialized organizations instead of highly specialized organisms. Companies compete for survival within their industries just as creatures compete for survival within their species. The more intelligent, adaptable, and responsive the organization, the better its chances of surviving in today's fast-evolving economic environment.

Paul Hawken: The Ecology of Commerce

Businessman/ecologist Paul Hawken, in his book *The Ecology of Commerce,* argues for a new system that:

■ reduces absolute consumption of energy and natural resources in the north by 80 percent within the next half century

■ provides secure, stable, and meaningful employment for people everywhere

■ is self-actuating as opposed to regulated or morally mandated

■ honors market principles

■ is more rewarding than our present way of life

■ exceeds sustainability by restoring degraded habitats and ecosystems to their fullest biological capacity

■ relies on current income.

■ is fun and engaging, and strives for an aesthetic outcome

Hawken ranges far and wide in searching out new models for components of the system. One, developed by the Global Business Network's Hardin Tibbs, refines the idea of an industrial ecology. Hawken suggests that "industrial ecology provides for the first time a large-scale, integrated management tool that designs industrial infrastructures 'as if they were a series of interlocking, artificial ecosystems interfacing with the natural global ecosystem.' For the first time, industry is going beyond life-cycle analysis methodology and applying the concept of an ecosystem to the whole of an industrial operation, linking the 'metabolism' of one company with that of others."

Tibbs suggests that the economic system must recalibrate its inputs and outputs to adapt to the carrying capacity of the environment. That would require an emphasis on "dematerialism," using less material per unit of output, minimizing inputs, and shifting away from carbon-based fuels to hydrogen. Creative new policies will be required to support these new ideas that "coherently align financial, economic and regulatory score-keeping on an international basis."

Another idea that Hawken advances is that of the manufacturer being responsible for the materials he or she produces in perpetuity. Essentially, manufacturers would have to consider their products "cradle-to-cradle," imagining "its subsequent forms even before it is made. Designers must factor in the future utility of a product, and the avoidance of waste, from its inception."

This is radical, Hawken says, and "because it gets down to the root causes of pollution and toxicity. Responsibility belongs to the maker, not merely the user, and certainly not with the victim." This idea is already in full bloom in Germany, he notes, with companies now designing products so that when they get them back after they have been used, they are easily dismantled and recycled.

Hazel Henderson: Paradigms in Progress

Hazel Henderson also tackles the larger problem in her book *Paradigms in Progress*. In a very broad, global way she identifies the major driving forces that support the status quo and proposes creative new frameworks for seeing the world in a different way. One of the central problems, she suggests, is the indicators we use to measure progress. At a time when money, the exclusive focus of classical economics, is losing its meaning as a measuring system for real-world production and value, new indicators are required that take into consideration the many other issues that contribute to the quality of life. She proposes a "Country Futures Indicator" instead of the now standard, gross national product. Her CFI would take into consideration such factors as:

- Population (birth rates, crowding, age distribution);

- Education (literacy levels, school dropout and repetition rates);

- Health (infant mortality, low birth weight, weight/height/age ratios);

- Nutrition (calories per day, protein/carbohydrate ratio);

- Basic services (access to clean water);

- Shelter (housing availability/quality, homelessness); and many more.

Hazel Henderson's broad thinking, along with that of Hardin Tibbs, Paul Hawken, Michael Rothschild, and others, is beginning the redefinition of economics to something that is friendlier to both humans and the planet. But the only way we can get from here to there is with governments, and that means politics, another sector fraught with change, as we will see in the next chapter.

Political Relationships:

Not the

Same Old Politics

Remember, democracy never lasts long. It soon wastes, exhausts, murders itself. There never was a democracy yet that did not commit suicide. It is in vain to say that democracy is less vain, less proud, less selfish, less ambitious, or less avaricious than aristocracy or monarchy. It is not true, in fact, and nowhere appears in history. Those passions are the same in all men, under all forms of simple government, and, when unchecked, produce the same effects of fraud, violence, and cruelty....
                                        —*John Quincy Adams*

There are two forces in tension in the political world today that will become even stronger and more in conflict in the next 20 years. As information technology explodes and exacerbates the have/have-not disparity, these two forces, one encouraging cooperation and commonalty and the other attempting to highlight the differences between groups, will increasingly be in open conflict. Although they are most often discussed in global and international contexts, they also are clearly at work within countries as well. These *integrationist* and *fragmentationist* forces, as Harvard's Samuel Huntington calls them in his book *The Third Wave—Democratization in the Late 20th Century,* manifest themselves in a number of places within most societies, but each has its central locus on opposite ends of the economic spectrum. In general, integrationists cluster in the developed world, and the fragmentationist message is more warmly received in less developed regions. In light of the trends we have examined so far in this book, it seems that there is good reason for this. The growth of information technology is increasing the interdependence of nations and groups. Economies blend with each other, boundaryless ideas move across borders, and people see that they are wedded to others in this world and cannot go it alone. In fact, they learn that there is a significant synergy and economy to working with other foreign governments, businesses, and academics. As the power and proliferation of information technology accelerates, it is likely that the trend toward integration will increase as well.

MAJOR POLITICAL TRENDS

But not everyone in the world is participating equally in the information revolution. Most of the world's residents, in fact, are not aware of the extraordinary trends and capabilities that you have been reading about here. They see (mainly through television) the effects of the underlying technology and education, and they often find it strange and threatening. Throughout history, the natural reaction to significant, unfamiliar change has been to search for stability by defending comfortable, well-known ideas and structures—and in so doing, discriminating one's own group from the larger society. This is the standard reaction to a lack of information accessibility, and it produces an inability to participate in change.

Let's use this polarity as the organizing structure for understanding the major political trends of the future.

Integrationist Trends

The trends toward integration are encouraging to observers in the industrialized world.

Democratization

Over 20 countries have given up their attempts to make communism work in the last dozen years. This has been the "third wave" of democratization in the world since 1974.

De-Ideology

A number of countries that became disillusioned with ideological communism have lost interest in ideology of any kind. China's Deng Xiaoping characterized that country's new orientation as "Chinese socialism," rather than calling their quest capitalism or socialism.

Multilateralism

An "evening-out" is taking place in the relative positions of major international political players; and, as a result of that and of growing interdependency, leaders are far more reluctant to go it alone in responding to major problems.

New concepts of broadened political community. Nations are beginning to take on democratic accountability for problems that transcend national boundaries. In both Iraq and Somalia, for example, many nations came together and jointly developed and contributed to a plan of action.

New ideas about world security. A new concept of national security is emerging, and at its center is the idea of interdependence. It is becoming clear that for the developed world, at least, the starting point must be with global or regional security, in order to begin to understand what is required for national security.

- The concept of sovereignty is changing, and the notion of political community is becoming broader.

- New, untraditional threats, like the global environment and the proliferation of weapons of mass destruction, must be considered.

- The need to become proactive rather than just reactive is becoming understood.

- New systems of cooperation are replacing the hegemonic models of the past.

Global Institutional Solutions. Some have talked about global solutions to transnational problems through institutional innovations, such as the creation of an international investment trust to recycle surpluses, a world central bank, an international debt facility, and a global environmental protection agency. A situation in which the United States, Japan, and Germany are the major political influences in the world could well evolve, particularly as the result of a profound catalytic event such as a major disaster. Continent-centered trading and security blocs, like the North American Free Trade Agreement, are, of course, being formed.

Demilitarization

A new collective security order may be on the horizon. Military planners believe that wars will be primarily small and regional, stemming from local antagonisms and the ambitions of third world rulers. Peace will be restored by the joint effort of the entire world community, as in the Gulf War. One indication of this trend is that developed countries are dramatically decreasing their military forces and defense budgets.

Fragmentationist Trends

In many parts of the world, sets of opposing pressures are at work: Leaders are working hard to extricate their nations and groups from the larger global community. In part this is a reaction to an inability of the groups to relate to and/or participate in some of the change that is going on in their areas. From our comfortable vantage point, these trends all look negative.

Ethnic Wars

Any number of the two dozen conflicts that are now in progress revolve around the attempts of ethnic groups to isolate themselves from or rid themselves of their neighbors. The former Yugoslavia is a tragic example, and other bloody conflicts are going on in Angola, Burundi, Sudan, Afghanistan, Georgia, and other locations around the world.

Ethnic Isolation

The breakup of the Soviet Union into 13 republics and of Czechoslovakia into two countries are good examples of the tendency of ethnic groups to isolate themselves rather than join together. In Russia alone, there are reported to be 16 different groups that want to break away and become independent countries.

A Reversion to Religious Fundamentalism

A worldwide Islamic revival threatens to put conservative fundamentalists in the leadership of an increasing number of governments, isolating them even further from the rest of the world. The main tenets of this trend are:

■ increased emphasis on viewing Islam as an all-encompassing way of life

■ the goal of a global Muslim community

■ heightened fundamentalism in values, ideals, and political solutions

■ organized movements mobilizing Islamic political power

A WORLDWIDE CRISIS OF NATIONAL IDENTITY

We are living through a time of transition—from the cold-war era to an era yet to be defined. One of the major characteristics of this time is realignment, in all areas of life. Politically, many relationships are shifting. Organizationally, new models are being designed. Since everything is in flux, old conventions that helped contain animosities and apprehensions have vanished. New concerns, influenced by technological and other forces, are being freshly generated. As a result, the definition and role of power is changing in all aspects of society.

The Diffusion of Power

Political power is diffusing away from strong national organizations. Consider the following points.

■ European countries are both strengthening their military and political unity and widening its scope.

- The USSR has been transformed from a tight, centrally controlled structure into a loose and voluntary confederation.

- Beijing has loosened its central control enough that capitalism is flourishing to the extent that it may well be the most significant threat to the continuation of the Communist government.

- Regional security accommodations are replacing previously superpower-dominated relationships.

- Corporations are becoming larger, non-national, and more efficient. Alvin Toffler raised the idea in his book *PowerShift* that as governments and intergovernment organizations become less responsive to business needs, it is likely that *transnational firms will end-run governments and demand direct participation in global institutions.* "It is not too hard to imagine," Toffler wrote, "a Global Council of Global Corporations arising to speak for these new-style firms and to provide a collective counterbalance to nation-state power." Already groups of corporations are taking over some of the traditional roles of government. In northern India, for instance, tea growers are raising an 8,000-member private army to protect their interests.

- Information technology is moving the world, step by step, toward a time when *individual people will have less and less need for many of the services supplied by the government* because they will have the capability and power to operate independently. Already it is predicted that many libraries, as we know them, will soon begin to close (or change) because computer owners will be able to access the information directly and more conveniently.

- As technology evolves, *both small groups and individuals will increasingly obtain the power to threaten established governments.* Nanotechnology and artificial life, for instance, may both ultimately allow individuals to menace whole nations, if not all of life itself. The early indicators are already here: a computer virus, designed by a youth, recently brought down whole industry segments and public service suppliers.

New Relationships

This fluidity has generated a worldwide crisis of national identity. Comfortable, familiar relationships have given way to searches for new relationships.

Proliferating Weapons

The proliferation of weapons clearly influences the political world as well as social values, as discussed in Chapter 10.

Lesser developed countries can buy advanced weapons systems from many sources. For example, Russian weapons plants have more than 200 combat aircraft and 1,000 modern tanks available for immediate sale. The result is that third world armies are equipped with some of the most sophisticated armaments in the world—supplied by the United States and Russia. That is bothersome not only because of the potential destructiveness, but particularly in light of the fact that American forces may someday face those weapons.

Some sources report that the CIA believes that tactical nuclear warheads are being sold by officials in some of the former Soviet republics to Middle Eastern groups. Iran has reportedly closed a deal to buy nuclear weapons from Kazakhstan. In 1992 there were over 100 attempts to smuggle radioactive materials out of Romania and the former Soviet Union. Then-Congressman Les Aspin's 1992 analysis of the security threat to the United States in the coming years determined that our number one concern should be terrorists with nuclear weapons.

The most ominous of this class of devices is biological weapons. A thimbleful of such an agent, dispersed by the wind, could kill most all of the inhabitants of a city like New York. There are no common antidotes for this threat. Saddam Hussein was working on biological agents—as, it is been rumored, have other third-world leaders.

U.S. intelligence analysts estimate that the number of countries with ballistic missiles capable of delivering a nuclear, biological, or chemical weapon over many hundreds of miles will double or triple by the end of the century. Almost all countries will be within reach of someone with this capability.

For the United States, the "new world order" has not yet materialized, and we have yet to decide what role we might play in the framework that ultimately evolves. We are being rapidly driven down an unknown path by new concepts in science, powerful new technologies, and a geopolitical situation that is undergoing rapid change.

Canada is struggling with serious national identity problems. Whether it will still be a country in ten years, with its familiar provinces, is now actively debated. The former Soviet Union, of course, is doing its best to transition to something new without an expansion of its already corrosive interrepublic and civil wars. At the same time, the United States has dramatically changed its opinions of and relations to a number of countries and regions.

THE ROLE OF TELEVISION

It is important to mention, briefly at least, the profound implications of television for promoting both integration and fragmentation trends.

In the last few years, with the advent of television repeater satellites, television has become a global communication device, moving images of people's lives, behavior, and fashions instantaneously among almost all nations and cultures.

This window on the rest of the world (primarily the Western world) is having a profound effect in promoting both integration (some think it will speed the integration of Europe) and fragmentation (the reactions of fundamentalist Muslims to the West is a by-product of TV images). Although it is hard to anticipate just what role this technology will play in future global politics, it is clear that we have entered a new era where images and sounds from distant cultures will increasingly find themselves inserted into our lives—wherever we live.

RUSSIA

Two major countries, Russia and China, are real political wildcards. The future of these countries could have a profound political influence on the rest of the world.

The former Soviet Union is in trouble. Big trouble. In broad terms, during a period when the developed world was embracing information technology as fast as it was produced, the USSR chose to try to continue to control information accessibility. While other societies were decentralizing, they maintained a tight, centrally controlled economy. Businesses in the West and in Japan were linking with each other at extraordinary rates, but not with the Soviets. Western nations refused to allow them to buy personal computers and other equipment that was freely available in other countries.

The net effect was that the developed world, enabled by information technology, began to move rapidly away from countries like the USSR. The tempo of development outside of Russia has become so much greater, that it is as if they are still deep in a hole, trying to get out, while the West is already half a mile away, running away faster and faster. One wonders if it is possible in the next two decades for Russia to even begin to catch up. The progress that they make will not be as much as that of others with whom they will compete politically and economically.

Some recent reports illustrate their problems.

"A U.S. business man in Moscow told me that the worst words in the world for him are instability and uncertainty," said the University of Chicago's Marvin Zonis recently. "Both are present in Russia. In fact, there is instability and uncertainty about virtually every aspect of life in Russia—the political, economic, legal, monetary and fiscal systems are either unknown or poorly established. As a result, many U.S. businesses are shying away from substantial investment."

In his 1992 report, *International Update,* Zonis cataloged the problems.

Illness and disease are sweeping Russia as its economy, water, medical, and public health infrastructures collapse. Pharmaceutical plants are shutting down. Water supplies are increasingly unhygienic with Moscow and Kiev joining St. Petersburg as unsafe. (The Russian government recently reported that 40 percent of all Russian hospitals do not have any running water while another 12 percent have no hot water.) Hospitals have run out of medicines, disinfectants, and soaps and infections are rampant. (When President Yeltsin's mother was hospitalized in Ekaterinburg, he flew her medicines from Moscow since none were locally available.) Illnesses, long thought to have been stamped out, have reappeared, in some cases in epic proportions. The birth rate has plummeted, the population is shrinking, and life expectancy has decreased.

In search of new sales, Russia dispatched recently its first military sales mission to the United Arab Emirates. Western governments fear new international arms races spurred by Russia's desperate search for hard currency earnings.

In its *Activities Update,* November 1992, the Jamestown Foundation reported similar trends in the political realm.

In short, the situation in Russia is very bad, and getting worse. We may have won the cold war, but as of today we're losing the peace.

In the best-case scenario, Russia and the other CIS republics will evolve into peaceful free enterprise democracies, contributing their wealth of human and natural resources to the betterment of the planet, and posing no threat to the world community.

In the worst-case scenario, Russia and the other CIS republics will disintegrate into chaos, and civil and interrepublic war, Yugoslavia on a horrific scale, but with the deadly difference which the possession of nuclear weapons makes—the potential for nuclear and ecological disaster.

The trend is in the wrong direction. The tide is now running in favor of autocracy and statism. The mood of the populace is ugly, and the political ramifications are dire. The statists and the "red brown coalition" are gaining strength daily. Yeltsin, in moves ominously reminiscent of Gorbachev, is attempting to appease them by retreating from his previous positions. Hardliners are moving into his cabinet. Reformers are leaving. Gaidar is gone. The reformist bloc in parliament is waning, as various factions and parties leave to join the growing statist bloc.

Time magazine, in late 1992, characterized Russia as,

undergoing the most severe economic hardships since World War II. State orders for unwanted factory goods have dried up, shrinking Russia's gross domestic product as much as 23 percent this year. The number of jobless workers has surged from 59,000 in January to 905,000 today. An estimated one-third of the population now lives below the poverty line. Russian economists believe inflation may hit a monthly annualized rate of 2,200 percent, further eroding faith in the ruble and threatening to scuttle reform.

A Severe Social Toll

The economic squeeze is taking a serious social toll. According to *U.S. News & World Report,* in December 1993, Russia's Interior Ministry announced that there were 32 percent more murders and attempted murders during the first nine months of 1992 than in the same period of 1991; 60 percent more armed robberies; and 51 percent more burglaries in homes.

These problems and changes have opened the door to elements that did not exist under Communist control. *Newsweek,* in October 1992, reported that in St. Petersburg and in every other big city in Russia, the mob rules. Gangsters are moving in on business, government, and the daily lives of the long-suffering population. Ministry of Interior investigators count almost 3,000 gangs across the country. With the help of well-armed "bulls," they extort millions of dollars and operate rackets from prostitution and drugs to the illegal export of billions of dollars' worth of Russian raw materials. In St. Petersburg, one top investigator estimates that 70 percent of the police are corrupt.

A new, ultraconservative political organization, Pamyat, is gaining adherents. In 1990 it claimed 30 branches around the Soviet Union, 20,000 members in Moscow alone. It is reported to have strong links to both the military and the KGB, as well as support from middle-level officialdom. Pamyat is facing criminal prosecution for spreading hate. It resembles the Black Hundreds movement, which organized pogroms under the Tsar at the turn of the century. Some of its membership call for a restoration of the Tsarist monarchy, linked to religious orthodoxy.

"Before *perestroika,* there were some ideals," says officer Sergei Selivonov, an expert in juvenile delinquency, "Now, these have been destroyed. People no longer know what to believe in."

But amid all of this darkness, hope still shines. One of Russia's premier sociologists and experts on public opinion, Leonid Keselman, has said: "I don't see a power strong enough to change the people's desire for a better society." His surveys, which are published in 15 newspapers and broadcast nationwide, indicate that most Russian citizens agree with him. Despite the deepening economic crisis in Russia, Keselman remains an optimist.

CHINA

China is a wildcard because it is so big and it is moving so fast. Its economy is booming, and the present rate of growth and development could be multiplied with a shift in governmental priorities, a very plausible possibility.

In December 1992, *Inc.* magazine characterized China in these terms:

> The 1980s may have witnessed Japan's global reach, but the 1990s belong to China. The Chinese are reshaping the world in everything from technology to manufacturing to finance.

Overseas Chinese—who account for the vast majority of foreign investment in China—already have transformed the mainland's southern coastal provinces of Guandong and Fukien, the ancestral homes of most Chinese abroad, into arguably the world's most rapidly growing economic region. Capitalists from Hong Kong employ more than 2 million workers in Guandong alone.

This slow process of economic integration with their capitalist cousins over time may do more damage to the Communists than the democracy movement itself could do. In the 1980s, China saw, in addition to its emergence as an economic power, the precipitous decline of its socialist structures, as the state-owned share of industry nationwide dropped from more than four-fifths of industrial production to barely half. In 1990, non-state-owned factories accounted for 70 percent of all industrial growth; the output from factories involving foreign investors, mostly Chinese émigrés, grew at nearly 20 times the rate for government-owned plants.

The increasing personal contact between mainlanders and their diaspora brethren could prove equally corrosive to the Communist order. With more than 300,000 Taiwanese alone visiting the mainland every year, more and more mainlanders have become aware of the enormous strides made by Chinese who live in places like Taiwan or North America, whose governments generations of mainlanders have been brought up to revile. If willing to capitalize upon their global experience, the Chinese, with their enormous human resources, historic flexibility, and entrepreneurial skills, have the potential to develop a worldwide presence not seen since the hegemony of the British.

From *Tribes* by Joel Kotkin. © 1992 by Joel Kotkin. Reprinted by permission of Random House, Inc.

THE UNITED STATES: NEW FORMS OF GOVERNMENT

America is facing some serious economic problems that are growing at an exponential rate. *During the next decade the major political concern of the country will be to get the domestic situation—economic and otherwise—under control.* There will be a shifting balance between America's global commitment and our domestic needs, resulting in a necessary decrease of U.S. regional security responsibilities.

Within the next decade, events will make it obvious that both the executive and legislative arms of our government, as presently structured, cannot effectively respond to the pace and composition of change. The organization of both business and education is rapidly changing to adapt to the new, information-rich environment. It is inevitable that government will as well—though, as usual, it will be the last to adjust.

The legislative side will have to link itself more effectively with its constituents. Although Ross Perot's and Bill Clinton's "electronic town meetings" will probably not be the ultimate form, the underlying idea—that the people will be more directly connected to the representative process by information technology—is correct.

The executive branch will also have to move information more quickly, push decision making to lower levels, cut out many layers of redundancy, and organize around different concepts if it is to remain effectively engaged. With the other major institutions in our society moving so much more rapidly and working so much more efficiently, government faces the very real risk of becoming even more reactive than it is, and ultimately finding itself under the "control" of external events and institutions. Major failures of the system may be required to generate the pressure needed to make these kinds of changes, but they are inevitable.

Effective organizations are responding to information technology by rapidly pushing decision making to as low a level as possible. There will be a pressure to do the same in government, with the federal sector granting the states control over matters previously maintained at the federal level.

If for no other reason than that centralized government will increasingly become unable to be responsive to the needs and problems of the country, the federal government will unload more and more of its responsibilities onto the states.

Similar decentralization trends are apparent in education, in organized religion, and in the "edge cities" that surround our major urban areas.

GENERAL TRENDS

The interaction of social, technological, and economic trends will produce some dramatic new political realities in the coming twenty years.

■ *The American government will be less able to deal with major shocks to the system,* like natural disasters. Except for the participation of the military, federal government agencies will be shown to be incapable of dealing with the events that require it the most.

■ *The American government will be reorganized.* There will be a new internal structure and method of functioning, and a new interface with the American people. By using information technology, people will be able to access government more easily at different levels. As fiber optic networks and other information infrastructure become ubiquitous, computer bulletin boards and other such message-moving mechanisms will become very important.

■ *The Boomer reaction will be a third political party.* The Thirteenerer generation sees the problem in far more fundamental terms; some of its members talk increasingly about a violent revolution being the only way to dislodge the deep tentacles of self-interest that characterize the present system.

■ *People will be increasingly informed and therefore powerful.* Information technology will make them far more knowledgeable about selected issues than they have been in the past, and they will demand more response from government at every level.

■ *Business will take an increasingly aggressive role in influencing the policy of governments.* Business is much more sensitive to environmental changes and has built-in incentives to respond and adapt. In times like this, they have much more to lose than government, and will respond accordingly. Many have grown to be larger in terms of annual sales than most countries' budgets. They are much better informed and more sophisticated than governments, and can act much faster.

■ *The mega-firms are non-national, and will respond in that way.* Large corporations are not international or transnational, they are non-national, and they will increasingly see economics and politics without a particularly national flavor.

■ *War, as prosecuted by the United States and other developed nations, will be increasingly oriented toward information war,* with information-rich approaches and an emphasis on very low exposure for friendly troops. Individual military groups will become more functionally specialized. They will be put together in "modular" ad hoc groupings based on the mission of the moment. The military will become much more flexible, agile, and adaptable.

■ *The developed nations may begin to practice triage,* deciding that some places, like Somalia, are beyond hope; that others will make it on their own; and that those who can be helped merit our attention and resources.

■ *The press will become stronger and more influential.* Because they are a business, they will react faster than governments and will have more advanced capabilities to access and analyze information. They will increasingly interpret and "shape" government (even more than they do now), because they control the configuration of the flow of information between the government and the people.

We have looked at 11 different areas of life and have identified a host of powerful and profound trends that appear to be on our horizon. But it is not enough to just know about them individually, for they all will operate together, developing synergistic interactions that in some cases negate themselves, and in others produce huge, unanticipated results. We must begin, in a very rudimentary way, to see it all as a system. In the next chapter we will pick and choose among the trends, mixing and matching them in a variety of ways that will begin to give shape to the general families of futures that might play out in the next two decades.

CHAPTER

13

Crosscuts and Wild Cards

*Distant ridges, far away clouds ... All events come
from a distance. With a high vantage point,
Foretelling the future is elementary.*
— *Tao Te Ching*

The future will be composed of
complex combinations of trends—
never a single "economic" or "transportation" event, but interaction
among various driving forces. A
good way to begin to communicate
the nature of this system is to
overlay major trends and look for
crosscuts—areas where combinations
of trends might interact together in
a significant way. We can create
mini-scenarios to look at how a particular crosscut might evolve, and
then we can begin to see how the
future might take shape.

Crosscut

Some revolutionary events, which we call *wild cards,* will inevitably occur. Wild cards have a low probability of occurrence but a very high impact. Although some wild cards are so catastrophic that they cannot be realistically planned for, we need to raise the possibility that they *can* happen and provide a framework from which to assess evolving events.

Wild Card

A FRAMEWORK FOR LOOKING AT TRENDS

It is helpful to begin to get an idea of where specific crosscuts and wild cards might be leading us. The Global Business Network (GBN), one of the world's leaders in scenario-based planning, has published its views as a set of broad potential futures. Using a rigorous process that takes into account many different inputs, the GBN staff has suggested that there are seeds of three different worlds on our horizon:

Market World

Market World posits that things become pretty rosy. Wonderful new technologies arrive to benefit business and society. Cooperation is the key in both economic and political terms. With the cold war over, nations ultimately begin to find positive ways to solve their biggest problems. Growth and development result. Innovation is unencumbered.

New Empires

New Empires has a less open view. Businesses and nations compete more stridently; possibly in closed, protectionist ways, or alternatively, in a largely free-trade mode. It is a picture of a regionalized world—a partly cloudy future.

Global Incoherence

Global Incoherence is "the sum of all fears is realized." It is a "world adrift"—lacking leadership and the motivating vision of the future that can propel societies forward. The weight of the past proves more powerful than the inspiration of any potential future. Weapons would take on a particularly influential role in this scenario.

The planning value of crosscuts and wild cards vary with how well they can be anticipated and what can be done about them once it is clear that they will happen.

Some will produce a situation in which a *positive reaction is possible.*

We will give humanity the benefit of the doubt and use this notation even in situations where both positive and negative outcomes are possible. In some cases, a *positive reaction is not possible.*

Most wild cards will be surprises, with *no early indicators.*

But again, we will be conservative and lean toward categorizing an event as having *early indicators available if at all possible.*

Figure 13-1 shows how we are going to be looking at these combinations of trends and surprises, and the framework that will be used. (Some of the wild cards are drawn from *Wild Cards: A Multinational Perspective,* published by the Copenhagen Institute for Futures Studies, the Institute for the Future and Bipe Conseil-Paris.)

Icons

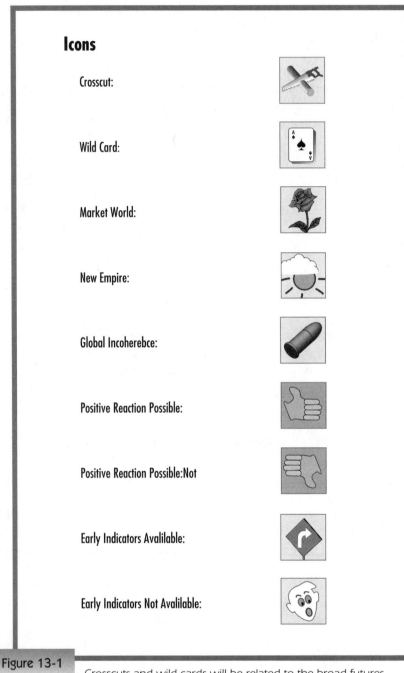

Crosscut:

Wild Card:

Market World:

New Empire:

Global Incoherebce:

Positive Reaction Possible:

Positive Reaction Possible:Not

Early Indicators Avalilable:

Early Indicators Not Avalilable:

Figure 13-1

Crosscuts and wild cards will be related to the broad futures that they contribute to and as to whether a positive reaction is likely to come from them

 MARKET WORLD

Fuel Cells Keep the Air Clean

By the year 2000, fuel cells become a major source of electricity. Technology permits a gradual buildup of fuel-cell use (using natural gas or coal gas and an electrolyte to convert the chemical energy of a fuel into electricity). The oil companies lose their tight grip on the world as fuel cells make a major breakthrough to achieve a safe, clean, and inexpensive technology.

This new fuel source revolutionizes the electric generation and transportation industries. The electricity obtained from the fuel cell can be used as an independent source of regular or standby power to drive traction motors in vehicles. These fuel cells operate safely at relatively low temperatures of about 600° Fahrenheit, have lower emission levels, run efficiently, give an uninterruptible supply of power, and use very little space.

Measures

■ The price of fuel cells drops to $1,500 per kilowatt hour—comparable to fossil nuclear fuels.

■ Fuel cells weighing one to three ounces or less per watt are developed.

■ One-half million vehicles in the United States are equipped with fuel cells.

■ Five billion watts of fuel-cell capacity are manufactured in one year (5 percent of new power capacity).

■ Import oil consumption drops in Organization for Economic Cooperation and Development (OECD) countries.

Implications

■ *Major prolonged power shortages are no longer an issue.* Companies are able to access power on demand—anytime, anyplace.

■ *In facilities where uninterrupted power supply is critical, such as hospitals and airports, the risk of exposure is reduced dramatically due to the inherent reliability of the technology.*

■ *Gas replaces oil as the critical fuel in the event of supply disruptions (such as during the Gulf War).*

■ *Activities in space (such as manufacturing) will pick up, since constraints on power supply and resupply are sharply reduced.*

■ *A major new fuel supply market opens for third world countries, where the power grid is inadequate or nonexistent. The Pacific Ocean archipelagos are the biggest beneficiaries, since they do not have grids.*

A Hydrogen Economy Evolves

Driven by the need to design pollution-free automobiles, manufacturers push hard to develop fuel-cell technology in order the meet the 1998 deadline for California. All indicators suggest that fuel cells will be much more efficient and have better operating characteristics than any other approach, as well as being completely pollution-free.

Since the natural gas infrastructure is already in place, it becomes relatively easy to supply this fuel to converters that produce the hydrogen for the fuel cells. About the year 2000, it becomes apparent that fuel cells are really going to work, and there will be a need for large quantities of hydrogen. Concurrently, molecular nanotechnology begins to produce its first usable products. It quickly becomes clear that an easy, clean way to generate hydrogen in large quantities is to use nanotech-based generating plants that produce hydrogen from seawater. Thus, by 2012, the ocean becomes an inexpensive fuel source for both developed and developing economies, eliminating much of the pollution that has attended the use of the automobile in the United States.

Education Revolutionized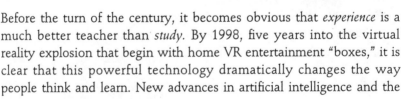

Before the turn of the century, it becomes obvious that *experience* is a much better teacher than *study*. By 1998, five years into the virtual reality explosion that begin with home VR entertainment "boxes," it is clear that this powerful technology dramatically changes the way people think and learn. New advances in artificial intelligence and the easy availability of the Cyc commonsense knowledgebase gives education technology designers the basis for developing a fundamentally new approach to learning.

Instead of checking out books in libraries, students find laser-disc VR "contexts" there, which allow learning to happen in a number of new ways. Mathematics is learned through a series of interactive games; students "walk" through certain periods of history; science involves moving virtual atoms and molecules while observing the reactions. In engineering, projects are designed using sophisticated computer-aided design programs and then the device is "tested" by using VR to run them through their paces. The rate of learning increases dramatically as it becomes far more interesting for students.

Computer Interface Becomes Transparent

As holographic neural technology matures, computers become able to interpret most any voice command. This capability is coupled with Cyc and other artificial intelligence programs to produce machines that understand common language. Logically, this capability is quickly moved into the interface with computer applications for control, analysis, and writing, resulting in machines that are operated completely with common voice commands and discussion.

Later on, success in transducing and translating brain waves allows people to interface with specific systems by thought, perhaps sensed through transducers in a headband or another such brain-machine connection.

New Understanding of National Behavior

Chaos theory opens up the opportunity to begin to better understand and perhaps predict how large dynamic systems, such as nations or cultures, might behave. If this theory was married to Cyc, and human common sense was added to the equation, it could well yield a tool of unusual analytical value.

Many "what if" scenarios could be run in order to build a broad understanding of possible behavior. The border between ordered and chaotic behavior might be able to be charted, thereby identifying when a group would go to war (either externally or internally), or shift from one state to another.

Understanding the Weather

The combination of chaos theory, far better techniques for monitoring the oceans, and significant increases in computing power suggest that sometime after the year 2000, our knowledge of how the world's weather works will increase substantially. This will not only allow better weather prediction, but will also generate a much better understanding of what contributes to our weather and changes in it.

Energy Breakthrough

Zero-point energy (ZPE) production is proved and moves into engineering and manufacturing. The methodology has absolutely no negative by-products, and the now free energy source exists everywhere and is unlimited. During the same period, breakthroughs are made in room temperature superconductivity, essentially making electricity transmission loss-free.

Measures

■ Research ongoing in Japan, Germany and the United States since the 1980s converges about 1996 to show incontrovertible evidence that energy can be extracted from the "ether." Increased environmental pressure causes significant investment in alternative energy sources.

■ Many researchers using both traditional experimental methods and new computational materials science come together to produce a material that superconducts at room temperatures and is relatively easily manufactured and configured. It can be shaped into wires and other forms, and is durable.

Implications

■ *All existing energy production methods become obsolete.* An immediate shift in research and development resources is made away from every existing energy generation method (both conventional and unconventional) and toward ZPE-based applications, both large and small. Electrical power generation devices, ranging from small batteries up to major power plants, are explored.

■ *An immediate shift in emphasis is made toward using electricity as a primary source for all heat and transportation energy.* The combination of ZPE and high-temperature superconductivity would make electricity far more cost effective than any other energy source.

■ *Fossil fuel-based conversion devices become obsolete.* An immediate shift in research and development resources is made away from internal combustion engines, and gas-, oil- and coal-fired furnaces and boilers, to electric motors and heating devices.

■ *The geopolitical structure is shaken.* The long-term value of oil and gas as a fuel plummets, with similar changes to the importance of countries that produce those materials.

■ *The amount of pollution that is produced by humankind begins to decrease precipitously* as new ZPE-based electrical power-generation plants come on line and transportation moves away from fossil fuels.

Micro-Devices Save Lives

Miniature devices allow medical professionals to monitor and control diseases by replacing malfunctioning organs, valves, or other body parts, and by monitoring and correcting bodily functions. Currently, micro-electromechanics engineering couples electrical and mechanical parts that are 100 nanometers or smaller (about the size of a human hair). These devices consist of servomechanisms operating mechanical devices in residence to electrical signals. Typical devices are motors, relays, pumps, and sensors.

In the future, these devices provide technological breakthroughs in health care. Small electromechanical devices implanted in the body monitor, enhance, or replace malfunctioning valves, joints, and tendons. Such devices perform several life-saving functions:

■ The miniature mechanisms of such devices mimic the functions of the body—opening and closing to regulate blood flow as a valve, controlling movement as part of a joint, even responding to electrical impulses of the brain.

■ The implanted devices monitor certain bodily functions, such as blood sugar level, blood pressure, and cholesterol level. If the micro-sensor receives an abnormal reading, it takes measures to correct the problem. If the problem is immediately controllable, the sensor automatically activates a micro-electromechanical pump that delivers a medication or otherwise corrects the problem. The sensor also can signal the person to take a pill or notify a medical professional that there is a problem that needs immediate attention.

▪ The devices deliver consistent, up-to-date information about the health status of an individual by transmitting data and other information to logical devices located inside or outside the body, to the physician, or to other interested parties.

Measures

▪ *Heart disease is no longer the number one killer.* The number of morbidity cases for diseases of the heart such as coronary disease, arteriosclerosis, and malfunctioning valves decreases, sending heart disease to the number two spot, behind cancer.

▪ *More people comply with doctors' orders* for treating diabetes, ulcers, and cholesterol, as measured by as much as a 50 percent decrease in the number of emergency room visits for diabetes, stomach, and heart-related problems.

▪ *Increased use of technology implants* replaces major surgeries such as heart, liver, and kidney transplants, and hip and knee joint replacements. The number of such transplants falls by 30 percent.

Implications

▪ *Lower morbidity and mortality.* The use of micro-devices to control or fix health-related problems inside the human body revolutionizes the practice of medicine. The incidence of major surgeries such as heart, liver, and kidney transplants decreases as more implanted micro-devices take control of bodily functions rather than replacing whole malfunctioning organs. Patients with arthritis have working micro-implants to replace failing joints. The devices are used to increase the effectiveness of fetal and infant surgery. The constant monitoring of disease conditions decreases unexpected problems. The ultimate result of micro-devices is decreased morbidity rates and a general increase in life expectancy.

▪ *More elderly people in developed countries.* Because the technology for creating such micro-devices is less accessible in developing countries, the use of these devices by highly skilled specialists also increases the age gap between developed and lesser developed countries.

Nanotechnology Takes Off

By 1998, it becomes clear that molecular nanotechnology will probably work. Global environmental problems have also become much worse, and there is rapidly growing pressure to find solutions to these mammoth issues. Governments and industry see nanotech as a way out of their predicament and begin to plow great amounts of money into all aspects of the discipline. The more work that is done, the more extraordinary become the possibilities for applications, and the more investment is made.

Measures

■ *Japan significantly increases its investment in nanotechnology.* As progress is made in research, Japan increasingly ups its $185 million budget for nanotech (established in 1991) and MITI begins to push the technology hard within corporate Japan.

■ *U.S. computer chip manufacturers' attempts to use nanotech as a process to move U.S. integrated chip production into a new era appears encouraging.* The initial foray by a group of 12 computer component manufacturers into the nanotech area shows signs of paying off; and the principles (and possibilities) of the technology become much better known in Silicon Valley and throughout American industry from the increase in technical papers and articles.

■ *Germany, India, Taiwan, Korea, and Russia begin to become seriously involved in the area.* As the value and potential of nanotech becomes more widely apparent, other developed countries and those with significant intellectual capital become involved in the race for development.

Implications

■ *Solutions to seemingly intractable problems become apparent.* Great hope and effort would be invested in the new technology. A rapidly growing segment of public and high-tech industry would see its revolutionary potential and push hard for faster development.

■ *Existing manufacturing companies are seriously threatened.* Nanotech would clearly threaten the status quo, and all of the interests that are vested in the world's existing manufacturing infrastructure. A great political "war" would ensue between the proponents of the future and the defenders of the past with heated arguments about jobs, sunken costs, and so on.

Some companies, of course, would see the writing on the wall early enough to shift their focus from the old techniques to the new ones. Many others would find it very hard, if not impossible, to change from being fabrication oriented, with its heavy emphasis on machinery, to being design-centered, which revolves around intellectual skills.

As long as the marketplace prevailed, the economic differential between the old manufacturing and molecular nanotechnology would be so great that there would be no question about nanotech quickly replacing significant industrial segments.

▪ *A huge, rapid "torque-ing" of developed societies would take place as they reconfigured their whole notion of how things are made, and the infrastructure that is required to support that industry.* This shift would be very painful for many people; displacing many manual laborers, restructuring huge sections of society, changing values (both for things and people), retraining many people, changing education, restructuring economies, and so on. Knowledge workers would be greatly enfranchised, causing a greater gulf between the information haves and have-nots in societies.

▪ *National social psyches would be turbulent.* Great hope would attend this new way of solving huge, global problems. A new era would loom on the horizon. However, shifting to the new mode would not be easy for those who cannot change easily and quickly. This would produce great despair for many.

▪ *The geopolitical landscape is reoriented.* Countries whose economic health depended on their natural resources would suddenly be threatened, as junk yards and garbage dumps became very valuable (and convenient) "mines," producing most every raw material required for feed stock. Oil would retain some of its value as a feed stock, since it is rich in carbon and therefore could easily be converted into diamond structures.

 # NEW EMPIRES

Major Fight Over Genetic Information

Although a majority of Americans believe that people found to carry a genetic disease or a defective gene do not have a right to absolute privacy about their condition, this attitude could change. In the future, a significant political conflict could ensue over who should have access to this knowledge: spouses, family members, insurance companies, employers, or no one?

The public is currently extremely optimistic about the progress of gene therapy and other experimental approaches to taming inherited diseases, and believes that the more open we are about genetic disorders, the more quickly all will benefit. If insurance companies, employers, and even family members were thought likely to use this information against the interests of the individual, however, the battle would begin.

American Cultural Influence Increases

As the intercontinental transmission of television becomes ubiquitous and the global information network becomes mature (allowing international subscribers access to a huge amount of American-based knowledge), American culture—our most powerful export—will grow in influence. This will have both positive and negative effects. It is likely to broaden the links of commonality among the younger generations of the developed world, while at the same time threatening and further alienating the United States from more conservative cultures.

End-of-Century/"New Age" Attitudes Blossom

A combination of end-of-the-millennium fixation, growing general apprehension about perceived social erosion, consciousness-is-causal ideas rapidly becoming accepted, and a growing search for meaning in the face of exploding information, are—with the help of both old and new information technology—responsible for a significant shift in attitudes of a sizable fraction of Western societies.

These new ideas, representing a newly emergent social value paradigm, move into the mainstream media through a series of films, books, and television programs. New archaeological findings give ancient credence to some of the concepts, and the battle is joined between this new group and the conservative religious and scientific communities who vociferously defend the status quo.

Education and Parenting Changes

As the underlying understanding of reality changes in a growing segment of a society, it will manifest itself in changes in both parenting and education. Inevitably, this will be a cultural battleground in the future.

The consciousness-is-causal philosophy focuses around personal responsibility. It argues that we have within ourselves the basic ability to change our reality. A corollary to this approach says that we are all interconnected, and individuals have a responsibility to contribute to the greater good (because everyone will affect it, one way or another).

The current social framework, on the other hand, puts much more emphasis on society than the individual, and attempts to assign some of the problems that an individual might have to society's reaction to the individual. The remedy to personal problems lies more with getting others to change their behavior rather than the "victim" changing his or hers.

As more people join the emerging paradigm segment, they will begin to question the principles being taught in schools to their children, who have been raised with quite a different perspective on how life works and one's responsibility to it.

This movement will be congruent with some of the conservative characteristics that should be exhibited by the Boomer generation as it continues to take over society in this decade.

Euthanasia Grows

The aging of the populations of the developed world, coupled with the growing belief that the mind exists apart from the body, and the fact that the support systems for health care will be increasingly stressed, suggests that more elderly will opt to control the time and conditions of their death than in the past. The activity of people like Dr. Jack Kevorkian, and new legislation like that in the Netherlands legalizing euthanasia, point to a liberalization of this activity.

The End of the Nation-State

International agencies become more effective in resolving interstate issues. That and the globalization of the media create a global village with a growing demand for nation-states to cede not only power but responsibility to supranational processes and organizations.

The effectiveness of the United Nations (UN) as a global conflict manager leads to an increasing level of responsibility for the most important international issues, such as health care, the environment, and population movements. What follows is a new predictability in the resolution of global problems. The populations of the nation-states adjust their world view to the regional and the international level. The nation-state, languishing at a superfluous midpoint, is functionally eliminated.

The UN's acceptance and administration of a wider variety of interregional affairs create a collateral increase in the adoption of international statehood by smaller regions, which feel less compelled by the former safety of the large nation-state. In the United States, there is a marked movement away from national administration, following 20 years of multi-issue devaluation from national to local government responsibility. The Articles of Confederation are revisited and, in some instances, taken further. In all regions of Europe, there is a move to dissolve large national structures in favor of smaller, historic regions. In Germany, for example, the Lander seize complete independence from the national government. In Asia, multiple states are created on the basis of local handicraft or technological production.

What starts with the increase in UN power and acceptability continues as a trend for global regionalism. The model of the Czech and Slovak republics becomes the norm. This trend allows for an effective nationhood based on religious, economic, or political allegiances. Groups as diverse as the Kurds and the Greens can have limited statehood. Common interest becomes the defining principle for a new series of smaller ideological states and closer ties between competing international treaty groups.

On the private level, some organizations achieve nation-like sovereignty, with representation in international agencies. Private entities are nominated and internationally accepted (for example, the International Committee of the Red Cross) as legally functioning international stakeholders whose interests are managed in the same manner as the newly formed regional states.

Measures

- ▪ *The world map becomes colored according to a layered, micro-regional plan.*

- ▪ *The UN, as the de facto beneficiary of the emerging supranational structure, expands its role* to include financial arbitration between member states. There is a 30 percent increase in the UN budget, beginning in the late 1990s.

- ▪ *Sovereignty is granted to multiregional economic or ideological nations,* despite their lack of physical territory.

- ▪ *UN membership undergoes a change* as many microstates join.

Implications

- ▪ *Sovereignty spreads* among many smaller, semiautonomous physical and ideological regions. This reduces large-scale conflict, but ultimately leads to special interest warfare.

- ▪ *The current high levels of trade continue to grow* at rates more than double that of the GDP.

The Group of Seventy

By the year 2000, trading blocs have taken over from national governments as the new focus for international trade. With the Asian, American, and European trading blocs firmly in place, the old Group of Seven leading industrial countries has given way to the new Group of

Seventy that has come to dominate the global negotiations over terms of trade. They exert enormous influence over the GATT agreements that are forged in the late 1990s, and they are an active lobby in global discussions involving the intersection of energy, environment, and development.

Measures

An early indicator of the emerging Group of Seventy is *Business Week's* Global 1000. The U.S.-based business publication publishes an annual list of the world's largest global firms ranked by market value. Morgan Stanley Capital International compiles the data, which are based on the current market value of the companies on the world's stock exchange. In 1992, the Global 1000 had sales of $7.7 trillion, exceeding the U.S. GNP by 30 percent and close to the combined GNP of the United States and Japan.

The top ten companies have sales that approximate the GNP of Belgium or Denmark, and revenues that exceed the GNP of all Latin American countries except Brazil. They are big economic players today, and as their global clout grows, they will flex their muscles increasingly in the international arena, in some cases overriding the sway of national governments. This is particularly true because they are concentrated in industries subject to domestically oriented regulations: telecommunications, pharmaceuticals, and financial services. Together these three industries account for 40 of the top 100 global firms ranked by market value:

- *Telecommunications.* Telecommunications accounts for 14 of the top 100, and includes the giants Nippon Telephone and Telegraph (NTT) and AT&T, as well as all seven Regional Bell Operating Companies.

- *Pharmaceuticals.* Pharmaceutical companies account for 13 of the top 100. This industry is becoming totally global, with Swiss, British, and American firms having multiple representation in the top 100. These companies may become increasingly active in shaping the national health policies of the countries in which they operate. As a result, they become agents of global harmonization in health systems, which traditionally have been influenced by national culture and history.

- *Financial services.* Banks and other financial services companies also account for 13 of the top 100. An astonishing seven of the top 26 global companies are Japanese banks. They will have disproportionate clout on the world financial scene because of their sheer scale. The globalization of financial services will be fueled by the increasing trend toward diffused global ownership and management of companies, and it will be enabled by the telecommunications and computer systems that will encourage continuous 24-hour global trading.

Today, the top 100 global companies include the oil companies and the giants of the industrial era. But they also include some surprise companies that represent new industries with global influence. Software, utility companies, franchised retailing, and environmental services may become huge global players in the next decade.

Implications

The rules for the new global economy are shaped more by companies than by governments. Some of these companies have global ownership and global management. Others, like the Japanese firms, play on the global stage with strong national interests at stake. The challenge for U.S. and European companies is to determine which stakeholders they are serving—their global shareholders, their domestic workforce, or the nation in which they are headquartered.

A No-Carbon Economy Worldwide

Rising temperatures, caused by greater concentrations of greenhouse gases in the atmosphere, are scientifically proven in the mid-1990s. At the same time, world climate deteriorates (more droughts, cyclones, heat waves, and so forth). Public awareness of this situation grows, bringing with it a greater understanding of the limitations of development based on abundant and cheap energy.

The European Economic Community (EEC), at the forefront of the issue ever since the "green tax" was mooted in the early 1990s, is the first to levy a tax on fossil fuels to discourage their use by means of a market signal (price) rather than by quotas. The new tax starts at $10/barrel in 1997, gradually reaching $100/barrel 30 years later, making the use of fossil fuels prohibitively expensive. The goal is to achieve a carbon-free economy by the year 2050, the only way to ensure that temperatures return to their previous levels.

Measures

Two indicators are used in the 1990s to determine whether the introduction of this tax is inevitable:

■ *Confirmation of global warming.* Advances by scientists in modeling the effects of higher concentrations of greenhouse gases in the atmosphere settle once and for all the debate about whether this phenomenon has a climatological effect. Confirmation of global warming, a northward shift by plant species, and growing public awareness of ever more frequent climatic accidents, finally force political officials to take vigorous steps.

■ *Politics restricting greenhouse gas emissions fail.* Concentrations of greenhouse gases in the atmosphere increase sharply as a result of rapidly rising energy consumption due to relatively inexpensive oil.

Implications

■ *The United States and some developing countries oppose the no-carbon economic agreement.* The EEC proposes the adoption of a global agreement aimed at the long-term elimination of fossil fuel use through a tax. The other European countries (including the Eastern ones) support such an agreement, as does Japan, which fears reprisals involving imports. However, the United States (where per capita CO_2 emissions are twice as high as in the EEC or Japan) rejects out-of-hand this plan that it feels will deal a death blow to its industries, claiming the ability to achieve the same result more gradually through tax incentives and funding of research into renewable energy sources and rational energy use. The countries of the former USSR—particularly Russia, the leading world energy exporter—react the same way. In less developed countries, there is disagreement among those who already have moved beyond the primary industrialization stage with their high-energy consumption industries and support the European project (newly industrialized countries, China, South American countries) and among those who reject it, citing their right to industrialize and their proportionally small contribution to the problem (sub-Saharan Africa, the Middle East, India). The tax, therefore, is adopted by a group of countries representing more than 60 percent of the world economy. These countries introduce a special border tax on imports, based on the fossil energy content of imported goods, to prevent imports from nonsignatory countries from being substituted for local products on which the fossil fuel tax is levied.

■ *Fuel is more expensive.* The use of automobiles begins to decline. With air traffic also hard hit, aircraft manufacturers find themselves with a serious problem. Electricity prices increase significantly, but more slowly than fossil fuel prices. New life is breathed into nuclear power programs in Europe: Hydropower resources not previously developed become a viable proposition under the new price system. Some industrial sectors (metallurgy, mechanical engineering) disappear almost completely, while others (chemicals, construction materials) undergo in-depth restructuring. A return to collective housing, which is less energy intensive, is inevitable for low- and middle-income households. Mass transit develops, to the detriment of the automotive industry.

■ *Nuclear power grows.* The public accepts the construction of new nuclear power plants, giant tidal power stations, and the burial of nuclear waste. The budget neutrality of the "green tax" is abandoned. Tax cuts (in particular, VAT) are restricted in scope and cover carbon-free products only. The socialization of earnings increases, and the state is more interventionist and coercive.

■ *More international research leads to a new industrial revolution.* The bulk of the portion of tax revenues not offset by a drop in taxation of other products is used to finance major international research programs on new energy sources, storing electricity, new materials, and nuclear power plant safety. These programs produce qualitative leaps of knowledge in numerous fields: Miniaturization of batteries enables electric cars to be developed; development of a maglev train whose speed is competitive with that of aircraft on a continental scale; substitution of new materials (composites, "green" plastics) in almost all applications where metals previously were used; a revolution in air transport, with conventional aircraft replaced by orbiting devices (on the space shuttle principle), the rocket launching of which does not cause greenhouse gas emissions; marked improvement in nuclear power plant safety and commercial operation before the mid-twenty-first century of breeder reactors; progress in the area of solar power, mainly affecting households (home heating and electricity); and so forth. A new industrial revolution takes place because most industrial processes have to be replaced.

■ *America finally signs the no-carbon economy agreement.* Although most of these research programs and the conversion of production facilities take several decades, all signatory countries to the carbon-free economy agreement benefit. The United States finally realizes this, and joins them five years after the agreement comes into force. Nevertheless, the technological lag that built up contributes to the decline of the American economy, and the country loses its position of leadership. The other countries that have signed the agreement see their standard of living rise to nearly that of the most developed countries. They benefit tremendously from the international scientific and technical cooperation necessitated by the scale of the problems to be resolved and from voluntary assimilation of new technologies.

■ *A changed system of values comes into being.* The recession caused by the tax gradually gives way to a new phase of development based on a changed system of values. The external cost of human activities increasingly is taken into account by economic agents. A sense of shared interest and frugality replaces the worship of abundance and individual freedom.

■ *The balance of economic power is altered.* The holdouts—those developing countries that, for the most part, were already lagging far behind the others—succumb irremediably as their nascent industries disappear with the closing off of markets in developed countries. The uncontrolled population growth causes the major urban centers in these countries to explode. The resultant chaos stimulates the population to return en masse to the land, which divides the world into two relatively self-contained parts: developed countries that have found a new mainspring for more harmonious and sustainable development, and the have-nots living on international handouts, firmly entrenched in under development.

Hong Kong Takes Over China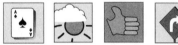

Great Britain relinquishes control of Hong Kong, but the joke is on China. Hong Kong, Taiwan, and the five special economic zones of mainland China become the supernova of the late twentieth century, gobbling the Chinese Communist dinosaur and blasting the possibilities of another Tiananmen Square into the prehistoric mists.

The establishment of the Shenzen Economic Zone in China's Guangdong province creates a vital free market in the coastal area surrounding Hong Kong. The special economic zones offer foreign businesses lower tax rates and special investment facilities and attract numerous joint ventures, particularly in oil, textiles, and telecommunications equipment. Throughout the rest of the decade, these zones proliferate, strengthen, and grow roots. By the turn of the millennium, Chinese capitalism is alive and well, thriving on the Soviet demise and on Western desires to jump on the Asian Russian/Central Asian economic bandwagon.

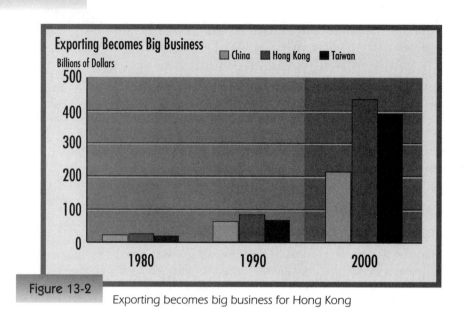

Figure 13-2

Exporting becomes big business for Hong Kong

Measures

▪ *By the year 2000, Hong Kong is serving as the main conduit for Chinese exports.* Mainland China's average annual growth rate stays constant due to a lack of infrastructure, while Hong Kong's exports jump from $82.2 billion in 1990 to $430.2 billion in 2000. Taiwan's exports increase from $67.1 billion in 1990 to $382.1 billion in 2000, as shown in Figure 13-2.

▪ *Direct foreign investment in China,* via Hong Kong and Taiwan, spirals upward from $14.6 billion (January to June 1992) to $100 billion in 2000.

▪ *Taiwan's exports to Hong Kong* (as the main entry point to China) have experienced an average annual growth rate of 28 percent since 1985. In 1997, China becomes a de facto open market, and the average annual growth rate of Taiwan's exports leaps to 33 percent (see Figure 13-3).

Implications

▪ *A weakened China subjugated to a financially strong and influential Hong Kong* serves as the economic hub of the proposed Tumen delta trade zone and changes the world balance of power.

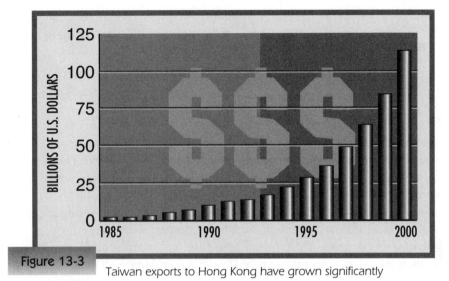

Figure 13-3 Taiwan exports to Hong Kong have grown significantly since 1985

■ *A Chinese-Russian-Korean-Japanese economic alliance* completely eclipses the United States and Europe (both too busy with regional preoccupations) and offers an attractive new trading partner for the developing world.

■ *A new (or strengthened) drug- and arms-trafficking network emerges.*

■ *The removal of traditional "Great Game" rivalries* provided by economic alliances completely changes the strategic politics of the Central Asian steppe, Iran, Turkey, Pakistan, India, Nepal, Mongolia, Tibet, and Afghanistan, not to mention the smaller East Asian countries.

■ *New areas of investment open up*—particularly in oil services, textiles, printing, dyeing, transportation and infrastructure, apparel, consumer electronics, fast food, and telecommunications.

■ *Corruption runs rampant on the out-of-control Shanghai and Shenzen stock exchanges,* and a whole new spate of sophisticated Chinese Michael Milkens arises (with a little help from Taiwanese, Hong Kong-based, and Western "advisors").

Big Business Disappears

The era of the large industrial enterprise is over. For the past 200 years, large enterprises have had a real advantage because of economies of scale in production, financial clout, and international contacts. But more affluent and educated consumers are changing the character of markets: More purchasers are switching from buying necessities to discretionary items; more products are turning over quickly on the basis of styles and fashion; and more advertising is aimed at individual consumers with tailored products.

New information technologies, with emphasis on quick product turnover and informal alliances, smash the power of the large firm. Medium-sized firms that bring together entrepreneurial and management talent gain access to finance and distribution channels as easily as large companies, and they can turn over products at a much quicker pace. Medium-sized firms using effective partnerships and alliances become the new kings of the hill.

Measures

▪ *By the year 2000, the share of medium-sized firms employing fewer than 1,000 people will increase* market share by an average of 40 percent at the expense of large firms. The largest gains will be made by manufacturing and distribution firms that provide specialized consumer and business products.

▪ *The rates of new product introductions will increase* in consumer electronics, apparel, food selections, autos, home furnishings, communication and office information equipment, and styles of service delivery.

Implications

▪ *The vast majority of the increases in both consumer and business spending* is on discretionary items tailored to the needs and tastes of individuals and companies.

▪ *The more successful marketing and distribution channels respond quickly to changing trends* among affluent consumers, and force very rapid product responses to these changes.

▪ *Partnering and alliances among smaller and medium-sized firms make international operations much easier for them;* the share of international business goes up for most successful smaller and medium-sized firms.

▪ *Successful firms can respond quickly to new opportunities* with a mobilization of substantial resources.

Services Become Automated

Rapid development of automated processes in the services industry reduces the number of jobs by more than 20 percent. Over the past few decades, developed countries have relied heavily on the automation of the manufacturing industry. Robots, computer simulation, automated assembly lines, and Total Quality Management (TQM) concepts help increase productivity. With fewer productivity gains in manufacturing, countries look to other industries for the application of these automated technologies. Since the services industry accounted for more than 32 percent of U.S. jobs and 18 percent of the U.S. GNP (second only to manufacturing) in 1990—typical for most other developed countries—it seems ideal for automation.

The automation of the services industry includes automated payments and expert systems in the financial services industry; remote retail shopping from home; customer capability to tailor products through technology rather than people (choosing sizes, colors, styling, pricing, and delivery times without salespeople); and more embedded capabilities in hardware, which reduces the number of software, legal, and business services people. As the services industry becomes more automated, the number of workers needed declines. More automated processes encourage more profitable and competitive companies. As profit soars, the services industry begins to account for a growing share of GNP.

Measures

▪ *New automated developments applicable to the services industry* are increasingly implemented.

▪ *The number of newly created jobs in business services, financial services, and sales declines* as the sales revenue per service worker increases.

Implications

▪ *The automation of the services industry* enhances the competitive nature of developed countries, as some are able to compete more effectively in the short run. In the long run, the number of displaced workers and increasing unemployment undermine the economies of these developed countries. Less developed countries, relying on developed countries for trade, finance, and economic aid, suffer immensely.

▪ *A more highly automated services sector requires shifts in education.* Not only are advanced education degrees in finance, economics, law, and other curriculum areas necessary to enter this newly transformed industry, but workers with computer, robotics, and other technical skills become highly desirable. Service automation provides new opportunities for aeronautics and defense engineers who face a declining industry with government cutbacks.

▪ *Intellectual property rights and technology transfers* that are intrinsic to the manufacturing industry are issues for the automated services sector.

Women Leave the Workforce

After three decades of constant growth in the number of women in the labor force, there is a turnaround. Tired of the "glass ceiling" effect and the high level of stress at work and home, women begin to put family values ahead of career aspirations. They leave the paid labor force in large numbers, and their participation rate declines to 1970 levels. Fewer women aspire to top management positions in private business, accept mommy-track career pathways, or fast-track in an attempt to break the glass ceiling. Women leave traditionally held "female" jobs such as nursing, teaching, legal, health, and business service positions. The pink-collar workforce shrinks drastically. Those women who remain in the work force tend to work for small businesses, especially in the service sector, and for women-owned businesses. Jobs women hold tend to be highly skilled, usually involving strong interactive management skills, orientation toward teamwork, and open communication.

Many women who turn away from the paid workforce pursue other rewarding and productive activities such as volunteering for a wide variety of organizations (educational, religious, cultural/arts, social service, and local enterprises); developing and managing community activities; and participating in local politics, lobbying groups, and other non-labor force activities. As women leave the paid workforce, men are forced to be the sole provider for the family. The average male salary rises as career opportunities increase. Because of their high education levels and work experience, the women leaving the labor force develop an active network of resources committed to social change, social policy, and improvement in the quality of life. These women form the social and political backbone of most communities; control an effective degree of power in the political and business communities; and are responsible for providing services that are exchanged through the network, ranging from child and elder care to educational and professional advice.

Measures

The United States has long been a leader in offering women career opportunities, but the late 1990s see a sharp reversal.

■ *In the early 1990s, the labor force participation rate for women reaches a plateau and then begins to decline.* The overall participation rate for women starts to dip into the low 50 percent range in 1997 for the first time in two decades, and the exceptionally high participation rates for baby-boom women really takes a plunge. The high level of participation by women between 35 and 54 falls from the low 80 percentile back to the 1980 level of about 65 percent. By the year 2000, the average participation rate for women is at a 35-year low of 45 percent.

■ *The major exodus from the labor force is driven by disillusioned baby-boom women,* many with children and with high levels of education. Their model of performing other non-labor force activities catches on among younger women in their late twenties and early thirties who remain in the work force for only a few years after graduation.

■ *Several occupations and industries are drastically affected.* Between 40 percent and 90 percent of these positions lack workers. The health and education fields feel the most impact as traditional female jobs, such as technicians, technologists, health assistants, and paraprofessionals, lose employees. Professional fields, such as business and law, also are hurt by a reduced administrative support and paraprofessional workforce. Sales workers and sales-related occupations are held predominantly by women, and these occupations feel the employment crunch from fewer women in the workforce.

Implications

Smart use of the workforce will be one of the key challenges for employers in the year 2000. They will have to reexamine the way they use technology to manage and provide goods and services, the way they hire and recruit new workers, their strategies for continually training and fine-tuning their core work staff, and how they may restructure their organizations to make the most effective use of their employees:

- *Use of labor and integration of technology are management issues of the future.* Fewer women in the workforce means that employers must develop ways to integrate technology into their work processes in order to operate with drastically reduced staffs. Companies have to learn to maintain production and increase productivity with a greatly reduced workforce. Massive labor shortages may be the driving force that pushes organizations from using information technology only as a replacement for routinized and automated tasks to using it as a tool to enhance workers' decision making, creativity, and innovation.

- *New strategies are required for hiring and retaining.* Incentives, rewards, and career mobility are key to hiring and keeping workers. Educating and training workers to take on new and growing responsibilities will remain one of the more critical challenges for companies to maintain their competitiveness. Women who leave organizations will take their experience and skills with them. Doing more with less will be the mantra of companies experiencing an outflow of women workers. Small core staffs will feel tremendous pressure to perform well and keep up productivity. Training is at a premium, as low-skilled jobs are automated on a wide scale and knowledge work becomes real. Minimally educated workers find themselves without any opportunities in the formal workforce.

In addition to management implications, other impacts on the economy and society arise from the decreasing participation of women in the labor force:

- *New definition of work.* Activities outside the traditional "employment" and "paid work" setting become highly valued in society. Local communities and governments get revitalized and take new shape as women devote more time and attention to these institutions. The political and civic power that develops outside of the paid workforce creates a new standard for valuing time and effort.

- *Decreasing average household income.* Families that no longer have two incomes team up to live within their economic means. Consumption of unnecessary products and services decreases, so marketers need to refocus their selling efforts to consumers who turn away from superfluous purchasing. A new source for resources develops within the women's network.

Life Expectancy Approaches 100

In the late 1990s, the genes that cause aging are isolated. A certain number of medical treatments are developed and put on the market. Life expectancy increases by about 20 years.

The percentage of people over 65 rises from 6 percent of the world population in 1990 to 12 percent in 2040. Distribution of the population by age bracket undergoes a fundamental change as the result of this sharp increase in life expectancy.

It is, nevertheless, the relationship between the working and nonworking populations that is of concern. In fact, medical progress makes it possible both to extend the duration of life and to modify the physical and intellectual capabilities of individuals. This affects the life cycle and delays all the principal stages of life (puberty, menopause, and so forth). Thus an increased lifespan does not constitute a social catastrophe. The challenge is limited to coping with a difficult period of transition before arriving at a new balance.

Measures

■ *Rising population growth in developed countries.* This goes toward reducing the discrepancy that currently exists within the southern hemisphere. The situation becomes easier to bear in the developing countries, since the reduction in mortality in part filters through to these countries, and the prospect of living to an older age leads to a reduction of the birth rate.

■ *Pensions finance housing and health.* The number of working-age people is not large enough to guarantee decent provisions for elderly people; so, to a greater extent, they would have to finance their own pensions. The transfer of housing by succession drops off considerably, and a serious housing shortage results. Other serious consequences, such as the financing of the health care system, soon make the situation unsustainable.

■ *Reorganization of the lifecycle.* The effect on our state of health allows a lifestyle at the age of 70 that is currently enjoyed at the age of 55.

■ *Prolonging working life.* We work from age 25 to 85, so a new form of job sharing takes shape to avoid unemployment and inactivity. It is almost impossible to do the same job for 60 years, so in-company training and reorientation make great advances and become the main considerations of educational systems.

■ *Shifts in family life.* It is unlikely that the housing shortage will lead to a regrouping of generations under the same roof, especially when prolonging life expectancy by about 20 years would lead to four generations living together. Female fertility lasts to age 60, so many births often are planned for about the age of 45 or 50. Moreover, life becomes a sequential process. Divorces multiply since it is inconceivable to some people to live 75 years with the same person, and parental relations become complex.

■ *Widening of the generation gap.* Dealing with the demographic transition becomes the primary short-term objective. It leads to a new balance between the working and non-working populations and between generations, since the age spread of the latter would be increased (having a first baby at the age of 45 or 50 is no longer exceptional).

Implications

The aging of the population alters the relationship not only between the working and nonworking populations, but also between young and old within the working population. The theory of human capital states that individuals accumulate a certain core of knowledge in the course of their career, and the increases in remuneration only reflect this acquisition of skills. The seniority model goes further, claiming that remuneration is lower than labor productivity for the youngest employees, higher for the longest standing, with the latter benefiting from the rights of seniority they have acquired during the first half of their career. This model is viable as long as the differences between productivity and remuneration balance each other out. The increased age of the staff leads to a worsening of companies' balance sheets. It therefore is indispensable, according to this scenario, that the accumulation of human capital be reflected in a major increase in productivity.

We can expect a series of crises initially in the domains of public finance, pensions, or possibly housing, and then a second phase, when new equilibrium is attained. For example, with 80 years to plan for, we could imagine new attitudes toward the payback of investments, which would be realized over a much longer period of time.

The new opportunities outweigh the transitional difficulties. The burden of the elderly does not become too great; the predominance of mentalities hostile to change does not occur. The quest for adventure and the joy of creating remain.

The End of Intergenerational Solidarity

The steady medical progress made in all countries of the world, especially in the OECD countries, has considerably improved life expectancy. This increases the proportion of elderly people in the overall population. At the same time, the drop in fertility observed in wealthy countries decreases the proportion of young people in the population, compounding the aging problem. The combination of these two phenomena radically changes the pyramid in the developed countries and becomes recognized as a demographic revolution.

Age differences cause a new set of conflicts. Older people are frequently rich and white. The generation conflict is becoming more intense and is crystallizing around three age brackets. The first group consists of young working people who often are recent emigrants suffering from cultural and economic disadvantages. At the other end of the scale, we find pensioners who hold on to their advantages: the "Grampa Bust." The middle group consists of the baby boomers who, because of their hedonistic desires, want to reduce compulsory contributions. Baby boomers are concerned about their approaching retirement, and they are in an arbitrator position because of their economic and social power.

Thus, without causing abrupt changes, the baby boomers have gradually reduced the material and moral conflict of older people while trying to prepare for their own future within the limits of the economic and social situation.

Measures

███ *Pension financing is a headache.* Most OECD countries finance compulsory pensions by the so-called sharing-out method (a formula by which pensions are financed by the contributions from the currently working population) rather than by capitalization (whereby the actualized value of all contributions for one age group is equal to the benefits it will get in the future—a system similar to insurance). Because these contributions are almost always charged to payroll costs, the future rate of such contributions increases excessively (see Table 13-1).

▪ *The average age of the working population goes up.* Wage agreements provide varying levels of higher wages as age increases, despite a drop in the retirement age. Thus the average salary will increase, lowering corporate profits.

▪ *Social security systems are affected.* The cash difficulties of health insurance and unemployment funds are already increasing. An increase in the number of older people means more treatment, care, and supervision expenses, exceeding the potential savings of a decreasing younger population.

▪ *The drain saps the vitality of developed countries.* Lower inventiveness— mathematicians are most creative before they turn 30—and the difficulty young people have in obtaining responsible corporate positions, because of the large number of older managers, will help to stifle society and foster social antagonisms based on age differences.

Year	United States	Japan	Germany	Sweden
1990	12.1	4.5	13.6	15.8
2010	12.0	12.9	18.6	16.3
2030	12.3	19.8	29.3	21.0
2050	16.4	23.0	28.9	20.1

Table 13-1. Contributions required for public pensions (percent of wages)

Source: Economie & Statistiques, No. 233, June 1990

Implications

Three remedies are implemented simultaneously to check the money drained by pension funds. Systems and acceptance differ from country to country:

▪ *Reduced benefits.* The reduction of services is organized gently and gradually. Under-indexation, compared to the rising cost of living, higher user fees, and higher income taxes, are burdening real income while superficially avoiding nominal income by factoring inflation.

■ *Postponed retirement.* People are encouraged to create savings funds, the effectiveness of which becomes apparent after many years when the large class of baby boomers reaches retirement age. The age at which people can retire with full benefits is regularly increased.

■ *Higher taxes.* The contributions by the working population are increased substantially.

None of these remedies prevents the material and moral conflict of older people from deteriorating compared to the existing situation. As a result of the generation conflict, older people are more frequently shunted aside, losing income or getting stuck in long-term unemployment. Some older people, veterans of the struggles of the 1960s, organize clandestine structures (White Panthers in the United States, Roten Armee Fraktion in Germany). Most withdraw into an ivory tower and decide to "eat it all." The disappearance of inheritances causes serious difficulties for young people struggling to improve their standard of living. The old-boy network of parents from the upper classes giving children their first job opportunities breaks down.

Deprived of the dynamism of a young working population, developed societies witness stunted economic growth while their world leadership is challenged by more authoritarian continents. China, which for thousands of years has been able to combine the dynamism of its merchants with the static structure of its family system, shows a remarkable capacity to recover domination of the world. The decline of the Roman Empire surely began the same way. As the old African proverb says, "We don't inherit the land of our parents, we lend it to our children."

Germany Moves East

With German reunification and the end of the Soviet Union, threats that were the basis of Europe's system of cooperation are dissolved. For most, the potential for a large-scale European war has been laid to rest. Thus the stage is set for this newly created power vacuum to be filled by historical forms of international relations. The concept of a single Europe acting as one entity becomes an unnecessary contrivance in the midst of new economic realities. The new reality is that of Russia as partner, both politically and economically, rather than as adversary.

While maintaining a weakening link to the EEC, by 1997 the German state embarks on an alliance formulation with key members of a revived Commonwealth of Independent States (CIS). This alliance focuses primarily on energy, infrastructure, and technology, and it is characterized by Germany as the big link between the EEC and Eastern Europe. This preempts any efforts by Japan and the United States to partner with Russia.

Through this strategy, Germany becomes an economic member of both the CIS and the EEC. The continuation of political linkage enhancement within the EEC is virtually halted by this alliance, leaving the other EEC partner states in a prolonged holding pattern. Germany's bargaining position within the EEC and internationally is unrivaled.

Measures

- *The level of German investment in the CIS* goes well beyond that offered by the United States and by the EEC.

- *The German GDP* begins to grow at a rate higher than the EEC average.

- *German investment* becomes a major component of total CIS investment.

Implications

- *The uncertainty of the international business community results in a period of low international investment.* While new customs and rules are sorted out, the economies not affiliated with the new trading blocs are devoid of investment.

- *All EEC members return to a national economy.* This results in localization of all finance policy to the exclusion of the centralized structures of the EEC.

- *The open market gradually closes as national barriers resurface in the wake of the new balance of economic power.* EEC members excluded from the new trading blocs return to a historical version of the national market.

- *Changes within the EEC eventually result in a reevaluation of investment in Pacific Rim activities.* The United States and Japan are strengthened by this return of investment and increase cooperation to combat the threat of a complete shift in global capital to the new alliance in Europe and the CIS.

- *Investors in southern European countries lose interest,* creating large holes in the economies of southern Europe and leading to greater political unrest.

Backlash Against AIDS Victims and Lifestyle

At the same time that the Boomer generation should begin becoming more conservative, reacting against the frustrations of policies and structures that haven't been working, the brunt of the AIDS epidemic will be hitting the United States. What had been a relatively small (in the opinion of most Americans) sprinkle of deaths will grow into what seems to be a thunderstorm.

The stress on the health care system will be very great, and may further threaten an economy that is ill from a combination of other blows (natural disasters, insurance company failures, restructuring around the information technology revolution, and so on). Americans will be looking for relief and solutions, and will see the deluge of AIDS costs as a major cause of the problem. The growing profile of the new paradigm tenet, that individuals are responsible for their own situations, will nest snugly with the similar emerging Boomer conservatism, and may translate into a backlash against AIDS victims and the lifestyle that is thought to encourage the disease.

Africa Unravels

If the situation in Africa looks bleak now, the high rate of population growth and slow to negative economic growth in the region suggest disaster before 2025. Without coordinated international efforts, Africa will be a teeming wasteland by 2025, an incubator of global plagues, and a harbinger of poverty and great military violence.

Africa's average growth in GNP per capita over the period of 1979 to 1989 was less than 1.7 percent. Unless measures are taken to increase average annual GNP growth rates in Africa above 3 percent, GNP per capita will plunge much lower than it is today.

While Africa had only 56 percent of the population of Europe in 1950, by 2025 it will have over 300 percent of the population of Europe.

The pressure upon most African environmental systems will be extreme because net capital flows will be, beyond doubt, insufficient to pay for imported energy and environmental technology. The developing world relies on bulk commodities to trade for hard foreign currency, and Africa is suffering from severe commodity deflation. For instance, in real dollar terms, a market basket of food items in 1989 cost only 61 percent of its cost in 1975. Timber, on the other hand, climbed on world markets, in real dollar terms, by over 80 percent in that period. Net result: logged-out forests; floods, because water run-off is so rapid without trees; and declining revenues from food production. Tropical forests are being decimated for firewood.

Because of high levels of debt and reduced commodity revenues, African nations will greatly suffer in the 1990s. The world's capital crunch is affecting the African continent more than is immediately obvious. Lack of capital means that the transportation infrastructure will remain very inefficient for food distribution. Mass starvation on an unprecedented scale could result.

As agriculture fails (due to war, depleted soil, and inability to afford fertilizers), a resultant migration of large rural populations to squatter communities near urban centers will put severe strain on urban political systems, water supplies, and sanitation systems (such as they are). Disease and political chaos will result. Millions will die of AIDS.

Genome Project Kills Health Insurance

Enormous predictive capabilities result from breaking the code of the human genome. A blood sample of an infant will allow the analysis of about 100 selected genes for flaws known to be prediagnostic for certain diseases. A potential life history of a person's health will be available at the push of a computer button. If a complete genetic map were available from every person, it is not unreasonable to assume that mandatory genetic screens would be standard before employment-based health insurance was issued. Jobs would not be offered to those with less than optimal genetic makeups, and insurance coverage would be denied for those diseases that genetic maps indicate individuals are most likely to get. It seems likely that, armed with this information, insurance companies will sell their services to those with the least risk for one price, and those with the most at another.

The Human Genome Project, therefore, raises the specter of differentiating our insurance groupings according to an assessment of genetic risk, a specter so unpalatable and unjust that our society could not tolerate it. A new system will necessarily evolve that provides access to anyone who is sick or who needs appropriate preventive services.

Major Information System Disruptions

The Clearing House Interbank Payments System, owned by 11 large New York banks, is an international computer network that automatically transfers more than $1 trillion—more than the entire money supply of the United States—throughout its system each day. Similar extraordinarily complex computer systems control regional and national telephone systems, electrical grids, global stock and commodity trading transactions, and other similarly important functions.

The complexity of these systems is accelerating—probably exponentially, like the rest of the information technology area—and therein lies the probability that there will be more, bigger system failures in the future. Already entire areas of the country have lost long distance telephone service because of program bugs.

As these systems expand, so does the opportunity for crime and mischief, if not just mistakes—all pointing toward more breakdowns.

The New Chernobyl

Nuclear energy is a key part of Western European energy policy, particularly in France. In 1996, a nuclear accident occurs in the Soviet-built reactor of Bohunice in Slovakia. This fulfills the prophecies of pessimistic experts who feared such a serious accident in the RMBK and VVER 440-230 models—the oldest and most unsafe power stations built in the former USSR.

Fueled by media broadcasts that followed the path of radioactive clouds above Western Europe, the disaster defines nuclear power plants in Western opinion as "an unacceptable hazard." Pressure from a frightened public, led by rising Green parties in Germany, Scandinavia, and some small countries inside the EEC, causes industrialized countries to totally abandon nuclear power.

Measures

The debate on nuclear safety is fierce. Most scientists stress the advantages of the nonpolluting nature of nuclear energy, as it is free from fossil fuel threats to the environment, acid rain, and global warming. But people's fears, increasing since the 1970s, are stronger about the problems of nuclear waste disposal and the possibilities of large-scale accidents (see Table 13-2).

▪ *All industrialized countries must revise their patterns of energy usage.* Increases in nuclear use and development programs are stopped. There is a strong push for a nuclear moratorium aimed at an immediate shutdown of plants worldwide. Most shaken are the countries that implemented ambitious nuclear development programs: France, Belgium, and Japan.

▪ *A dramatic political test for European cohesion.* The conciliatory solution advocates a balanced dispatching of shortages in Europe. But implementation creates a crisis; France unilaterally decides on an extended closure program lasting 15 years. Lack of solidarity results in a cacophony, and closure programs are voted on case by case, depending on the share of nuclear power of total energy production in each country. This occurs quickly in the United States, and slowly in France and Japan.

The Cleanest Energy	1984	1989
Renewable energies	52	43
Natural gas	18	21
Nuclear	10	10
Coal	9	7
Oil	4	2
No answer	8	18
Total	100	100
Nuclear Energy	**1984**	**1989**
Unacceptable danger	38	52
Without interest	7	6
Worthwhile	43	30
No answer	12	12
Total	100	100

Table 13-2. Europeans turning against nuclear (percent of respondents)

Source: European survey for the EEC Energy General Director, Energy and Environment, 1982, 1984, 1986, 1987, 1989

Implications

The worldwide uproar depresses financial markets, reactivates aggressive trade practices, and brutally breaks the momentum of the global economic recovery. Economic activity is depressed by the energy shortages. Vast campaigns promoting energy conservation are launched with some success as they meet the ecological concerns of the public. Of course, research on innovative solutions, especially on renewable energies, receives more credit. But because new energy sources—geothermal, wind, thermal, solar power—will not be available until after 2020, they do not represent a reliable short- or medium-term answer.

▦ *Oil is market-regulated.* A sharp rise in oil prices gives new negotiation power to the oil-exporting states.

▦ *Natural gas is popular for being the less-polluting fossil fuel, but production limits global growth.*

▦ *Coal, with its 200- to 300-year-old reserves, emerges as the great solution to the nuclear crisis.* Boosted activity goes along with progressively cleaner technical processes. In particular, fluidized bed combustion and combined cycle turbines with gasification are the big winners.

The Balkanization of Western Europe

Long before the introduction of the nation-state, Europe existed as a set of culturally distinct regions. These regions merged into the conceptual tool of the nation-state as a hedge against economic and political danger. The security of the national borders was viewed as far superior to those of the regions. This concept was extrapolated to the construction of the EEC for similar reasons. The EEC offered economic and political security.

By the year 2000, the regions of Europe decide to dismantle the nation-state in favor of strong regional representation in the EEC. The EEC still is seen as necessary to protect the interests of its founders, but the nation-state as an intermediate step in the hierarchy of decision making has been obviated over time. The EEC is less threatening to regional values when the nation-state is removed. The cost of two, often-competing centralized interests is no longer acceptable.

The motivation for this activity emanates from grassroots movements throughout the European regions. In much the same way as the restructuring of the late 1960s was brought on by a struggle of values, this European regional revolution is fought from common interest rather than from a desire for competitive advantage. In areas formerly boasting little or no indigenous local culture, there is a new tendency to invent a locality of cultural identities. These identities strengthen in all regions.

Measures

- *National parliaments dissolve in favor of regional and European parliaments.* The regionals become the key administrative units.

- *The regional revolution has its basis in cultural activities.* Thus most economic issues are decided at the EEC level. The key issues dealt with at the regional or decentralized level include culture, art, education, local planning and infrastructure, local environment, health, and social security. All other matters are addressed at the EEC level.

- *A new series of economic alliances forms across old national borders.* These alliances initially will be based on common cultural or religious compatibility and involve a common regional activity—for example, fishing, shipping, agriculture, heavy industry, or national resources. They are not operated on a basis of exclusivity, but on economic complementarity. Most regions carry on multiple trading/production arrangements with multiple patterns. The grid is quite large and multidimensional.

Implications

- *The open market functions more efficiently than it did as a national/EEC unit.* Regional trading strengthens both local and European economies.

- *The lack of national power structures results in the oppression of minorities within regions.* These conflicts are addressed by the EEC, but response is slow. Minor conflicts arise at a greater rate than under the national structure. The conflict resolution within the EEC is initially one of mediation and arbitration, followed later by internal peacekeeping forces.

- *Most companies must adapt their infrastructure to the regional trading concept.* The necessity for regional representation in all departments requires a more political allocation of funds.

> ▬ *The European decentralized system becomes a model for sustainable structural change in the southern hemisphere.*

China: Financier to the World

In 2002, China—having already taken its place in the G7 some years ago, and on its way to becoming the largest economy in the world—unleashes its great resource of saved capital and becomes the world's principal source of financing.

Measures

▬ Through the last seven years of the 1990s, China's economy continued to grow at the rate of 8 percent to 10 percent annually.

▬ The Chinese people continued to maintain the second highest saving rate in the world, close behind the leader, Liechtenstein.

▬ The Chinese version of capitalism flourished during the decade of the 1990s, and the government of China became more liberal after the death of Deng.

▬ The United States, Japan, and Europe continued to economically muddle through the last half of the 1990s, without any strong economic showing on the part of any of them.

Implications

▬ China becomes a major global economic and political influence.

▬ China begins to take significant equity positions in Western companies and uses its influence to draw the leading high technology to itself.

▬ China is the biggest market in the world for consumer products.

GLOBAL INCOHERENCE

First Contact Is Made with Extraterrestrials

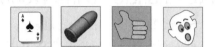

A team of volunteer researchers makes active contact with a UFO and videotapes the initial interchange with the extraterrestrial crew aboard their ship in 1996. The tape is widely broadcast around the world. The media, in following up the story, determines that this event is the culmination of a sophisticated international, multi-year strategy of a U.S.-based nonprofit group that has resulted in a number of earlier UFO contacts of increasing levels of interchange.

Measures

Although the mainline press had not lent much, if any, coverage to this story before its landmark event, after-the-fact research establishes that a well-organized international network of UFO researchers have been actively attempting to initiate the first official contact with extraterrestrials since 1991. Using a sophisticated strategy and unusual techniques, small teams from an international group of over 600 trained people first initiated contact with UFOs in 1992, when they were successful in drawing ships into their immediate neighborhoods in Florida and England, getting them to hover overhead, change their flying formation, reply to light signals, and in one memorable case, hover within 100 meters of the team.

After the initial encounters, the group's leader had been invited to a meeting with a very high White House official who had confirmed that the government had, for some time, confirmed extraterrestrial existence, most significantly from photographic data received from U.S. surveillance and reconnaissance satellites.

A much higher-profile, government-sponsored initiative, launched in 1992, had focused on using radio telescopes for listening in deep space for signals from other civilizations. This project, supported by an international group of well-known scientists, had so far not produced any significant results.

Implications

◼ *Pockets of wonder; pockets of panic.* For many in the majority segment of people in industrial societies who believe that UFOs are real, this event, though disquieting, was seen as opening up the window to a whole new world and reality full of immense questions—but not at all necessarily negative. There was wonder and questioning in the context of a desire to solidify relationships and learn more from these strange "people."

At the same time, pockets of people (and some governments) reacted as though acutely threatened. The assumption was that these beings were coming to take over, or unduly influence the world and that the appropriate response was to quickly build up corporate and individual defenses.

◼ *The world is shaken.* All societies with access to television are transfixed by this event. Never before seen levels of global excitement and anxiety are experienced. The implications of this event cause an ultimate change in most every aspect of life on earth.

◼ *Conservative theologians search for answers.* One of the hardest hit groups are conservative religious organizations, for whom this event does not fit into their relatively narrow explanation of reality. This, perhaps the biggest event in history, causes religious leaders to scramble to explain (and in some cases, modify) theology to fit this new situation.

◼ *New technologies give hope.* Although some groups see the benefit of the new visitors in terms of new technology that can be made into weapons, many others see it as a hope for solving some of the very serious, intractable problems the world is confronted with at that time. Energy production is of particular interest.

Major Shift in Global Weather–U.S. Insurance Industry Failure

Changes in the world's weather and increased natural disasters could easily come together to deliver a knockout punch to the American (and probably international) casualty insurance industry. The year 1993 was the worst year for claims in the history of American casualty insurance, most losses being the result of natural disasters.

Additionally, the social conditions within which the Los Angeles riot occurred (another big casualty loss), continue to exist and are getting worse as the disparity between the American haves and have-nots increases. If the economy does not respond to the stimulus of 1993 and produce significant new jobs, the possibility of additional urban unrest is not remote.

If hurricanes, earthquakes, and volcano eruptions increased and produced significant damage to developed areas (a big California quake could produce $60 billion in losses), the industry would likely fail.

Technology Increasingly Gets Out of Hand

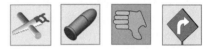

The extraordinary capabilities that technology is offering to society could well get out of hand because we were not able to control it or use it effectively. Already, for instance, experts are warning that our technical expertise may be advancing more rapidly than our ability to manage genetic information. Amniocentesis, widely used to detect genetic abnormalities in developing fetuses, also reveals the baby's gender, and doctors report a surge in the practice of eliminating children of an undesired sex through abortion.

Any number of other evolving technologies will become helpful or not, based on the values of the people who develop and use them. Because the technology is moving so fast, it is clearly possible that there will be increasing instances of technology being used negatively, and in ways not anticipated during development.

The Poor Know They Are Poor and Get Weapons

As the result of television, poor people understand how poor and disenfranchised they are. At the same time, the weapons manufacturers of the world are actively attempting to open new markets for their wares to offset the significant decrease in market associated with the end of the cold war. Nuclear weapons are also reported to be beginning to leak out of the former Soviet Union into radical hands. On a smaller scale, this trend can be seen in urban groups in our own country: The most disenfranchised are the most well-armed. This all suggests that increasingly more poor people will have the perceived reason and means to threaten others, and will probably do it.

Hard Times for the Fishing Industry

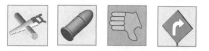

As outlined in the environmental section, the global fishing fleet has increased its catch systematically from 22 million tons in 1950 to 100 million tons in 1989. When catches plateaued in the 1970s, larger-yielding fishing techniques, including higher-technology sonars and driftnets, were instituted to restart the growth again in the 1980s. These larger and larger catches threaten many commercially important fish species and have forced fishing fleets to pursue far less valuable fish—because that is all that is available.

At the same time, the destruction of habitats and breeding grounds by coastal development, nutrient contamination of offshore waters from industrial effluents, agricultural runoff, ocean dumping, and litter contribute to the decrease in sea life. From 1980 to 2000, coastal urban populations are expected to increase by 380 million—about the 1990 population of Canada, the United States, and Mexico. The United States has already lost over 50 percent of its coastal wetlands; Italy had lost over 95 percent of its historic wetlands by 1972.

Ozone depletion is certain to increase in the coming years (because of CFCs already in the atmosphere) and may well begin to affect the phytoplankton, on which the ocean fishing industry is ultimately dependent.

The fishing catch has already begun to fall (down 4 percent in 1990 alone), which may be a harbinger of much worse times for commercial fishing in the future.

A Loss of Financial Underpinnings

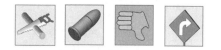

By 1996, there is a sharp reversal of the trend toward increased international financial interdependence that we have experienced during the past 40 years.

It is heralded by the complete collapse of the Japanese property market after rampant inflation. Even the Japanese have trouble meeting international payment obligations. The Japanese repatriate foreign investment at an incredible rate. The wide currency swing leads to a new era of mistrust. In the United States, this lack of trust leads to cries for a protectionist trade policy; it is compounded by the failure of the EEC to ratify the Treaty of Maastricht.

Investors lose all confidence in the concept of international enterprise, which creates a credit crisis in a wide range of dependent institutions. This financial crisis, in combination with falling material prices in industrialized countries, leads to unemployment rates of more than 15 percent in all OECD countries.

The "pull back to the border" mentality that is instilled by this immediate lack of international confidence acts to heighten an already notable return to nationalist policy and isolationism. There is a push for returning to the gold standard and away from electronic money. This move is also based on a new-found lack of trust in anything associated with international relations.

Measures

■ *Japanese property values continue their plunge.*

■ *The Japanese foreign investment figures drop by more than 15 percent annually.*

■ *Total international lending drops 3 percent to 4 percent each year through the 1990s.*

■ *German public debt increases dramatically until the year 2000.*

■ *Unemployment rates in OECD countries rise an average of 1.5 percent annually from 1992 levels.*

■ *OECD growth figures reflect a drop to less than 1 percent for the latter half of the 1990s.*

Implications

■ The legislative output from the mid- to late-1990s reflects a new era of national priorities. Trade legislation to limit the importation of Japanese and other foreign goods is passed by the United States and the EEC, and new financial controls on capital flows are planned.

■ Corporate reaction to the changes are reflected in the immediate downsizing of operations to account for the loss of a global market. In the United States, there is a new age of domestic strategic alliances.

The antitrust laws are restructured to allow for a more cooperative "Japanese" model to emerge. The year 2000 sees the advent of U.S. domestic business groups. This new domestic alliance mentality results in a renewed capability for internationally competitive development and production.

■ In Japan, the unemployment problem causes more internal strife than the country has seen since 1947 and results in three changes of government between 1995 and 2000. The cycle of low growth is perpetuated by domestic unrest.

■ In the EEC, the problem is unemployment, which already had been high prior to the collapse of international flows.

■ By the year 2000, there are wild fluctuations among world currencies.

U.S. Economy Fails

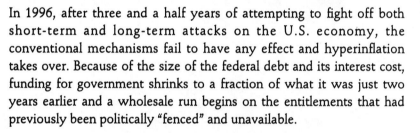

In 1996, after three and a half years of attempting to fight off both short-term and long-term attacks on the U.S. economy, the conventional mechanisms fail to have any effect and hyperinflation takes over. Because of the size of the federal debt and its interest cost, funding for government shrinks to a fraction of what it was just two years earlier and a wholesale run begins on the entitlements that had previously been politically "fenced" and unavailable.

Measures

■ *The federal budget deficit continues to grow during 1993 to 1996.* Attempts to build a serious bipartisan attack on growing budget deficits fails. Growth in programs more than offsets savings from cuts and increased tax income. Debt service consumes 70 percent of the total tax revenues of the country.

■ *Attempts to redesign the nation's health care system end with a poor compromise between the providers and government.* Threatened with a significant decrease in income, drug companies, hospitals, physicians, and others in the health care industry drag their feet and refuse to go along with significant system reform. A compromise is worked out that holds costs from rising significantly, but makes no material cuts in the nation's cost of health care.

■ *An increase in natural disasters strikes a body blow to both government and industry.* A major earthquake in California, a number of East Coast and Gulf Coast hurricanes, and the explosive reactivation of Mount Rainier come together with significantly increased flooding that accompanies much stronger thunderstorms to bankrupt the casualty insurance industry and put significant pieces of the U.S. economy out of business. Federal government disaster relief funds are exhausted.

- *The AIDS epidemic begins to peak, with 50,000 or more deaths per year.* The dramatically increasing costs of tending to the rapidly escalating AIDS death rate, then $15 to $20 billion yearly, offsets any savings that the health care reform process produced.

- *As the economy stagnates, failing corporations bankrupt the Pension Benefit Guaranty Corporation.* The federal government is forced to come up with $40 billion of the over $90 billion of the unfunded guarantees that the PBGC has amassed.

- *The trade deficit increases 50 percent.* China's economy continues to grow at 8 percent per year, and it overtakes Japan as the country with which the United States has the greatest trade deficit. The combination of Japan's slowly rising and China's rapidly rising exports increases the U.S. trade deficit almost 50 percent.

Implications

The domestic and international implications of this scenario are all negative, in most cases very much so. Not only would the U.S. economy be in extraordinary trouble, but such an event would shake, if not mortally wound, the global economy as well.

Third World Exodus

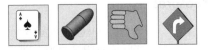

By the year 2000, the economy of the developed world has cured itself of the recessionary tendencies evident during the 1990s. The GATT talks have resulted in a world trade agreement more equally balanced among North America, Europe, and Asia. With the newly revived global economy comes an even greater disparity between the developed countries and the less developed countries. The latter, still struggling with very high population growth and low per capita income growth, are no longer able to hold their people back from the economic carrot of the North. The result is a mass exodus.

The Mediterranean becomes a veritable flotilla. The borders within Africa crumble into a patchwork of armed conflicts and emigration toward Europe. The economic and ethnic conflicts in Eastern Europe and the former Soviet Republics result in a similar, albeit smaller, influx of refugees to Western Europe. In Southeast Asia, there is a rerunning of the Vietnamese exodus, but at levels 1,000 times greater. The economically viable regions of Malaysia, Indonesia, and Thailand are overrun by this migration. In North America, the Mexican borders are compromised from all angles, with a spillover into the United States and Canada.

Illegal aliens can no longer be stopped by traditional border controls on entry roads and at airports. The desperation of the fleeing masses will be completely unanticipated, weakening the effectiveness of the response.

Measures

■ *Per capita GNP growth rates in less developed countries are barely measurable.*

■ *Per capita GNP growth rates in developed countries are between 3.5 percent and 4 percent.*

■ *Population growth rates in less developed countries continue to rise during the 1990s.*

■ *There is a distinct rise in the incidence of illegal alien populations along the fringes of the industrial world in Mexico, Southern Europe, and Malaysia.*

■ *There is an increasing integration of traditional military activities into border patrolling and planning.*

Implications

Initially, there will be mass incursions—of the Normandy type—by residents of poor countries. Lacking any other quick-fix solutions, this will require a military response. The brutality of responding militarily to economic hostility will not play well in developed countries. The media will be sending images of a new holocaust to the developed countries. Global public opinion requires a more humane and lasting solution. The failure of such a solution will allow this conflict to progress into the major cities of the industrial countries, where it will cause the absolute destruction of state-supported social services. The consequence to the North is the very destruction of its isolated economic system. The weapon of developing country population growth has proved more effective than advanced military technology in the battle for effective global policy.

There will be an immediate multilateral conference and agreement among developed countries to sacrifice growth for the effective placement of development aid into the less-developed countries. The range will be up to 9 percent of GDP. This will be seen as the only method by which a seemingly endless global North-South conflict may be averted. The cost to the developed countries will be small compared to the essentially continuous state of the global emergency having emerged as a consequence of the economic disparity between North and South. This will be the first truly effective policy of development aid, involving total developing country debt relief as well as a revision of all archaic infrastructures.

Urban Terrorism Comes to the United States

America has lost its national cohesion: The family is fragmented, the pace and complexity of life is increasing, there is increased loneliness and ever-encroaching impersonal technology, along with eroding moral standards. All tend to push those who are on the edge, over.

If the U.S. domestic economic situation is not controlled, the federal deficit could get out of hand, the government monetizes the debt, we have hyperinflation, millions of people lose their jobs, and we're back into a 1930s-style crash. But this time it would be a lot worse. There are more people, there's not the cohesive effect of shared spiritual/moral beliefs, a greater percentage of the population is near the breaking point, and even in "good" times the anxiety level is extremely high.

In such a "crash" climate, one can imagine desperate inner-city minorities who have nothing to lose in organizing and carrying out urban guerrilla activity against established authorities and commercial interests. It is a latent state that already exists in many of the hard-core inner-city areas.

Nuclear Terrorist Attack on United States

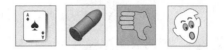

In 1996, a container ship brings a small nuclear device into New York harbor hidden in one of 2,000 containers on the ship. It is detonated by remote control, spreading a radioactive fog over all of New York city and eastern New Jersey. An Islamic fundamentalist organization claims responsibility for the blast, suggesting that this was just God's way of punishing America for its godless philosophy.

New York city panics and effectively shuts down all activities.

Measures

■ *It is confirmed that tactical nuclear weapons were sold by former Soviet republics to Middle East buyers in 1992 and 1993.*

■ *The global economic have/have-not disparity increases.*

■ *U.S. society makes a social decision that runs counter to deeply held Islamic teachings.*

Implications

■ *Extraordinary blow to the United States, its economy, and its national psychology.*

■ *A very serious, if not mortal blow to the global financial system. New York is the largest node in the global financial system. If it, and the financial institutions located there, were to suddenly be eliminated from the larger system, it would be extremely damaging.*

Clearly, extraordinary things can happen—and probably will. The question is, what should we do? The final chapter looks at some answers.

CHAPTER

14

So What

Should We Do?

*If we believe a thing to be bad, and if we have a
right to prevent it, it is our duty to try to prevent it
and to damn the consequences.*
—Lord Milner (1854–1925)

Two things are clear: One, a number
of new ideas, concepts, and ways of
behaving are interacting in complex
ways that are both exciting and
unnerving. And two, too many
trends—and they're big ones—are
going in the wrong direction. The
net effect of all of this is not
particularly encouraging.

In the end, the question is whether humans will get together and change the way they behave before it is too late. There certainly is a growing awareness of the big problems, but one wonders whether the critical mass of concern will coalesce before the expanding trends of fragmentation, pollution, and proliferation also unite to produce a revolution that can't be controlled.

WE MUST REDEFINE LIFE

As I wrote in the first paragraph of this book, we are living in an extraordinary period of time, unlike any other we know about. And therefore we have to learn, and learn very quickly. We have to leave the old ways and invent new ones. We virtually have to "redefine life." Every aspect of human existence will change markedly in the next few decades, so we must figure out what that new reality is going to be—or it's guaranteed that it will all be a surprise, followed by a surprise, and another surprise. If we just wait and do nothing, the shocks will come so fast and be of such magnitude that we will not be able to effectively deal with them. We will surely be pushed toward global incoherence.

But that is not the only alternative. I believe that it could all change for the better. Peter Drucker once told me that he thought that there would be big change, but that it would be driven by a "catastrophic, catalytic event" that would scare humanity into quickly moving in a new direction. It could be an environmental disaster, or a series of natural disasters, or maybe something really far out, like contact with extraterrestrials. Who knows? But one just hopes that it happens sooner, rather than later, because the trends that must be changed have enormous inertia.

This set of problems is not about technology, or energy, or population. It is about human behavior, which is driven by human values. If the values change, so does everything else. More specifically, it's about security. Since all of our other decisions are made on the basis of what we think we need to be secure, if we change our idea of security, we will change the way we live, vote, and spend our money. If we could believe that global as well as national security was at stake here, we would quickly shift to seeing the world in a new way.

We must begin to envision the future implications of some of these trends and understand that what we are doing now will determine what kind of future we and our children will have. And this time, we have a much narrower window within which we must act to extricate ourselves. The magnitude of the trends we have already put in place will soon be so great that any attempts to change them will be in vain. We must act quickly.

WE NEED OLD AND NEW THINKING

Perhaps the key lies with a combination of some very old thinking and some new thinking. The Industrial Age brought the belief that happiness and satisfaction could be gained from money. Our economic and political systems are biased that way. That is how we keep score. But we are at a time when we must change the incentives. We must add new elements to the equation on which we build our lives—things like our environment, our families, education, our cities, and so on. We must embrace some of Hazel Henderson's and Paul Hawken's ideas, understanding that if we don't, the future picture will not be pretty.

We should also learn from the principles of quantum mechanics. At the time that I am writing this, one of the best-selling books in the United States is Deepak Chopra's *Ageless Body, Timeless Mind.* Dr. Chopra takes the principles of quantum mechanics and applies them to health and aging. He starts with a set of assumptions that are at the same time both amazing and true:

■ There is no objective world independent of the observer.

■ Our bodies are composed of energy and information.

■ Mind and body are inseparably one.

■ The biochemistry of the body is a product of awareness.

■ Perception is a learned phenomenon.

■ Impulses of intelligence constantly create the body in new forms every second.

■ Despite the appearance of being separate individuals, we are all connected to patterns of intelligence governing the cosmos.

■ Time is not absolute. The underlying reality of all things is eternal, and what we call time is really quantified eternity.

■ Everyone inhabits a reality of non-change lying beyond all change. The experience of this reality brings change under our control.

■ We are not victims of aging, sickness, and death. These are part of the scenery, not the seer, who is immune to any form of change.

Quantum mechanics says these assumptions work for anything—and everything. Just change the word "body" to environment. Change "aging, sickness, and death" to pollution.

If this is really true—if these ideas better describe reality than our historical, Newtonian perspective—then if we begin to change our minds about what constitutes security and an acceptable future, that process alone will begin to realign and reshape the world in which we live. In practical terms, we will do things differently. But there's a larger concept that is frankly quite hard to fathom. (If you'd like to explore these ideas further, I'd suggest you start with Fred Alan Wolf's *Taking the Quantum Leap: The New Physics for Non-scientists.)*

We are in an predicament that is both exciting and extraordinary. We will need to use extraordinary methods to provide new direction to this world. We have the opportunity to build a new human civilization. We should get about it.

APPENDIX A

Trend Matrix

In order to understand the broad systemic nature of the rapidly evolving environment, it is necessary to take an aerial view above the whole landscape and see how different trends might interact. This matrix is a simple tool that can be used to facilitate that perspective.

Science/Technology

Quantum mechanics
Artificial life
Artificial intelligence
Global information network
Chaos theory
Complexity
Virtual reality
Virtual prototyping
Nanotechnology
Biotechnology
Holography
Robotics
Holographic neural technology
Cyc
Biotechnology
Bioelectronics
Bioelectromagnetics

Space

Communications
GPS
Messaging
Remote sensing
Russia/China launch

Environment

Greenhouse gases
Ozone depletion
Phytoplankton
Wetlands
Rain forests
Acid rain
Habitat loss
Fisheries
Drinking water
Desertification
Weather change
Ocean knowledge
Smog
Toxic waste/nuclear waste
Garbage
Biodiversity

Health

Biotech
Organ replacement
Life extension
AIDS
Mind/body
Virulent diseases
Economic load
Human genome

Social Values

Boomers
Conservative
Responsible
Generational revolt
Culture war
Community
Television influence
Values-laden
Paradigm shift
Consciousness is causal

Population

Global teens
Global growth
Urban migration
Immigration
U.S. ethnic diversity
Rich/poor disparity
Aging
Immigration
Fertility
Single parents
Value loss
Youth stress

Economics

New definition required
World recession
China
Possible depression
Trade balance
U.S. debt
Insurance weak
Pension funding
Education system
Health care
Bionomics
Global finance markets

Transportation

Maglev
High speed trains
SST
MHD drive
Fuel cells
Intel
Vehicle/highway system
Intermodalism
Electronic market

Energy

Oil
Natural gas
Coal
Nuclear power
Photovoltaics
Wind
Efficiency
Superconductivity
Zero-point energy
Nanotechnology
New perspectives

Politics

Integrationist
New party
New government
Power diffusion
Demilitarism
Multilateral
Fragmentation
Weapons trade
Weapons of mass destruction
Islamic revival
Identity crisis
TV Influence
Less sovereignty

APPENDIX B

Projected Special Forces Technology

The U.S. Special Forces projects that there will be a large number of exotic new systems available to the military by 2020.

2000

Miniaturized resuscitation and stability kit
Voice translators
Modular food systems
Advanced clothing and individual systems
Chamelogical camouflage
Chemical ballistics and agile eye protectors
Advanced sniper weapons
Optical laser weapons
Selectable yield munitions
Enhanced explosives
Nonballistic weapons systems (hypervelocity weapons)

2010

Multispectral vision devices
Pharmacological performance sustainability enhancement
Human sensory enhancement
Applied skin protection
Broad spectrum immunity to most biological agents
Injured tissue adhesives
Exoskeleton armor
Small remotely guided agile destruction systems
Directional explosives
Hand/tactile guided virtual presence weapons
Nonlethal, incapacitating micro-minaturized munition clusters
Unmanned air resupply
Deceptive signature generators
Multispectral decoys and mimics

2020

Whole blood replacement
Multispectral invisibility
Soft tissue regeneration
Handheld medical diagnostic equipment
Robotic weapons (large and small)
Families of micro-robotic war-fighting systems
Hybrid mechanical-biological robotic vehicles
Agile individual and crew multipurpose vehicles land/sea/air
Biogenetic sensor systems with genetically engineered biological electromagnets
Emplaced multipurpose autorobotic modules
Handheld multisensor fusion system
Surreptitiously acquired DNA identification
Microchip destabalization

Other Projections:

By the year 2000, 15 percent to 20 percent blood doping will be proven to provide up to 25% enhancement of a soldier's performance in a variety of environments.

By the year 2000, special operating forces will have commercially available voice translation devices weighing less than 1 pound.

Vehicles will use vapor from exhaust of vehicles to provide a clean water source.

Source: U.S. Special Forces Technology Seminar, November 1992

APPENDIX C

Crosscut and Wild Card Matrix

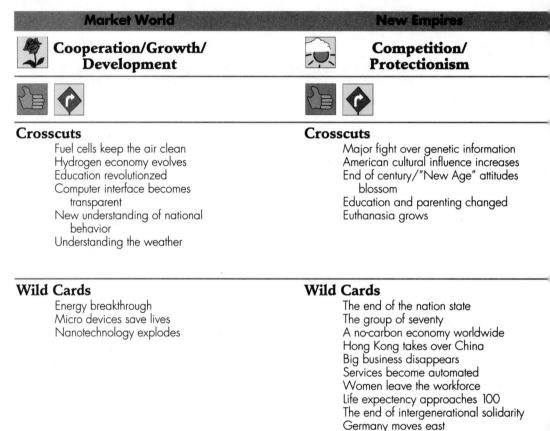

Market World	New Empires
Cooperation/Growth/ Development	**Competition/ Protectionism**

Crosscuts

Fuel cells keep the air clean
Hydrogen economy evolves
Education revolutionzed
Computer interface becomes
   transparent
New understanding of national
   behavior
Understanding the weather

Crosscuts

Major fight over genetic information
American cultural influence increases
End of century/"New Age" attitudes
   blossom
Education and parenting changed
Euthanasia grows

Wild Cards

Energy breakthrough
Micro devices save lives
Nanotechnology explodes

Wild Cards

The end of the nation state
The group of seventy
A no-carbon economy worldwide
Hong Kong takes over China
Big business disappears
Services become automated
Women leave the workforce
Life expectency approaches 100
The end of intergenerational solidarity
Germany moves east

Crosscuts

Crosscuts

Backlash against AIDS victims
Africa unravels
Genome project kills health insurance
Major information system disruptions

Wild Cards

Wild Cards

The new Chernobyl
The Balkanization of Western Europe
China financier to the world

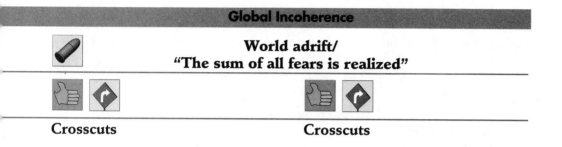

Global Incoherence

 World adrift/
"The sum of all fears is realized"

Crosscuts

Crosscuts

Wild Cards
   Official contact is made with
     extraterrestrials

Wild Cards

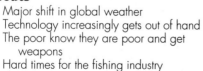

Crosscuts
   Major shift in global weather
   Technology increasingly gets out of hand
   The poor know they are poor and get
     weapons
   Hard times for the fishing industry

Crosscuts
   Urban terrorism comes to the
     United States

Wild Cards
   A loss of financial underpinnings
   U.S. economy fails
   Third world exodus

Wild Cards
   Nuclear terrorist attack on the
     United States

BIBLIOGRAPHY

These books may be of interest to those who would desire to pursue these subjects further:

American Future, The, Wm. VanDusen Wishard; [Washington, D.C.: The Congressional Institute, 1992]

American Renaissance, Marvin Cetron and Owen Davies; [New York: St. Martin's Press, 1989]

An Atlas of Planet Management, Norman Myers; [New York: Doubleday, 1984]

Art of the Long View, Peter Schwartz; [New York: Doubleday Currency, 1991]

Artificial Life: The Quest for a New Creation, Steven Levy; [Pantheon, New York: 1992]

Bankruptcy 1995, Harry E. Figgie, Jr.; [Boston: Little, Brown & Co., 1992]

Beyond the Limits, Donella H. Meadows, Dennis L. Meadows, Jorgen Randers; [Post Mills, VT: Chelsea Green Publishing, 1992]

Bionomics, Michael Rothschild; [New York: Henry Holt & Co., 1990]

Birth of a New World, Harlan Cleveland; [San Francisco: Jossey-Bass, 1993]

Borderless World, The, Kenichi Ohrnae; [New York: Harper Collins, 1990]

Disappearing Through The Skylight—Culture and Technology in the Twentieth Century, O. B. Hardison, Jr.; [New York: Viking Penguin, 1989]

Earth in the Balance, Al Gore; [New York: Houghton Mifflin, 1992]

Ecocide in the USSR, Murray Feshbach and Alfred Friendly, Jr.; [New York: Basic Books, 1992]

Ecology of Commerce, The, Paul Hawken; [New York: Harper Collins, 1993]

Engines of Creation, K. Eric Drexler; [New York: Anchor Doubleday, 1986] *Unbounding the Future,* K. Eric Drexler, Gayle Pergamit, Chris Peterson; [New York: Wm. Morrow, 1991]

Future, The, Ronald D. Rotstein; [New York: Carol Publishing Group, 1990]

Future Mind Artificial Intelligence, Jerome Clayton Glenn; [Washington, D.C.: Acropolis Books Ltd., 1989]

Future Worlds, Norman Myers; [New York: Doubleday, 1990] GAIA

Generations, William Strauss & Neil Howe; [New York: Wm. Morrow, 1991]

Global Mind Change, Willis Harman; [Indianapolis: Knowledge Systems, Inc., 1988]

Knowledge-Value Revolution, The, Taichi Sakaiya; [New York: Kodansha Intl., 1991]

Last Oasis, Sandra Postel; [New York: W. W. Norton, 1992]

Megatrends, John Naisbitt; [New York: Warner Books, 1982]

Megatrends 2000, John Naisbitt & Patricia Aburdene; [New York: Wm. Morrow, 1990]

Mind Children, The Future of Robot and Human Intelligence, Hans Moravec; [Cambridge: Harvard University Press, 1988]

New Realities, The, Peter F. Drucker; [New York: Harper & Row, 1990]

Paradigms in Progress, Hazel Henderson; [Indianapolis: Knowledge Systems, Inc., 1991]

Popcorn Report, The, Faith Popcorn; [New York: Doubleday Currency, 1991]

PowerShift, Alvin Toffler; [New York: Bantam Books, 1990]

State of the World 1993, [New York: W. W. Norton, 1993]

State of the World 1994, [New York: W. W. Norton, 1994]

Strategic Planning and Forecasting, William Ascher & William H. Overholt; [New York: John Wiley & Sons, 1983]

Taking the Quantum Leap: The New Physics for Non-scientists, Fred Alan Wolf; [New York: Harper & Row, 1981]

Third Wave, The, Alvin Toffler; [New York: Bantam Books, 1980]

Virtual Reality, Howard Rheingold; [New York: Summit Books, 1991]

War and Anti-War, Alvin and Heidi Toffler; [New York: Little Brown, 1993]

Whale and the Reactor, The, Langdon Winner; [Chicago, University of Chicago Press, 1986]

2020 Visions, Richard Carlson & Bruce Goldman; [Stanford: Stanford Alumni Association, 1991]

RESOURCES

Chapter 2 New Ideas in Science

Consciousness Is Causal:
> For further information about ongoing research in this area, contact the Institute for Noetic Sciences, 475 Gate Five Road, Suite 3, Sausalito, CA 94965; Fetzer Institute, 9292 W. Kalamazoo Ave., Kalamazoo, MI 49009; and *Brain/Mind Bulletin*, P.O. Box 42211, Los Angeles, CA 90042.

Artificial Life:
> See Steven Levy, *Artificial Life*, and his "A-Life Nightmare," in *Whole Earth Review*, Fall 1992; and "Creatures Get a Life," *New York Times*, October 13, 1992.

Chapter 3 Extraordinary Technology

Cyc:
> Contact the MCC Corporation, 3500 West Balcones Center Dr., Austin, TX 78759

Holographic Neural Technology:
> Contact the AND Corporation, 10 George Street, 4th Floor, Hamilton, Ontario, Canada L8P 1C8

SimNet:
> Contact the Simulation Lab, Institute for Defense Analysis, 1801 Beauregard, Alexandria, VA 22311-1772

Virtual Prototyping:
> Contact the Advanced Research Projects Agency, Arlington, VA

Nanotechnology:
> Contact the Foresight Institute, Box 610058, Palo Alto, CA 94306

Condensed Charge Technology:
> Contact the Institute for Advanced Research, 4030 Braker Lane West, Suite 300, Austin, TX 78759

Holography:
> Contact the MIT Media Lab, Niesner Building, Massachusetts Institute of Technology, Cambridge, MA 02139

Philosophy of Technology:
> Good practical thinking on this subject can be found in Neil Postman's Technopoly; Langdon Winner's *The Whale and the Reactor;* and the writings of William VanDusen Wishard at World-Trends Research, 1805 Wainwright Drive, Reson, VA 22090

Chapter 4 Environmental Alert!

Industrial Ecology:
> You can reach Hardin Tibbs, one of the foremost thinkers in this

field at Global Business Network, 5900-X Hollis Street, P.O. Box 8395, Emeryville, CA 94608

Not Valuing Pollution:
Amory Lovins of the Rocky Mountain Institute in Snowmass, Colorado, has done some of the most creative thinking in this area. Rocky Mountain Institute, 1739 Snowmass Creek Road, Snowmass, CO 81654-3851

Chapter 6 Energy: Big Shifts

Zero-Point Energy:
Contact the Institute for Advanced Research at Austin, 4030 Braker Lane West, Suite 300, Austin, TX 78759

Energy Policy:
Contact the Natural Resources Defense Council, New York, NY

Chapter 7 Transportation: Moving in New Directions

Zero-Emission Automobiles:
Some of the most impressive theoretical work in this area has been done by the Rocky Mountain Institute in Snowmass, Colorado. Their study on supercars is probably the best work on this subject. Rocky Mountain Institute, 1739 Snowmass Creek Road, Snowmass, CO 81654-3851

Chapter 8 Space: Linking Everyone Else

Space:
One of the best sources for information in this area is the newspaper *Space News;* Times Journal Company, 6883 Commercial Dr., Springfield, VA 22159

Chapter 9 Health: Serious Threats ... and Gains

U.S. Health Care Problem:
A good summary was contained in "Crisis in U.S. Health Care," *International Update,* June 7, 1992, Marvin Zonis and Associates, 4942 S. Ellis, Chicago, IL 60615

Chapter 10 Changing Social Values

Paradigm Shift Model:
Contact Applied Futures, Inc., 2101 Crystal Plaza Arcade, Suite 233, Arlington, VA 22202

INDEX

Books have a substantial influence on the destruction of the forests of the Earth. For example, it takes 17 trees to produce one ton of paper. A first printing of 30,000 copies of a typical 480-page book consumes 108,000 pounds of paper which will require 918 trees!

Waite Group Press™ is against the clear-cutting of forests and supports reforestation of the Pacific Northwest of the United States and Canada, where most of this paper comes from. As a publisher with several hundred thousand books sold each year, we feel an obligation to give back to the planet. We will therefore support and contribute a percentage of our proceeds to organizations which seek to preserve the forests of planet Earth.

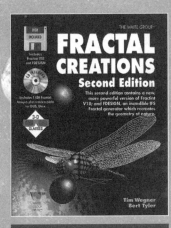

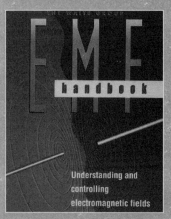

SATISFACTION REPORT CARD

Please fill out this card if you wish to know of future updates to
The Road to 2015: or to receive our catalog.

WAITE GROUP PRESS™

Company Name: _____

Division/Department: _____ Mail Stop: _____

Last Name: _____ First Name: _____ Middle Initial: _____

Street Address: _____

City: _____ State: _____ Zip: _____

Daytime Telephone: (_____) _____

Date Product Was Acquired: Month _____ Day _____ Year _____ Your Occupation: _____

Overall, how would you rate *The Road to 2015*?

☐ Excellent   ☐ Very Good   ☐ Good
☐ Fair   ☐ Below Average   ☐ Poor

What did you like MOST about this book? _____
_____
_____
_____
_____
_____
_____

What did you like LEAST about this book? _____
_____
_____
_____
_____
_____
_____

Is there any subject you would like to see The Waite Group cover in a similar approach? _____
_____
_____

Where did you buy this book?
☐ Bookstore name: _____
☐ Discount store name: _____
☐ Computer store name: _____
☐ Catalog name: _____
☐ Direct from WGP   ☐ Other _____

What price did you pay for this book? _____

What influenced your purchase of this book?
☐ Recommendation   ☐ Advertisement
☐ Magazine review   ☐ Store display
☐ Mailing   ☐ Book's format
☐ Reputation of The Waite Group   ☐ Topic

How many other Waite Group books do you own? _____
What is your favorite Waite Group book? _____

Additional comments? _____
_____
_____
_____

Send to: Waite Group Press, Inc.
Attn: *The Road to 2015*
200 Tamal Plaza
Corte Madera, CA 94925

☐ Check here for a free Waite Group catalog   *The Road to 2015*